# The Only Guides You'll Ever Need!

THIS SERIES IS YOUR TRUSTED GUIDE *through all of life's stages and situations. Want to learn how to surf the Internet or care for your new dog? Or maybe you'd like to become a wine connoisseur or an expert gardener? The solution is simple: just pick up a K.I.S.S. Guide and turn to the first page.*

*Expert authors will walk you through the subject from start to finish, using simple blocks of knowledge to build your skills one step at a time. Build upon these learning blocks and by the end of the book, you'll be an expert yourself! Or, if you are familiar with the topic but want to learn more, it's easy to dive in and pick up where you left off.*

*The K.I.S.S. Guides deliver what they promise: simple access to all the information you'll need on one subject. Other titles you might want to check out include: K.I.S.S. Guide to the Unexplained, K.I.S.S. Guide to Yoga, K.I.S.S. Guide to Photography, and many more to come.*

## GUIDE TO

# Dreams

### LISA LENARD

Foreword by Stephen LaBerge, Ph.D
Lucid dreaming researcher and author

DK Publishing

LONDON, NEW YORK,
MUNICH, MELBOURNE, DELHI

**DK Publishing, Inc.**
**Senior Editor** Jennifer Williams
**Editorial Director** Chuck Wills
**Publisher** Chuck Lang

**Dorling Kindersley Limited**
**Project Editor** Jane Sarluis
**Project Art Editor** Kelly Meyer
**Senior Editor** Caroline Hunt
**Managing Editor** Maxine Lewis
**Managing Art Editor** Heather McCarry
**Production** Rita Sinha
**Picture Research** Anna Grapes
**Jacket Designer** Katy Wall
**Jacket Editor** Beth Apple
**DTP Designer** Mike Grigoletti

**Produced by**
**Dorling Kindersley India Limited**
**Project Editors** Ranjana Saklani, Rimli Borooah
**Project Art Editor** Kavita Dutta
**Managing Art Editor** Aparna Sharma
**DTP Designer** Sunil Sharma

First American Edition, 2002
02 03 04 05 10 9 8 7 6 5 4 3 2 1

Published in the United States by
DK Publishing, Inc.,
375 Hudson Street,
New York, NY 10014

**Library of Congress Cataloging-in-Publication Data**

Lenard, Lisa.
  K.I.S.S. Guide to Dreams / Lisa Lenard.
    p. cm. – (Keep it simple series)
    Includes index.
    ISBN 0-7894-9199-0 (alk. paper)
    1. Dreams. 2. Dream interpretation. I. Title. II. Series.
  BF1091 .L525 2003
  154.6'3–dc21

                                                         2002073496

Color reproduction by Colourscan, Singapore
Printed and bound by MOHN Media and Mohndruck GmbH, Germany

See our complete product line at
# www.dk.com

# Contents

# Foreword

IN DREAMS, WE LIVE another life, nightly traveling to a too-often forgotten land of fabulous possibilities. As with any journey, a guidebook and maps are essential, and such is the purpose of this book. Let's start by dispelling some of the misconceptions clouding our vision of dreams. The standard dictionary definition of "a dream" as a series of thoughts, images, or fancies passing through the mind during sleep, fails to capture the compelling reality of dreams. Hellish, heavenly, or prosaic, our dreaming time is as much a part of our life experience as our waking time.

My scientific work has led me to propose that consciousness – our experience of being alive and aware – is, in fact, a dream. While awake, we use the information from our senses to build a model of the world. In dreams, however, sensory input is greatly reduced, setting our brains free to experience worlds unconstrained by what is "real." However, to make the most of the freedom dreams offer, we must know we are dreaming at the time! Gravity, the impenetrability of solid objects, the rules of social life, remain real in dreams as long as we believe in them. However, in lucid dreams, knowing we are dreaming, we can fly, pass through walls, or experience anything imaginable.

While exploring the uncharted frontier of dreaming, I advise you to "Keep It Simple, Sleeper!" Don't believe anything without proof. Although dreams go beyond reason, they will never contradict it. Dreams can show you much about yourself, but remember that no one is better qualified to understand your dreams than you are. Like the author of KISS Guide to Dreams, I believe that dreams are not so much messages as they are improvised plays or poems, composed of the elements of your experience: your fears, desires, expectations, and so on.

You have in your hands a simple, but effective, guide to dreams. It aims to be the first, rather than the last word on this profoundly fascinating realm. This book touches on most of the dizzying array of current and past theories, dogmas, belief-systems, and techniques of dream-work and play. Think of it as a menu of menus, summarizing the offerings of more restaurants than you could patronize, specializing in cuisines as varied as the cultures of the world.

You will find that you get out of your dreams what you put into them, with interest. To reap the greatest return from these most personal creations, you must learn from your dreams themselves what dreaming is, what value dreaming life offers you, and what may be found beyond the dreams of both sleeping and waking.

*SœBerge*

STEPHEN LABERGE, PH.D
Lucid dreaming researcher and author

# Introduction

*TO SLEEP IS TO DREAM, and to dream is to explore a world both different from and similar to our waking world. If you're like most people, you can't help but wonder about the world of dreams. I wrote the K.I.S.S. Guide to Dreams to begin to answer some of those ineffable questions.*

*I can remember dreams from before I had the words to articulate them, and, according to friends who I went to school with, I've been interpreting them for others for nearly as long. I'm neither a psychologist nor a psychic, however: I'm a writer, and as a writer, I understand how important the stories we tell ourselves when we are asleep are to our waking lives.*

*Whether you want to learn about the biology of dreams or their psychology, whether you want to understand your own dreams or interpret the dreams of others, this book will provide you with tools for exploring dream elements and imagery. This book is not a dictionary reducing every dream symbol to one meaning (as you'll soon find out, I don't like or use the term "symbol"). Instead, it's a way to help you get in touch with your own unconscious, and learn what it is you're trying to tell yourself.*

It's my belief that our individual dreams actually connect us far more than many of us imagine. Dreams offer us fleeting glimpses of our human interconnectedness and a shared imagery that we're only now beginning to understand. So, if you're ready for the next frontier of human adventure, the K.I.S.S. Guide to Dreams can act as your compass.

*Lisa Lenard*

LISA LENARD

# What's Inside?

*THE* K.I.S.S. GUIDE TO DREAMS *is designed to teach you everything you need to know about dreams and dreaming, including techniques and exercises you can use right away to help you understand and interpret your dreams. Besides helping you learn more about your dreams, these techniques will also help you learn more about yourself, and have fun in the process.*

## Part One

In Part One you'll learn the basics about sleep and dreams. You'll learn how Freud, Jung, Perls, and others interpreted dreams. I'll show you some ways to remember and record your dreams, as well as methods for separating the imagery and the people who "live" there.

## Part Two

In Part Two you'll learn how to interpret the stuff of dreams. Sample dreams throughout this section will help you see how different dreamers' dream imagery is both similar to and different from your own. In this part I'll also give you the tools to begin to understand and interpret your own dream imagery.

## Part Three

In Part Three you'll learn about different types of dreaming and whether they are simply variations on the same theme. I'll show you how to dream creatively or lucidly, and we'll take a look at angels and spirit guides who appear in dreams, as well as ask the question whether people can visit you after they have died. In addition, we'll explore astral projection and dream flying, as well as out-of-body experiences and dream telepathy.

## Part Four

In Part Four you'll learn how to begin to work with others on both your and their dreams. I'll explore the future of dreaming, including some new uses for your daydreams, the possibilities of collective and shared dreaming, and how forensic dreaming can help you achieve your greatest potential. Dreaming doesn't end when you awaken in the morning, and working with your dreams doesn't end when you finish this book: both are only the beginning.

# The Extras

*STARTING AT THE BEGINNING of this book and reading it through will give you a basic and thorough guide to working with dreams. Once you have read it through, you'll likely want to go back to areas that you found particularly interesting. For that, I've provided icons that will simplify your search. You'll find four of these icons in the margins throughout the book. Next to each, you'll find some text in bold print – that's the text directly related to the icon.*

### Very Important Point

This icon will point out information that I believe deserves your careful attention. Be sure you don't miss these.

### Complete No-No

This is a warning symbol pointing out something you should avoid at all costs.

### Getting Technical

Sometimes you just need to know the details. These may get a little technical so read carefully.

### Inside Scoop

These are bits of my personal experience – learning of my own that I'd like to share with you.

You'll also find boxes that contain information that's useful or simply fun.

### Trivia...

*Here's where I'll share interesting tidbits of information about dreams.*

### DEFINITION

*I'll try not to use confusing or **unfamiliar terms**, but if you run across one in the text, you'll find the term explained in a box right on the same page.*

### INTERNET

### www.internet.com

*In these boxes, you'll find specific addresses on the World Wide Web. The Internet can be a great resource into the world of dreams!*

# PART ONE

## Dream Basics

FROM ANCIENT ORACLES TO contemporary psychoanalysts, dream interpreters have sought to understand the stuff of dreams. Here you'll learn the basics about dreams, and how to start exploring dreams and their imagery.

# Chapter 1

# Dreaming Defined – Past and Present

ARE DREAMS MESSAGES from our ancestors or from the gods? Are they visions of a parallel reality? A way for our unconscious minds to communicate with our conscious minds? Tools for us to understand ourselves and thus change and grow? There is something mystical about dreams that fascinates even the most logical of us. They unfold like stories we don't yet know, and thus appeal to our inherent desire for storytelling. Because we humans have been telling stories as long as we've been communicating with one another, it makes sense that we begin by exploring some of the stories about dreams.

## In this chapter...

✓ A dialogue with the gods

✓ A parallel reality

✓ Body and mind, mind and spirit

✓ A psychological tool?

EUGÈNE DELACROIX'S PAINTING OF JACOB WRESTLING WITH HIS DREAM ANGEL

# A dialogue with the gods

*WHEN I WAS FOUR or five years old, I dreamed that I was 40, that the little girl I saw sleeping was my young self, and that the life that girl would live would in reality be a dream. When I was 40 (having by then forgotten the earlier dream), I dreamed that I visited my little-girl self as she lay sleeping, and told her that it hadn't been a dream after all. I told her that I (she?) had lived that life thus far, and we would now continue the journey together. These dreams still have the power to awe me as I write this. Which one was "real"? Which life is the "dream"?*

## Defining dreams

More to our point, what are **dreams**? Are they, as some scientists insist, the mind demanding a "story" from what is actually the random firing of neurons? Or are they, as suggested by my own dreams described above, messages from a larger universe than we ordinarily consider as we live our day-to-day lives?

My own answer is that dreams are both these things – and much more as well. Some call dreams "a dialogue with the gods," and if you consider that dreams indeed reveal things outside the ordinary, this is a rather lovely way of defining them. In fact, humans have been fascinated with dreams as long as we've been able to communicate them; in other words, for a very long time. So let's begin with a tour of dream theory through time, starting with our most ancient ancestors.

> **DEFINITION**
>
> **Dreams** *are narratives experienced while one is asleep, consisting of a mixture of "real" and "unreal" events. Webster's New World Dictionary calls a dream "a sequence of sensations, images, thoughts, etc., passing through a sleeping person's mind."*

## Ancient dreamers

It shouldn't surprise us to discover that the first lengthy record of dreams is also the first recorded story: the chronicle of Gilgamesh. Recorded on clay tablets in Assyria in the seventh century BC, Gilgamesh's adventures begin a tradition that continues to this day: what mythologist Joseph Campbell called "the Hero's Journey."

■ **The Epic of Gilgamesh,** *a recorded dream, describes the adventures of the legendary warrior king Gilgamesh, who changes from tyrant to a great hero in the course of his search for immortality.*

*The Hero's Journey is an archetype for life itself. Beginning with a call to adventure, the journey continues through a series of challenges and struggles to victory. I'll be referring to the Hero's Journey throughout this book.*

Epics from *Gilgamesh* to the *Odyssey* to Shakespearean tragedies to present-day films follow the formula of the Hero's Journey – as do many of our dreams. We have recorded evidence of dreams from the ancient Babylonians and Sumerians. Like the Assyrians, these peoples took the predictive power of dreams for granted. It's clear that even this early in human history, systems of dream imagery and symbolism had been developed.

One example of such a system comes to us in the tale of Gudea, a Sumerian king who lived about 2200 BC, which has been preserved on clay tablets. An interesting aspect of this tale is that, in his dream, Gudea sees symbols which he doesn't understand, whereupon he is immediately presented with more imagery, which confuses him further!

## So the Bible says

When we arrive at the era of the Old Testament, it is a singular God who now speaks to humans in their dreams. If you were raised in the Judeo-Christian tradition, chances are you're familiar with some of these Biblical dreams. In Genesis, for example, Jacob wrestles with a dream angel, who rewards him with a new name – Israel – and the promise of him fathering a nation. His son, Joseph, was skilled at interpreting dreams, as recorded in Exodus. In Kings, King Solomon is given his wisdom in a dream, while in Prophets, Daniel's dream interpretation saves him from death in the lions' den and earns him a permanent position at Nebuchadnezzar's palace.

■ **Joseph** – *the central figure in the relief shown here – was an interpreter of dreams. Sold by his brothers to some passing traders, Joseph ends up in Egypt, where his ability to interpret dreams endears him to the Pharaoh.*

## Early Christian beliefs

The New Testament is less reliant on dreams, perhaps because Christianity has often viewed dreams as messages from demons rather than from God. Traditional Christianity holds that visions from God come while awake rather than asleep. Examples of waking dreams include the story of St Paul – until his visions, an ardent opponent of Christianity – who "saw a light from heaven" while on his way to Damascus to suppress the new religion. Early Eastern Orthodoxy took a slightly different tack: pagans may receive messages when asleep, but only because these messages encouraged them to convert to Christianity.

## It's all Greek to me

By the time we arrive in ancient Greece, the stuff of dreams has become multifaceted. Artemidorus of Daldis, for example, wrote the *Oneirocritica* (The Interpretation of Dreams), considered the first **dream dictionary**. Arranged categorically, it decodes dream omens, predictors of the future. Artemidorus divided dreams into three categories: symbolic dreams, visionary and oracular.

The Greek philosopher Plato (427–347 BC) studied the emotional impact of dreams on one's waking life. His student Aristotle (384–322 BC) furthered Plato's ideas, rejecting the idea of divine inspiration and proposing that dreams were the result of external stimuli, which could also affect waking life via the dreams.

> **DEFINITION**
>
> *Alphabetically arranged, a* **dream dictionary** *connects dream images to specific symbols. Dreaming of a baby, for example, might signify pregnancy. While modern dream theory holds that dream dictionaries are far too reductive, the books continue to enjoy strong sales.*

## The Greek physicians

Hippocrates (469–399 BC), considered the father of modern medicine, also had a dream theory. He believed that the physical body was in control when one was awake, and that the soul took over when one was asleep. Like Artemidorus, he divided dreams into three categories: prophetic, diagnostic, and revealing.

Galen, a Greek physician who lived nearly 500 years later, took Hippocrates's ideas about diagnostic dreams further, using their prognostications as the basis for surgical operations.

■ **Ancient Greeks** *built temples, called Asclepieions (shown here), honoring the physician Aesculapius. It was believed that sick people who slept in these temples would be sent cures in their dreams.*

# A parallel reality

MEANWHILE, IN THE yet-to-be-"discovered" Americas and Oceania, native peoples had been developing equally intriguing concepts about dreams. Whether the **dreamtime** of the many Australian aboriginal tribes or the religious traditions of the equally diverse Native American tribes, native peoples share a reverence for dreams that seems to be untroubled by the vagaries of "rational" thought.

> **DEFINITION**
>
> **Dreamtime** *is the name given to the heroic parallel reality from which Australian aboriginals come and to which they return. Rituals performed in the present life reenact these heroes' journeys in order to keep the connection between past, present, and future realities one.*

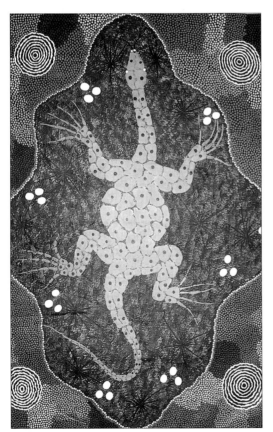

■ **Australian aboriginal art** *depicts a large number of myths associated with dreams. Shown above is* Goanna Dreaming, *a 1996 painting by aboriginal artist Michael Jabanardi.*

## The aboriginal dreamtime

The basic construct of Australian aboriginal dreamtime is that past, present, and future coexist. These parallel realities are accessed through dreams, which thus can reveal not only things that have happened in the past, but things that will happen in the future, because, according to this concept, "all time is now."

It stands to reason that there is far less discontinuity between sleeping and waking for these eternal dreamers than is experienced in western cultures. In addition, not only are their dream experiences applied to waking life, but waking events often presage dream ones.

## Varied beliefs

Specific beliefs within this larger framework vary widely among the more than 500 distinct Australian aboriginal tribal groups. Many tribes believe that spirits of the dead or ghosts visit the dreamer, while others hold that the dreamer visits other places and other times. Still others are certain that when one snores, the spirit leaves the body.

## Native American dreamers

As with Australian aboriginals, beliefs about dreams vary from Native American tribe to tribe. Consistent among these various beliefs, however, is the importance attributed to the dream experience itself.

*Among Native American tribes, dream experiences are not only accorded equal billing with waking life, they are often used to determine the specific life role an individual will play within the larger tribal framework.*

Many tribes believe that the world began in dreams, and that dreams continue to presage what will happen in the world. A well-known example of this is the dream which predicted the killing of the buffalo, the arrival of white people, and the ultimate subjugation of the Native American tribes. The Iroquois of upstate New York believed that an individual's dream held significance for the entire tribe. Important dreams were reported to tribal leaders so that appropriate action could be taken by all members of the tribe.

A remarkable Native American construct is that of the "Dreamcatcher." Made of a web of strings strung across a ring, from which dangle feather, beads, or shells, it is said to filter through good dreams while holding back the bad ones.

■ **According to Navajo legend,** *a spider wove the dreamcatcher so that good dreams could pass through the small holes while bad dreams became entangled in the web.*

## DREAM WORK AMONG THE SENOI

The Senoi people of Malaysia are a particularly intriguing subject for dream study as dream control is an intrinsic part of their daily lives. Until World War II, when many of them were killed by Japanese forces, they remained isolated from the rest of the world. According to the Senoi, the dream-soul leaves the body during sleep and encounters other dream-souls, whether of people, animals, natural elements, or otherworldly beings. The information the dream-souls bring back is often prophetic or healing, and is treated very seriously, although a differentiation is made between significant and insignificant dreams. Training in dream control and understanding begins at a young age in this culture, and discussions of dreams are a part of the daily routines of both children and adults.

# SHAMANIC DREAMS AND DREAMERS

Psychologist and dream researcher Stanley Krippner, PhD, calls shamans "the first dreamworkers." That's because one of the jobs of these tribal religious leaders was to dream for the tribe as well as interpret the dreams of others. Found in tribes throughout the world, shamans are particularly adept at bringing on the dream state at will, with or without the use of psychedelic drugs. Even how a shaman is selected is determined by a dream – usually on the part of the future shaman himself. In Part 3 of this book, I'll explore some of the traditional shamanic methods in more detail.

■ **Shamans** *use dream states to heal, mediate between the world of the living and the spirit world, or guide the soul into the afterlife.*

## Dreaming and the Cree

Let's look at another Native American concept about dreaming. The Cree, Canada's largest native group, see no difference between waking life and dreaming. Jayne Gackenbach, PhD, a past president of the Association for the Study of Dreams, has been working with the Cree in Central Alberta to explore what she calls "the difference between dreaming and not dreaming."

Because the Cree don't draw the lines between dreaming and waking that North Americans of European descent do, what scientists and theorists have perceived as two very different states actually becomes a much murkier and more ambiguous area – excellent fuel for Dr. Gackenbach's ideas.

It is worth noting that contemporary European-descended North Americans, hoping to reconnect with their own spirituality, sometimes appropriate the ideas of Native American tribes without understanding the much broader cultural context from which these ideas originate.

*Don't try to adapt ideas about dreams from other cultures without understanding the context in which they are embedded.*

**INTERNET**

**www.sawka.com/ spiritwatch/bio.htm**

*This web page is a good introduction to dream researcher Jayne Gackenbach's work on dreams.*

# Body and mind, mind and spirit

*IF YOU WERE EVER part of a late-night discussion during your college years, you probably pondered the "who's dreaming who" question. Because dreams pose as many questions as they answer, they're often the subject matter when we ponder the imponderables. And just like late-night student philosophers, dream researchers explore dreams from many different angles.*

■ **Dreams can help** *us transcend day-to-day existence via connections to both the larger world and the inner self. Shown here is the painting* The Wanderer above the Sea of Clouds *by Casper David Friedrich.*

## Exploring the connections

What's the connection between the body and the mind, for example? Do we dream so that the body can go about its nightly work of self-regeneration? Or do we sleep so that we can dream and thus renew the spirit? Is it possible that spirits do visit us as we sleep – or that we visit others?

Whether philosophers, psychologists, or psychics, theorists are drawn to dreams because of both their possibility and their mystery. While Plato may have been the first to posit the separation between the waking and dreaming states, other thinkers have long been considering the connection between body and mind, and mind and spirit.

# The "New Age" dreamers of the Middle Ages

Contemporary New Age thinkers concern themselves with questions of mind, body, and spirit, using a whole range of approaches, from mysticism to meditation to holistic medicine. According to James R. Lewis's *The Dream Encyclopedia* (see *Further Reading* at the end of this book), the not-so-new ideas behind today's New Age movement are:

- The self is divine
- Personal transformation is possible
- Broad cultural transformation is possible
- Occult arts, such as astrology, the tarot, and psychic healing, can be used to bring about these transformations

The "New Age" dreamers of the Middle Ages, however, were less hopeful about the occult arts. In fact, it was believed that anyone practicing an occult art was under the influence of the devil. Dreams, too, were labeled as Satan's temptations. In *Our Dreaming Mind*, Robert D. van de Castle, PhD, quotes a sixteenth-century Jesuit priest: "The devil is most always implicated in dreams, filling the minds of men with poisonous superstition and not only uselessly deluding but perniciously deceiving them."

■ **Reading the Tarot** *is a popular way of shedding light on dreams. Many look upon it as a path to self-realization.*

*According to the experts of the day, the devil did most of his dirty work in dreams through his minions – incubi and succubi – demons that assumed human form in dreams to seduce mere mortals. They certainly helped assuage the guilt of monks and nuns who had erotic dreams!*

■ **In the Middle Ages,** *dreams were believed to be the work of the devil. This carved relief shows the devil tempting a student of divinity.*

■ **Artists have long been fascinated** *by the connection between the individual and the creative imagination. Henri Rousseau's* The Dream *(1910), for example, depicts "Yadwigha peacefully asleep" enjoying "a lovely dream," according to a poem written by the artist.*

## What do the philosophers say?

Greek philosophers were the first to separate the dreaming life from the waking one, an idea that western philosophers have been exploring ever since. In the seventeenth century, young René Descartes evolved his philosophical theory of dualism, which holds that while humans' physical bodies function as other animals' bodies do, their minds are controlled by a nonphysical soul, after a dream suggested to him that he needed to develop a way of understanding the body and the spirit.

Also in the seventeenth century, Thomas Hobbes posited a different approach. Dreams, Hobbes suggested, are caused by a connection between emotions and the dream. According to Hobbes's theory, if you dream you're hot, you may be very angry, while if you dream you're cold, you may be frightened. Like Descartes's ideas, Hobbes's theory continues to have its followers.

*Trivia...*

*The oft-quoted phrase "life is a dream" comes from the sixteenth-century philosopher Blaise Pascal, who said "Life is a dream, a little more regular than other dreams."*

By the eighteenth century, writers had begun to use dreams to highlight the connection between the individual and the creative imagination. In the nineteenth century, Henri-Louis Bergson proposed that time, not being, is the ultimate reality, and argued for a study of dreams that included not only their biological basis but their relationship with memory. This tied in with his philosophy: that we do not forget anything, that all experience is imprinted on our memory, and thus is material for our dreams.

# A psychological tool?

*THE MODERN APPROACH to dreams can be said to have begun in the nineteeenth century when philosophers such as Johann Gottlieb Fichte and Johann Friedrich Herbart began to regard dreams as revelations of our unconscious fears and desires.*

It was with the publication of Sigmund Freud's *The Interpretation of Dreams* in 1900 that the revolution in dream theory started in earnest. By the end of the nineteenth century, much of dream theory had entered the realm of the new field of psychology. That's where we'll be heading in Chapter 2. Dreams were now increasingly regarded as a tool for change, growth, and well-being.

*While there can be a host of approaches to the study and interpretation of dreams, ultimately you will discover that working with dreams is as individual as you are.*

## A simple summary

✔ Dreams are narratives experienced while one is asleep – a mixture of "real" and "unreal" events.

✔ Ancient and Biblical dreamers believed that dreams were divine messages.

✔ Australian aborigines believe that past, present, and future coexist within an always-now dreamtime, while Native American tribes hold that the world began in dreams, and that dreams can presage events in one's waking life.

✔ In the Middle Ages, it was thought that the devil tempted and misled humans in their dreams.

✔ Faced with the seeming separation between the waking state and the dream state, philosophers came up with theories like dualism (Descartes) and the idea that life itself is a dream (Pascal).

✔ Since the nineteenth century, especially in the wake of Sigmund Freud's work, dreams have been studied as an aspect of psychology.

# Chapter 2

# The Psychologists Check In

AT THE END OF THE 19TH century, Sigmund Freud's study of the links between neuroses and the unconscious – which he called the field of dreams – caused a marked change in ideas about dreams. At about the same time, Carl Jung developed his own theories about dreams and the unconscious. Others soon followed with equally intriguing ideas. In this chapter, in addition to Freud's and Jung's theories, we'll briefly explore those of Alfred Adler, Medard Boss, and Fritz Perls.

## In this chapter...

✓ **Freud and the unconscious**

✓ **Jung and the collective unconscious**

✓ **Adler and the social unconscious**

✓ **Boss and the existential unconscious**

✓ **Perls and the Gestalt theory of dreams**

# Freud and the unconscious

*"IN THE FOLLOWING PAGES I shall prove that there exists a psychological technique by which dreams may be interpreted, and that upon the application of this method every dream will show itself to be a senseful psychological structure which may be introduced into an assignable place in the psychic activity of the waking state. I shall furthermore endeavor to explain the processes that give rise to the strangeness and obscurity of the dream, and to discover through them the nature of the psychic forces which operate, whether in combination or in opposition, to produce the dream."*
– Sigmund Freud, The Interpretation of Dreams (1900).

■ **Sigmund Freud's** *seminal work established the study and interpretation of dreams as a legitimate part of psychoanalysis.*

## Freud's early work

Dr. Freud (1856–1939) is considered the father of psychoanalysis, and his revolutionary book, *The Interpretation of Dreams*, is one of his earliest works (see *Further Reading* at the end of this book). It heralded the important role that dreams would play in the new field – and the new century.

*Although* The Interpretation of Dreams *was ready for publication by late 1899, Freud took the unusual step of withholding it until 1900, as he considered it a work for the new century.*

Freud began his career working with the French neurologist Jean Charcot, whose "cure" for hysteria was hypnosis. He then moved on to work with the Viennese physician Joseph Breuer, with whom he developed the technique of ***free association***. They used this technique with patients whose neuroses seemed to have psychological rather than physiological roots. However, the relationship between the two men became strained as Freud explored what he believed to be the sexual roots of neuroses (mental disorders that can give rise to symptoms such as anxiety, compulsion, phobia, or depression).

# The "id" has it

Freud's work soon led him to believe that the bases for neuroses can be found in early childhood. He posited that the suppression of sexual instincts in order to conform to societal rules led to repression – the psychological mechanism by which we withhold unconscious information from our conscious minds. This in turn led to adult neuroses. Freud proposed that every personality is comprised of three parts:

**1** **Id,** the unconscious part. The portion of the *psyche* concerned with pleasure and desire. Freud believed this was the realm of the unconscious

**DEFINITION**

*The word* **psyche** *(from the Greek word for soul) refers to the whole complex entity of the human mind.*

**2** **Ego,** the conscious part. The portion of the psyche that experiences the external world

**3** **Superego,** the censoring part. The psyche's censor, which enforces moral codes for the ego, and blocks unacceptable impulses of the id

Only in dreams, Freud went on, did the superego let down its guard so that the primitive desires of the id might become known. He believed dreams are the acting out, in fantasy form, of these desires. In fact, his study of dreams began with a dream of his own. When an associate, Otto, implied that Freud had failed to cure a patient, Irma, Freud dreamed that Irma's problem could be traced to an error of Otto's. This, he said, was because he had felt humiliated by Otto, and wished to show that he was a better diagnostician than Otto.

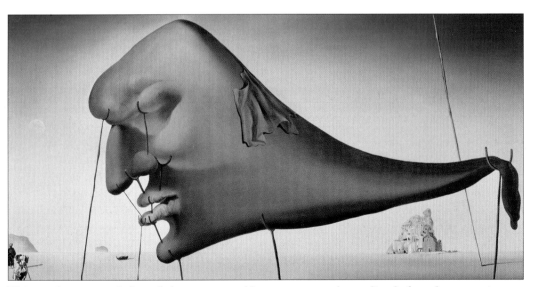

■ **Surrealist artists believed** *that it was possible to transpose a dream directly from the unconscious to the canvas, without the intervention of the painter's conscious mind. Shown above is* Sleep *(1937) by Salvador Dali (1904–89).*

# THE FIVE PSYCHOLOGISTS AT A GLANCE

This chapter discusses the dream theories of five psychologists. Here, I have condensed this information and compared their ideas to make it simpler for you.

| Psychologist | On the unconscious | On human beings |
|---|---|---|
| ● Sigmund Freud (1856–1939) | It is an area of the human psyche concerned with desire and pleasure. Freud called this the "id" to distinguish it from the conscious, which he called the "ego." | They are a bundle of repressed desires that they keep from themselves. Sexual desire and its repression forms much of human personality. |
| ● Carl Gustav Jung (1875–1960) | It is not an area of animalistic desire but of a unique wisdom that can help the conscious self achieve its potential. | They are the repositories of profound wisdom via their "collective unconscious": a storehouse of knowledge, common to all humanity, expressed in myths, symbols, and themes. |
| ● Alfred Adler (1870–1937) | Did not make a distinction between the conscious and unconscious selves. | They are motivated by the need to achieve control and power in their society. |
| ● Medard Boss (1903–1990) | Posited an existential unconscious, wherein an individual chooses to be what he or she is. | They create their own reality though they may stifle themselves by suspicion or a desire to be in control. |
| ● Fritz Perls (1893–1970) | Did not talk in terms of an unconscious. Believed in "Gestalt psychology" wherein all aspects of a personality work together to create a coherent structure. | They need to integrate memory, experience, facts, events, ideas, beliefs – all aspects of their selves and lives – into a healthy whole. |

| On dreams | On interpretation | On dream therapy |
|---|---|---|
| They are a kind of wish-fulfillment of unconscious desires – desires that we cannot otherwise acknowledge or indulge due to social codes. | What the dreamer "saw" is not the meaningful aspect of the dream. There is a hidden or "latent" meaning which can be brought out with the help of an analyst. | Repression of desires leads to psychological illnesses called "neuroses." An analyst can uncover the hidden meanings in dreams, and thus, the hidden desire at the root of the illness. |
| They articulate the shared symbols and ideas of humanity. They put the dreamer in touch with the collective unconscious and are an important vehicle for personal growth. | What the dreamer "saw" is very important as is the dreamer's own interpretation. There is no one "correct" way to interpret a dream, and the analyst is not essential. | The psyche is essentially healthy. Dreams are not needed to "treat" us for an illness but to help us realize our potential better. |
| They were not central to his analysis. He saw them as something that could provide impetus to the waking self. | It is easy to interpret a dream (for example, flying signifies ambition); there are no hidden meanings. | Dreams can give pointers on how to solve a problem (in fact they only occur if one has a problem that needs solving). |
| They are not mysterious manifestations of an unconscious mind but simply reflect the dreamer's life. | The dreamer should plainly see the dream images (not look for symbols or hidden meanings) and let them speak for themselves. | Dreams are a simple vehicle to help us understand our situation in life and therefore understand what is wrong or right and act accordingly. |
| They are an intensely personal projection of the dreamer's self and do not emanate from a collective unconscious or a universal symbolic language. | The dreamer should narrate the dream, describe dream objects in the first person, act out the dream playing the various roles, and discuss the dream with the therapist. | Through Gestalt therapy the dreamer can get in touch with his or her deepest feelings and work toward a more well-rounded self. |

## Freud and his contemporaries

The problems that contemporary psychologists and dream theorists have with Freud are many. But Freud also had disagreements with his own contemporaries, most famously with Carl Jung, whose ideas we'll explore in the next section of this chapter. Part of the problem lay in Freud's own insecurity, which led him to insist that his was the only possible solution. But many of Freud's theories were based on supposition, much of which later research has found to be flawed.

## It's all about sex

Freud believed first and foremost that sex was at the root of everything. In early childhood, according to Freud, little boys have an unconscious desire to have sex with their mothers (the Oedipus Complex) and are jealous of and wish to compete with their fathers. Similarly, little girls desire to be the love object of their fathers (the Electra Complex). It is the repression of this sexual desire that is the basis of all neuroses, Freud said.

■ **The Freudian term** *"Oedipus Complex" comes from the myth of the Theban king Oedipus, featured here in Jean Auguste Dominique Ingres's painting. He unknowingly kills his father and marries his mother.*

## Dreams and sleep: who's the guardian?

Another problem that contemporary psychologists have with Freud's dream theories is his belief that the function of dreaming was to guard sleep. Freud contended that if the desires expressed in dreams found their way to the conscious mind, the dreamer would be profoundly disturbed by them. In fact, contemporary dream research has found the opposite to be true. As Dr. Ann Faraday notes in *Dream Power*, "Sleep, in fact, is the guardian of dreams."

*Dr. Ann Faraday notes that Freud's contention that dreams provide a safety valve for our repressed desires is flawed. Most dreams are not the id-fueled dramas Freud imagined them to be but trivial pursuits.*

# Freudian dream tools

As we've noted, Freud believed that all dreams begin in a desire for wish fulfillment, a desire he called the "latent content." The latent content, however, lay hidden beneath the dream's manifest content, that which is visible to the dreamer upon awakening. According to Freud, five processes are at work when we dream:

- **Displacement** is the process by which a desire for one thing or person is symbolized by another
- **Condensation** contracts an urge into a brief dream image or event
- **Symbolization** is a dream way of acting out suppressed desire metaphorically
- **Projection** is the tendency of the mind to propel our own desires onto another
- **Secondary revision** is the way in which the mind organizes an incoherent dream into an organic narrative

> **Trivia...**
> "A thing is a phallic symbol
> If it's longer than it's wide,"
> wrote singer/ songwriter
> Melanie in a late 1960s
> spoof of Freud.

*Freud called the unconscious dreaming mind function the primary process, and conscious thought the secondary process.*

Freud had a name for the process by which the mind turns the primal desire into a dream symbol – "dream work" (this should not be confused with the more contemporary term dream work, which refers to working toward understanding one's dreams). He considered dream work to be a form of self-censorship. The role of the psychologist, then, would be to help the dreamer, via free association, to uncover the many layers that lay between the latent dream and the manifest dream. According to Freud, the latent dream contains the dreamer's repressed desires, while the manifest dream contains mere surface meaning.

■ **The Eiffel Tower** *as a phallic symbol may sound like an absurd idea, but Freud's preoccupation with sexual dysfunction meant that he considered almost everything, from a cigar to the Eiffel Tower, to be a phallic symbol.*

## How Freud interpreted dreams

Freud called dreams "the royal road to the unconscious." Now that you understand something of how Freud believed the mind (on all its levels) worked, it's easy to see why he would think this was so. In the Freudian view, the conscious and unconscious minds did constant battle between morality and desire. However, unconscious desires could – and often did – emerge in other ways, and it was when the resulting neuroses became debilitating that the analyst would step in to walk "the royal road." Because Freud believed that without the tempering effects of the ego and superego the id is at best an animalistic gratification machine, his method of dream interpretation existed solely to uncover just what the desires of a particular id were.

*Freud believed the ego and superego, the rational parts of the psyche, were superior to the instinctual id.*

## The importance of being Freud

While many of Freud's theories have been largely discredited or discounted, it's important to remember that:

**1** He was the first to make the connections between dreams and desires

**2** He was the first to help patients discover what those desires were

**3** His free association methods continue to be helpful in a variety of venues today

**4** It may not all be about sex, but, as Freud first told us, dreams are a way for us to discover ourselves

*Free association has often proved a valuable tool for discovering a way for the unconscious to communicate with the conscious mind. So, as with any multifaceted theory, it's important we don't "throw out the baby with the bathwater."*

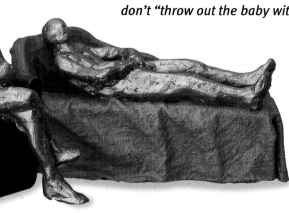

■ **Freudian dream interpretation** *is typically represented by a patient lying on a couch relating a dream while a therapist takes notes and periodically utters, "Hmm."*

# Jung and the collective unconscious

*LIKE FREUD, CARL JUNG (1875–1960) believed the psyche consisted of a conscious and an unconscious mind, and, also like Freud, he believed* **depth psychology** *was the clearest path toward understanding individual neuroses. But this is where their similarity ends.*

> **DEFINITION**
>
> **Depth psychology** *involves probing the unconscious to discover the roots of conscious behavior.*

## The Freud-Jung difference

Freud saw the unconscious as an area teeming with animalistic desires and unchecked urges whereas Jung believed it housed an intriguing combination of instinct and spirit. Further, Jung felt that the purpose of dreams was to communicate rather than conceal, and that the particular wisdom the unconscious possessed (and could communicate via dreams) could help the conscious self achieve its potential.

*For a brief time early in his career, Jung was a student of Freud's. During this time, Freud referred to Jung as his "son," and it was ultimately that very paternalistic attitude that Jung could no longer tolerate.*

Although the two men parted ways because of Freud's dogmatic insistence that his way was the only way, Jung throughout his long life acknowledged his debt to Freud and his ideas.

## Jungian concepts

Jung's division of the psyche differed from Freud's in a number of ways. First of all, Jung viewed the ego as one's sense of self, and suggested that we each possess a sort of "counterego" as well. Jung called this the shadow, a term that refers to personality traits opposite those we reveal via our persona. He thought it not evil in itself, simply "somewhat inferior, primitive, unadapted and awkward." The shadow is an aspect of Jung's concept that all things can be viewed as paired opposites, such as male/female, good/evil, and light/dark.

■ **The shadow** *is Jung's term for the dream representation of those aspects of our personalities that we don't wish to acknowledge.*

Other components of the ego, according to Jung, include the *anima*, which refers to the psyche's female personality traits; and the *animus*, which refers to the psyche's male personality traits. Lastly, Jung called the side of our ego we show to others our persona – the mask we wear for the world.

Opposing this conscious ego, Jung posited an unconscious consisting of a personal unconscious and the **collective unconscious**. According to Jung, we connect to a universal repository of myth and history via symbol and imagery, both in our waking lives and in dreams (these universal symbols are the language of the unconscious and hence, of dreams). Rather than everything being about sex, in other words, Jung asserted that some greater meaning is communicated via dreams.

> **DEFINITION**
>
> The **collective unconscious**, *according to Jung, is the universal storehouse of myth and idea shared by all of humanity. It acknowledges the universal symbolism found in myths from diverse cultures.*

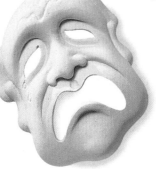

■ **The persona**, *according to Jung, is the mask we wear in society.*

## Personal versus collective unconscious

Jung's view of an unconscious wisdom in each of us is a marked departure from Freud's assumption that we are seething bundles of insecurities that we keep from ourselves. Because Jung's explorations of dreams led him to believe that their purpose was to reveal rather than conceal the workings of the unconscious, he said, "I was never able to agree with Freud that the dream is a 'façade' behind which its meaning lies hidden . . . To me dreams are a part of nature, which harbors no intention to deceive."

There's a decidedly New Age touch (*see p.21*) to Jung's theories. He believed, for example, that every individual could achieve personal transformation, and that dreams were an important vehicle for doing so. In addition, Jung refused to draw boundaries around the various areas of the psyche he defined. In other words, while the personal unconscious and collective unconscious are opposites, they are not in opposition. Rather, these opposites work together to achieve a common goal of holistic health.

*Carl Jung was the first to describe the theme of the Hero's Journey, later developed in more depth by mythologist Joseph Campbell. Jung discovered many such common themes in his study of the mythological base of the collective unconscious.*

## How Jung interpreted dreams

As I've suggested, Jung held that dream images are attempts by the unconscious to communicate with the conscious self. For this reason, Jungian dream interpretation looks at these images to discover what they might reveal about our selves, our relationships with others, and events in our lives. Unlike Freud, Jung approached a dream with no pre-suppositions. Rather than assume that there was one "correct" way of interpreting a dream, Jung insisted that whatever meaning ultimately felt right to the dreamer was the most important.

■ **What your dream reflects** *is, according to Jung, up to you and your interpretation of it.*

*Jung believed that we can interpret our own dreams without the help of an analyst, and suggested conducting "inner dialogues" with dream characters to discover their messages.*

When it came to dream interpretation, Jung liked to quote the Talmud: "The dream is its own interpretation." Not surprisingly then, Jung found a dream's manifest content just as revealing as its latent content. He also asserted that dreams dealt with present problems, not those rooted in infantile repression, and so found that discussing what was going on in the dreamer's life could hold important clues to a dream's meaning.

## Making personal analysis possible

Most important to Jung's method of dream interpretation was his confidence in an individual's unconscious wisdom. Jung firmly believed that we all possess the resources for solving our own problems within our personal and collective unconscious, and that dreams provide blueprints for our conscious to follow. Unlike Freud's insistence on an essentially unhealthy psyche, Jung said that the psyche is quite healthy. Dreams provide prescriptions so that the conscious can remain that way.

Today, there are far more who subscribe to Jung's ideas about dreams and dream interpretation than to Freud's. It's easy to see why: Jung did not insist, as Freud did, that his ideas were an end in themselves or the only way of seeing things. At the same time, Jung's ideas allow the dreamer to participate in dream interpretation and make personal judgments about his or her dreams. Jungian psychologists, then, are less paternalistic than Freudian psychologists, and hence far more accessible.

**INTERNET**

**www.dreamweavers.org**

*Get your own Jungian dream analysis online at the Dream Weavers web site. You can also learn more about Jungian dream analysis and interpreting your own dreams here.*

# MEET THE ARCHETYPES

Jung noted that certain "types" could be found in our mythic dreams, and coined the term "archetype" to describe them. He called archetypes "mythological motifs," symbolic ideas that arise from the collective unconscious and appear repeatedly in story, myth, and dream.

*Jung believes we have archetypal, or "great," dreams at life's turning points. These make us feel as if we have "discovered" something crucial, which we have: our link with all of humanity via the collective unconscious.*

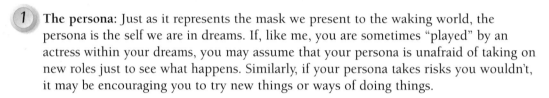

Jung also sketched out seven major archetypal characters, which I'll discuss in more detail in Chapter 5. You might want to think of a film you've seen or book you've read, and see if you can identify a character for each of these archetypes:

1. **The persona:** Just as it represents the mask we present to the waking world, the persona is the self we are in dreams. If, like me, you are sometimes "played" by an actress within your dreams, you may assume that your persona is unafraid of taking on new roles just to see what happens. Similarly, if your persona takes risks you wouldn't, it may be encouraging you to try new things or ways of doing things.

2. **The *anima* and the *animus*:** As we've discussed, the *anima* and *animus* are the female and male sides of each of us, containing all of human potential between them. Mythologically, they are represented by couples like Adam and Eve, Eros and Psyche, and Romeo and Juliet. Dream representations are often commanding people of the opposite sex, a motif which suggests that the dreamer should not ignore his or her "other side."

3. **The divine child:** The divine child symbolizes our true self, innocent and unaware, all too susceptible to the outer world's nastiness. In dreams, the divine child is often represented by an infant or a very young child, who can be thought of as the self we aspired to be before we encountered the world and became cynical.

■ **Adam and Eve** *are classic representations of Jung's concepts of* anima *("feminine" qualities) and* animus *("masculine" qualities). Lucas Cranach the Elder's painting is featured here.*

**4** **The shadow:** In Jung's words, we "have no wish to be" what our shadow represents, so this is the side that we do our best to repress or ignore. In dreams, however, the shadow may assume the role of a frightening antagonist, often someone of the same sex, who thwarts our desires at every turn. Dream shadows often leave us frightened or angry – and so do those shadows we encounter in our waking life. In fact, when we feel anger toward someone else because of a specific personality trait, it is usually because this trait is a shadow trait of our own.

**5** **The trickster:** You'll find the trickster in cultures from ancient Greece to Native America, assuming personas from Mercury, the quicksilver messenger, to Coyote, the wily escape artist of Navajo myth. The trickster aspect often plays subtle – and not-so-subtle – jokes to keep the ego from taking itself too seriously. At the same time, the trickster is a changeling – capable of altering his form at will. He often appears in our dreams when we overreach or misjudge.

■ **Coyote,** *in Native American mythology, is a mischievous, cunning, and resourceful trickster who has many stories associated with him.*

**6** **The wise old man:** Often represented by a teacher, father, or other authority figure, the wise old man appears to show the dreamer that his or her own wisdom lies within. People who report frequent mythic dreams often develop "relationships" with their wise old man; some even give him a name.

**7** **The wise old woman:** Perhaps most familiar to Westerners in her role as Mother Nature, the wise old woman (also called the great mother or old crone) appears across all cultures as the source of fertility and abundance. Because this archetype represents the mystery of birth, however, she also represents the mystery of death and destruction, the opposite side of the great cycle of life. Interestingly, studies have shown that pregnant women often dream of their mothers, possibly signifying this very cyclical nature.

# Adler and the social unconscious

*FREUDIAN AND JUNGIAN dream theories are the mere tip of the iceberg. Those who have explored dreams since these two pioneers almost always use the ideas of one or both of them as takeoff points, then posit some intriguing additions of their own.*

■ **Dreams of flying**, *according to Adler, suggest ambition. Adler made such connections because he believed that what one dreamt was directly connected to one's life.*

Alfred Adler (1870–1937) was, like Jung, briefly closely associated with Freud. While Adler did not give dreams the same level of importance in his psychological theories, he nonetheless had some intriguing ideas about them. Where Freud said everything was about sex, Adler said it was about power. In fact, Adler posited, control is the driving force of the individual, and society the driving force behind the need for control. Dreams are part of one's preparation for mastery over one's life; their function is to prepare the dreamer to meet his future.

Adler's dream theories have influenced many who followed him. That's because he felt that there was a direct connection between the waking life and the dream life rather than the separation Freud suggested.

## Individual Psychology

Adler grouped his theories under the name Individual Psychology. In his view, the conscious and unconscious are not separate; rather, we have the same personality whether awake or asleep. Dreams, therefore, serve as an impetus to waking action; in short, they are problem-solving devices, and nothing more.

*According to Adler, if one's life is relatively problem-free, he or she isn't likely to dream very much. In fact, Adler believed that the less one dreamed, the healthier one was psychologically!*

Adler did not spend much time developing his dream theories, and in fact, unlike other psychological dream theorists, recorded few dreams of his own. Still, his ideas, like those of Freud and Jung, are important starting points for those who followed.

## ADLER'S INTERPRETATIONS

Adler's interpretations of dream imagery were direct. Some examples:

- Falling dreams represent a fear of falling from one's current social status
- Flying dreams signify ambition
- Naked dreams suggest a fear of public ridicule
- Dreams of paralysis show that the current problem is without solution

# Boss and the existential unconscious

*MEDARD BOSS (1903–1990) suggested a connection between dreaming and existentialism – the idea that we each create our own reality. Because existential theory assumes the ability of the individual to make his or her own choices, the dream in this view is a simple vehicle toward making those choices.*

Boss resisted the idea of any symbolic content in dreams or elsewhere, employing instead a WYSIWYG ("what you see is what you get") approach. He considered the dream itself a phenomenon rather than a manifestation of a separate, unconscious mind or self. "In reality there is no such thing as an independent dream on the one hand, and a separate waking condition on the other," he wrote.

Boss's existential unconscious works with the existential conscious to help the individual make the choices that govern his life. In Boss's view, there are no secrets, and ultimately, no mysteries, as to what a dream or its purpose is.

■ **According to Boss,** *a dream has no "layers of meaning" but, like a mirror, simply reflects the image of the dreamer and her existence. Shown here is Peter Layzell's* Reflection.

# Perls and the Gestalt theory of dreams

*FREDERIC ("FRITZ") PERLS (1893–1970) founded the school of Gestalt therapy, which subscribes to a holistic view of the individual. In Perls's view, the mind naturally strives toward an organizing principle, a Gestalt, in other words. To cite Perls's own example, when we see an incomplete series, such as an alphabet with some letters missing, our minds will naturally "fill in the blanks."*

## Perls on dreams

"The dream," Perls wrote, "is a message of yourself to yourself." Perls believed that everything in a dream was an aspect of the dreamer, and every person some aspect of the dreamer's self. Your mother, then, would represent your own maternal instincts (assuming she's a mothering type); your father, your own authority. A chair might represent your tendency to refuse to get up, an airplane your desire for flight.

## Gestalt dream interpretation

Gestalt therapy involves retelling the dream in the present tense. Next, the dreamer describes the characteristics of dream objects as if they are the dreamer him- or herself. If the dreamer dreamed of a garden, for example, he or she might say, "I am lovely and fragrant," or, "I am neglected and overgrown."

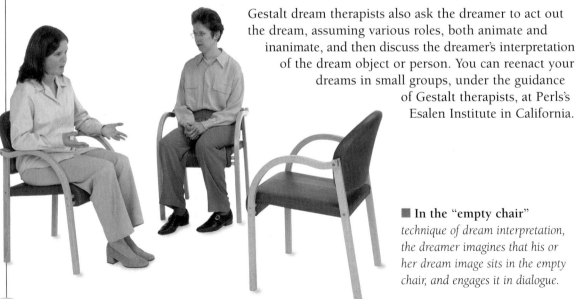

Gestalt dream therapists also ask the dreamer to act out the dream, assuming various roles, both animate and inanimate, and then discuss the dreamer's interpretation of the dream object or person. You can reenact your dreams in small groups, under the guidance of Gestalt therapists, at Perls's Esalen Institute in California.

■ **In the "empty chair"** *technique of dream interpretation, the dreamer imagines that his or her dream image sits in the empty chair, and engages it in dialogue.*

## Your dream, your story

Gestalt dream interpretation also encourages the dreamer to engage in a dialogue with a dream object, with both the object and the dreamer explaining their feelings to each other. In this way, Perls believed, the dreamer can get in touch with his or her deepest feelings and bring them out into the open.

*Perls viewed dreams as "emotional holes" in the dreamer's own unfolding story. Dream symbols, it followed, were generated from the dreamer's life rather than from any collective unconscious.*

# A simple summary

✓ Sigmund Freud was the first to delineate between the conscious and unconscious minds. He believed that dreams were designed to conceal the unconscious's primitive thoughts from the conscious self.

✓ Freud's approach held that all dreams are wish fulfillment brought on by repressed desires. This is now largely considered too reductive.

✓ Carl Jung suggested that we possess both a personal unconscious and a collective unconscious comprised of universal motifs. According to him, dreams used the symbolic content of the collective unconscious to communicate with the conscious mind.

✓ Jungian dream interpretation allows the dreamer to uncover and explore the meanings of his or her dreams.

✓ Alfred Adler believed that all strive toward control over their lives, and that dreams help us achieve that power.

✓ Medard Boss viewed dreams as mirrors of a self which has control over life and its possibilities.

✓ Fritz Perls, creator of Gestalt therapy, suggested that everyone and everything in one's dream is actually an aspect of the dreamer.

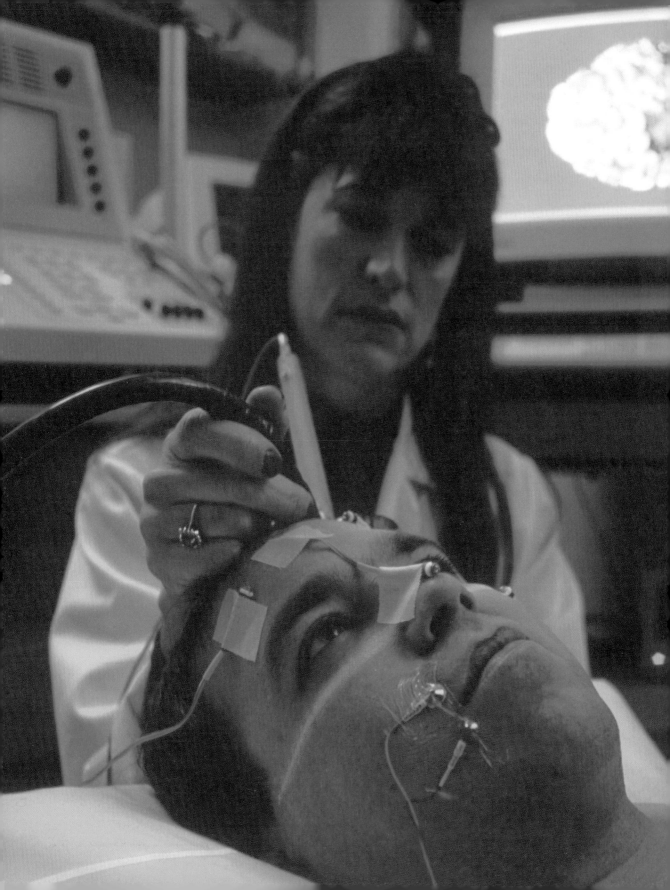

# Chapter 3

# The Dream/Sleep Connection

W HAT HAPPENS WHEN we sleep? Why – and how – do we dream? It's only in the last 50 years that scientists have begun to understand some of the answers to these questions. The "discoveries" of REM (rapid eye movement) and NREM (non-rapid eye movement) sleep, and of the five stages of sleep, have led to a better understanding of "good sleep" versus "bad sleep," and to new ways of helping you sleep – and dream – more soundly. Dreams, too, are being delineated by researchers, and in this chapter, I'll discuss several types of dreams.

## In this chapter...

✓ **The biomechanics of sleeping and dreaming**

✓ **Good sleep, bad sleep**

✓ **Good dreams, bad dreams**

# The biomechanics of sleeping and dreaming

*MAYBE YOU'VE HAD this experience, too. As I lay tossing and turning in bed last night, I went over the reading I'd done yesterday as I prepared to write this chapter. Was I headed for yet another sleepless night? Through my open window, I listened to the first quiet rain of the high desert summer. At the same time, my mind moved rapidly over the events gone by.*

## The hyperactive brain

I reviewed the party I'd thrown and then considered my husband's weekend visit (he lives and works in northern California, while I am in New Mexico). I touched on some friends who'd come to visit, went on to my daughter's still-pending application to an arts' school, and then thought of a house we are considering purchasing. Then I went over a phone call I'd got informing me I'd won a prize for one of my novels. I considered whether I should call the gardens where I'd purchased my none-too-healthy pond plant. This led me to the koi that had recently died, and the dead koi to some of my dogs who have died over the years. That's when I told myself, "Enough!"

*This nighttime routine, when your mind runs over a litany of events that have happened, or may happen, has a name: severe initial insomnia.*

There are many suggestions for curtailing the litany that ends my days: following a bedtime ritual, taking a before-bed bath, unwinding with a series of yoga stretches, reading myself to sleep, or making love. Unfortunately, as noted in the previous paragraph, the last, most attractive option, was unavailable. Instead, I turned on the light and selected a book on my nightstand. I read for close to an hour, during which at some point the rain ceased. I read until I was no longer paying attention to what I was reading. When that happened, I closed the book, turned out the light, and again lay down. Soon, I was asleep.

■ **Yoga is a good way** *of relaxing your body and mind at the end of a busy day. It should help you fall asleep more easily.*

## Charting brain waves

In order to fall asleep, my brain (and yours) needs to, quite literally, slow down. Scientists have charted four levels of brain waves whose level of activity determines waking and sleeping:

- **Beta waves**, which pulsate at 14–30 cycles per second, indicate that we are wide awake and fully mentally engaged
- **Alpha waves** occur when we are awake but relaxed. They pulsate at 8–13 cycles per second
- **Theta waves** occur in a state of light sleep or daydreaming, at a rate of 4–7 cycles per second
- **Delta waves**, at 1–3 cycles per second, indicate deep and dreamless sleep

The phrase "fall asleep" is actually more than a metaphor. To pass from being awake through sleep latency, the period of time between going to bed and falling asleep, into sleep, our brain wave activity must quite literally "fall." Sleep latency normally lasts about five minutes, during which time we move from relaxed alpha waves to light theta waves. While sleep latency occurs only once during the night, the rest of our sleeping time passes through 90-minute cycles, each cycle comprising five stages. During a typical night, we will cycle through these stages five times, for a net sleep of about seven and a half to eight hours.

## Sleep stages – the early research

In the early 1950s, Eugene Aserinsky, a young graduate student at the University of Chicago, noted while conducting an unrelated study that when sleeping infants shifted position during sleep, a period when their eyes could be seen moving under the closed lids immediately followed. Under the direction of physiology professor Nathaniel Kleitman, Aserinsky measured these eye movements using an electro-encephalograph (EEG) and an electrooculogram (EOG), and soon ascertained that the movements were both periodic and cyclic.

■ **The REM breakthrough** *in sleep research happened during Eugene Aserinsky's study of sleeping infants.*

**DEFINITION**

**REM sleep** *is the period of sleeping during which our eyes move rapidly. This period is often when our most vivid dreams occur.*

Intrigued, Aserinsky conducted the same experiments with adults. Everyone, he soon discovered, exhibits the same behavior during sleep. Aserinsky and Kleitman called this period of sleep "rapid eye movement" or ***REM sleep***, and believed it was linked to dreaming. Sleep, they further noted, can be divided into REM and NREM, or non-rapid eye movement, periods. It was found that a sleeper woken up during a REM period could recall his dream very clearly.

## Why do we need REM sleep?

Recent evidence strongly suggests that during REM sleep the mind processes the new information it has acquired during the day. Even during a quiet day spent at home you discover new things: the spot on the wall that needs a touch-up of paint, the time of day your mail is delivered, the most comfortable position for curling up with a good book. During REM sleep, your mind organizes the day's new material and processes it into your larger mental system. This might connect to the fact that children, and infants in particular, sleep longer than adults: they have far more new information to process each day.

# THE FIVE STAGES OF SLEEP

William Dement, who charted the stages of sleep, noted that there are five of them, each characterized by specific changes in brain activity, eye movement, and muscle tone. The first stage is when we fall asleep, but a cycle of the next four stages is repeated a number of times during the course of the night. Brain activity during the different sleep stages can be measured by an EEG, in which electrodes attached to a sleeping person's head measure the level of electric activity in the brain. These can be studied as graphs.

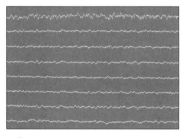

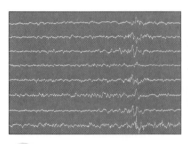

**1** Stage 1

*In stage 1 sleep, brain waves shift from alpha to theta. It takes anywhere from 30 seconds to seven minutes, and we pass from waking into dreaming. The actual "passing" takes less than a second, occurring when serotonin is released to activate the slumber system. Pulse and respiration slow down while the muscles relax, and body temperature and blood pressure fall. Stage 1 sleep occurs only once during the night, unless we wake up.*

**2** Stage 2

*In stage 2, brain waves continue in theta. This is the deeper sleep that follows stage 1 and that begins each subsequent cycle during the night. During stage 2 sleep, our pulse, body temperature, and metabolic activity decrease. The first stage 2 cycle of the night lasts about 50 minutes, and it's still quite a light enough sleep, so that we may be awakened by exterior stimuli – light or sound. The last stage 2 cycle lasts only 25 minutes and is a deeper sleep.*

**Because stage 1 sleep often feels like falling or floating, we are sometimes jolted awake by the sensation.**

## Mental regeneration during REM sleep

Another function of REM sleep seems to be processing creative and visual information. These, and other, right-brain activities are more noticeable during REM sleep than when we are awake or at other times when we are sleeping. Some researchers believe that we go through some emotional fine-tuning during REM sleep as well, and that it helps us tackle stress. Researchers have found that REM sleep deprivation causes over-sensitivity, lack of concentration, and memory loss. Deprivation of REM sleep seems to cause more lasting damage than lack of NREM sleep.

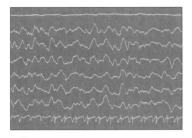

■ **The body regenerates** *during non-REM sleep, while during REM sleep the mind gets revitalized.*

### 3 Stage 3

*Stage 3 has slow delta waves. During this deep, dreamless sleep, researchers believe, our immune system sets to work repairing the day's damage, the endocrine glands secrete growth hormone, and blood is sent to the muscles so that they can be reconditioned as well. This sleep lasts from seven to fifteen minutes during the first two or three sleep cycles only.*

### 4 Stage 4

*Slow delta waves continue in stage 4. This is the last stage of NREM sleep, a deeper sleep than even stage 3 sleep. Recent studies have demonstrated that the more regeneration a body requires, the longer the period of stage 4 sleep. Typically, however, this stage lasts about 12 minutes and occurs only during the first two or three sleep cycles.*

### 5 Stage 5

*This is the stage known as REM sleep, when much of our remembered dreaming occurs. Its onset can be noted by a change in body position or even a sudden jerk of the body. After this movement, the involuntary muscles are paralyzed for the duration of REM sleep. The first REM cycle of the night lasts a few minutes; the last and longest can be as long as an hour.*

*The difference between stage 3 and stage 4 sleep, both states of deep relaxation and physical revival, is that during stage 4 sleep, all metabolic levels are very slow, so that the sleeper is entirely isolated from the world.*

### Discovering the dream/sleep connection

When REM sleep was first discovered, researchers believed that it was the only sleep stage during which dreaming occurred. A number of things about REM sleep led them to this conclusion: the increased brain activity and eye movement, erratic changes in blood pressure and pulse, and rapid, often short, breathing.

*It's now clear that we dream during each sleep stage, but because the mind is bombarded with images, feelings, and sounds during the REM stage, the resulting dreams are more vivid and thus more likely to be recalled upon waking.*

On a more technical level, studies have shown that more vivid dreams occur during REM sleep because the rapid firing of neurons required during the daily information processing in turn releases electrons that generate hallucinations. In other words, these dreams occur as new memories enter our minds. So, many dream researchers believe it's possible that what we know about dreams now is still just the tip of the iceberg.

# Good sleep, bad sleep

*WHILE IT'S NOW CLEAR that sleep recharges the body and mind, one recent study has explored the possibility that stage 3 and stage 4 sleep may in fact be part of the immune system, which protects the body from disease. Some researchers have even suggested that sleep, fever, and the immune system work together against everything from cancer to the flu, which would explain why all we want to do is sleep when we don't feel well.*

### A good night's sleep

Good sleep is good for you, in far more ways than you may have previously considered. That makes getting a good night's sleep every night all the more important. If you're like me, however, getting a good night's sleep may often sound like, well, a dream. Keep reading for help!

■ **Insomnia is not limited** *to difficulty in falling asleep but also refers to waking up repeatedly or very early.*

## The many guises of insomnia

There are many reasons we don't fall asleep or stay asleep, but we can divide them into a few broad categories:

- **Sleep onset insomnia:** This is the inability to fall asleep in the first place
- **Delayed sleep phase insomnia:** If you wake up again and again during the night, you may have delayed sleep phase insomnia
- **Unfinished sleep insomnia:** This refers to the condition when you fall right to sleep, and then wake up way too early
- **Disturbed sleep insomnia:** This is what you have if nightmares are disturbing your sleep

## How to try and get a good night's sleep

You can increase your chances of getting a good night's sleep by following some simple steps:

**1** **Go to bed only to sleep:** No matter what your sleep problem, this is the first cure. Going to bed only to sleep means you should not watch television nor (alas!) read in bed. Further, if you do not fall immediately to sleep, you should get out of bed and go elsewhere in your house. After a few nights of not sleeping well because of this enforced getting out of bed, chances are you will get into a routine of going to bed and falling asleep quickly.

**2** **Don't go to bed until you're tired:** For years, I've teased my mother about meal times: even when we've had an earlier mid-afternoon snack, at 6 o'clock she'll insist it's time to eat. I, on the other hand, eat only if I'm hungry, and have been encouraging my mother to tune in to her internal sensors rather than relying on external ones (like clocks) for determining meal times. Sleep disorder specialists apply the same logic: you retire when you're tired, not just because it's "bedtime." Once you've established a bedtime routine, this will usually be about the same time each night.

■ **Getting a good night's sleep** *may be as simple as establishing a bedtime routine, similar to the bedtime rituals often created for children.*

**3** **Always get up at the same time:** You'd be surprised how many people don't do this, but, it turns out, if you get up at about the same time every day, you'll fall asleep at about the same time every night with a minimum of tossing and turning. It makes good sense to work with your body's natural rhythms, not against them.

4 **Relax!** Just as sleep restores both mind and body, not sleeping affects every aspect of how you feel. You can help avoid a bad night's sleep by de-stressing before you go to bed, instead of waiting until you're lying there trying to fall asleep and at the same time, trying to dredge up the day's problems. In fact, most sleep disorders are a direct result of not being able to let go of those problems. Meditation, deep breathing, yoga, a warm water bath – all can help you relax before you lie down to try to sleep.

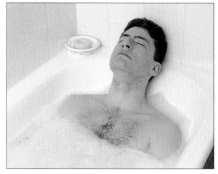

■ **A soak in the bathtub** *might be just the thing to induce sound sleep.*

5 **Thou shalt not nap!** This may break your heart as much as it breaks mine, but the truth is that if you nap, you're fragmenting your sleep instead of concentrating it into one period, which is the body's natural way of sleeping.

*If you feel like napping in the afternoon or early evening, go for a walk around the block instead. Eating lighter meals seems to counteract the urge to nap as well.*

6 **Go to a sleep disorder clinic:** Finally, if your condition is chronic, you may want to consider a sleep disorder clinic. At these facilities, you are first interviewed to find out the nature of your problem. You'll then work with a sleep disorder specialist to create a more effective sleeping routine – and learn how to get a good night's sleep every night in the process.

## Health disorders: snoring and sleep apnea

Sleeping difficulties can have a mind or body basis – or both. It's important to rule out physical causes of insomnia. Some, like snoring, are simple – and simply cured. Others, like sleep apnea, can have more dire consequences than not sleeping well.

**INTERNET**

**www.sleepfoundation .org**

*Want to know more about sleeping or not sleeping? Go to the National Sleep Foundation's web site for up-to-the-minute information on research and resources.*

a **Snoring:** If you're a snorer, you probably know how much you're disturbing others. What you may not realize is how much you may be disturbing yourself. Snoring can indicate a serious disorder, such as sleep apnea, which I'll discuss in a moment. Research has shown that the vast majority of snorers (who in turn make up 25 percent of adults) are middle-aged, overweight, sedentary males. Thus, you may snore because you're out of shape. And snoring, in turn, may be keeping you from getting a good night's sleep.

# STOP SNORING NOW!

Research has shown that adopting a healthful lifestyle cures the vast majority of snorers. What can you do now? You already know what I'm going to say, but I'll state the obvious anyway:

**1** **Lose weight**

*Say no to that second helping of creamy dessert.*

**2** **Quit smoking**

*One cannot overstate the dangers of smoking. Smoking and health – never the twain shall meet.*

**3** **Curb your alcohol intake**

*Cutting down on alcohol is bound to have positive effects on your health.*

**4** **Exercise daily**

*Regular exercise is one way of keeping snoring, among many other problems, at bay.*

 **Sleep apnea:** If your snoring wakes you up, you may have sleep apnea, a disorder that is potentially fatal, because you actually stop breathing while you are sleeping. At its most benign, sleep apnea prevents a good night's sleep because you never move beyond stage 2; you keep waking up instead. But sleep apnea is seldom benign and can even be potentially life-threatening. Doctors note six warning signs of sleep apnea; if you have even one, you should consult your own physician as soon as possible:

- Headache and dryness in throat upon awakening
- Exhaustion, confusion, lethargy, irritability, or other signs of mood change
- Memory impairment or difficulty with hand-eye coordination
- Abrupt nighttime awakening accompanied by shortness of breath
- Daytime fatigue
- Impaired sex drive or impotence

*Sleep disorder clinics can be found in just about every major city. Look in your telephone directory under "Physicians – Sleep disorders" to determine if there's one near you.*

# Good dreams, bad dreams

*WHETHER "ORDINARY" OR "GREAT," all dreams arise from the same source – you. Dreams are classic autobiography, written about you, by you, and for you. Understanding the source of all your dreams is the first step in understanding the dreams themselves. In the chapters that follow, I'll be exploring dreams from several angles. But before I do that, let's look at some of the more common types of dreams that you've likely experienced many times.*

## "Ordinary" dreams

Ordinary dreams are the ones that deal with the everyday: you're waiting at a stoplight, you're brushing your teeth, or just walking down a road. Often, ordinary dreams encompass nothing more than day residue – random details left over from the day's events, whether concerning events or people, situations or feelings. Each of us has our own brand of ordinary dreams. If you begin to keep a dream journal (more about journals in Chapter 4), you'll soon begin to note your own patterns.

*Some dreams that you may consider less-than-ordinary are actually ordinary as well, whether it's making love to someone you don't know or being involved in a car accident or fleeing from someone.*

## "Great" dreams

Great dreams, as defined by Jung, are archetypal. When you wake up from a great dream, you feel as if you now have some profound, previously undiscovered, knowledge – whether about yourself or about the world. It might even change your life forever. Great dreams often feature archetypal characters and scenarios (as I discussed in Chapter 2), and there is often an "aha!" moment within the dream itself:

*I am repeatedly climbing a ladder up to the attic to put away boxes full of stuff, and am annoyed because my brothers keep shaking the ladder. Suddenly, I realize I don't need to put the stuff in the attic – I could use it every day.*

*This is one of my own "great dreams." I woke from this dream knowing I'd realized something very important: that I could use the "stuff in my attic" in my everyday work, writing. My brothers are the archetypal tricksters here, a role they assume in many of my dreams.*

■ **Some frightening dreams** – *of being adrift on a stormy sea or lost in a forest – may be self-preservation dreams, suggesting that you have the means to find your way out of a difficult situation within yourself. Shown above is the painting* The Red Boat *by Odilon Redon.*

## Self-preservation dreams

Self-preservation dreams feature the persona of the dreamer in a dire situation, with no apparent way of escape. They come very close to being nightmares. However, in a flash of insight, the persona will realize that he or she can rescue him- or herself – and does. My dental hygienist told me this marvelous self-preservation dream:

> *I was underwater, chained to the bottom of the ocean. Somehow, I could breathe, but I was caught and I knew I had to get away. Suddenly, I remembered that I'd hidden a knife in the ocean floor. I dug it out, cut the chains, and swam away.*

## Signal dreams

Signal dreams may offer solutions to waking problems, but unlike great dreams, they will not feel profound or life-changing. Here's one such dream narrated to me by a friend:

> *I dreamed I was at a crossroads, uncertain which way to turn. Then I saw a sign with an arrow – "Boston, 31 miles" – and I knew which way to go.*

For this dreamer, who'd been trying to decide whether to accept a job in Boston, the message of the signal dream was clear. Signal dreams show the way for some problem you have encountered in your daily life.

■ **Colors and shapes** *are often seen as we fall asleep or just before we wake up.*

## Hypnogogic and hypnopompic dreams

As we go off to sleep, our minds fill with hallucinatory visions, which Frederic W. H. Myers, author and one of the founders of the Society for Psychical Research, gave the name hypnogogic dreams. Similar visions occur just before waking, and Myers called these hypnopompic dreams.

Artists, writers, and visionaries have reported everything from tiny bright dots to cartoonish characters, as well as waves of color, patterns, shapes, and designs in this brief period of stage 1 sleep. Some have seen writing in languages they do not know; others note archetypal images, as well as mirror and reversed ones. I myself have often almost grasped a hypnogogic image I've seen since I was quite young, which I call "the smoothness." There's no describing this sensation/ sight/feeling – but there is comfort in knowing that what I've sensed is not unusual.

## Recurring dreams

A recurring dream is defined as any dream or dream theme that appears regularly. A 1979 study conducted by dream analyst and author Rosalind Cartwright found that the average duration of recurrent dreams was 8.2 years. Often disturbing in nature, recurring dreams seem to signal some unresolved conflict – though whether of a conscious or unconscious nature is a matter that psychologists continue to debate. Most agree, however, that once the issue is resolved, the dreams will stop as well.

■ **Waking tensions** *and fears may cause us to dream of beasts and fiends, as captured by Goya in* The Sleep of Reason Produces Monsters.

## Nightmares and night terrors

Why do we have nightmares? Research suggests that **nightmares** begin when, as children, we first begin to encounter the larger world and the fear and anxiety that accompany it. There is evidence that children's nightmares are far worse than adults', possibly because children can't put a name to what has frightened them. Of course, as we know, adults do not outgrow nightmares, especially if childhood fears of abandonment, strangers, or dying are not resolved as we grow up.

> DEFINITION
>
> **Nightmares** *are dreams filled with terror and anxiety that the dreamer is unable to resolve within the dream.*

*Some psychologists believe that nightmares are the mind's way of forcing the dreamer to come face-to-face with such unresolved issues, eventually moving beyond the terror toward resolution.*

# A simple summary

✔ Brain activity is recorded in beta, alpha, theta, and delta waves. During sleep, brain wave activity is quite slow, except when we are dreaming.

✔ Sleep occurs in five-stage cycles throughout the night.

✔ The most vivid dreaming occurs during REM (rapid eye movement) sleep, when the mind processes the day's new information.

✔ Body and immune system renewal occur during NREM (non-rapid eye movement) sleep.

✔ Sleeping difficulties can have a mind or body basis – or both. Getting a good night's sleep may be as simple as establishing a bedtime routine or de-stressing before you go to bed.

✔ All dreams arise from the same source – you. Understanding the source of all your dreams is the first step in understanding the dreams themselves.

✔ Recurring dreams and nightmares often deal with unresolved issues in the dreamer's life.

# Chapter 4

# Capturing Your Dreams

MANY ADULTS DON'T remember their dreams simply because they aren't part of a social milieu where dream recall is important. If you're reading this book, you have probably already discovered ways to improve your own dream recall. In this chapter, I'll discuss tried-and-true ways for remembering more of your dreams and for keeping a dream journal, as well as show you how you can start exploring your dreams for personal meaning.

## In this chapter...

✓ **Your dream journal**

✓ **Preparing for dream-sleep**

✓ **Remembering and recording your dreams**

✓ **Reviewing and interpreting a dream**

# Your dream journal

*THE FIRST STEP in getting serious about dream interpretation is to begin keeping a dream journal. You don't need anything fancy – a straight-forward notepad and a pen will serve the purpose: I keep a college-ruled spiral notebook and pen in my nightstand.*

## The equipment

You could use that lovely journal that you hesitated to mar because it was so pretty. Some people prefer to use binder paper that can be inserted into a three-ring notebook, while others keep a tape recorder (voice-activated ones work very well) next to their beds. Bear in mind that this latter method could be disruptive to your sleeping partner, however.

*When I teach writing classes, I often discourage students from buying beautiful journals, because these can discourage spontaneous garble from which good writing emerges. But when it comes to dream journals, it sometimes seems that the more decorative the book, the better.*

To record dreams in the middle of the night, many dream researchers keep simple *light-pens* by their beds, although a small flashlight can work as well. Turning on your nightstand light may literally cast too much light on the subject and cause you to lose part or all of the dream – and it may disturb your sleeping partner, too.

## Six simple do's and don'ts

The most important consideration in recording your dreams is to do so immediately upon waking. With that in mind, here are more pointers for your dream journal:

1. **Don't get out of bed:** Move as little as possible, in fact, as anything that alerts your body to its waking state tends to get in the way of dream recall

2. **If you're in a hurry, make a few notes:** These may be enough to jog your memory later, when you have time

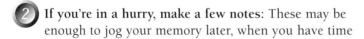
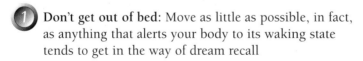

■ **A notebook,** *plain or fancy, and a pen are all you need to get your dream journal going.*

**3** **Record as many details as you can:** Don't judge what's important and what's not – that seemingly throwaway detail may turn out to be the most revelatory aspect of your dream. Include any numbers, colors, clothing, weather, or any other details you can recall

**4** **Note feelings and other sensations:** Everyone processes information differently, and if your memory is not visually oriented, you may recall your dreams less visually as well. Even if you do have a visual memory, try to recall if you felt warm or cold, or angry or elated, or any other feelings or sensations

**5** **Draw pictures:** Even if you're not an artist, a simple line drawing can help you remember a dream later. When it comes to dreams, pictures can be worth a thousand words – or more

■ **A simple sketch** of *your dream will help you recall it later.*

**6** **Include dream fragments, however small:** Even if you can't remember an entire dream, record what you can recall. Dream fragments often lead to the rest of the dream when you review them later

*I can't tell you how many times I've jotted down a few notes about a dream, only to go back to those notes later and have absolutely no recollection of them. But the more you record your dreams, the better you'll get at this.*

## Helping recall

While you won't remember a dream every single day, the dreams you do remember will usually be the last ones you have before waking in the morning. Of course, you may remember a dream if you wake up during the night (it may even have been what caused you to awaken). If so, as quietly as possible, record the dream in your journal. With the routine of writing upon waking, your mind will learn to pay attention to what you're thinking just before you wake up, which is precisely what you desire. The simple fact of keeping a dream journal will help you to remember more of your dreams.

**INTERNET**

http:/www.nauticom.net/ www/netcadet/nltjk.htm

*Run by an ASD-affiliated "dream journalist," this page is on Long Term Journal Keeping and links you to useful articles such as "advice on writing your dreams."*

# Preparing for dream-sleep

*WHILE IT'S CLEAR THAT EVERYBODY dreams, some of us remember our dreams more easily than others. A large part of learning to capture your dreams involves making yourself more receptive to doing so. I've already mentioned the first step, keeping a dream journal. Now let's take a step backwards, to the time just before you fall asleep. Ensuring that your body, mind, and soul are prepared to dream when you go to sleep can enhance your dream recall still more.*

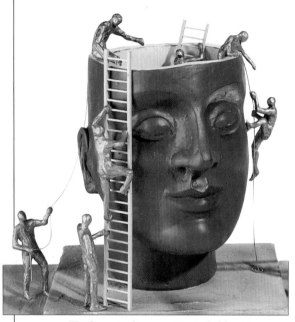

■ **The mind's capacity** *to hold petty as well as significant information is immense. The most trivial to the most profound thoughts can keep you awake.*

## "Monkey mind"

If you can't fall asleep, you can't dream. And chances are, if you can't fall asleep, you're a victim of what Zen practitioners call "monkey mind" – the relentless clutter of trivia that stands between your conscious and unconscious. My own "monkey mind," for example, likes nothing better than to review not only the day's events, but my entire life, and then to worry about the future as well.

## Goodbye to monkey mind

Creating the right dream-sleep environment starts with getting rid of "monkey mind" before you go to bed. Be aware that various daytime factors can affect your ability to sleep and dream:

- Stress
- Fatigue
- Medication
- Alcohol

*Alcohol is a big no-no for a dream "setting" because it disrupts your sleep patterns, and can wake you up in the middle of the night. If you want to have an alcoholic drink, have it well before bedtime.*

# PREPARING BODY, MIND, AND SOUL TO DREAM

Dream researchers have discovered a number of ways to relax the mind (and the body and soul) before you lay your head on your pillow. Chances are, you'll find one (or more) you can adapt to your own purposes.

### 1 Have a warm cuppa

*Once again, Mother was right: preparing your body to sleep may be as simple as drinking a warm glass of milk before you go to bed. If you're lactose-intolerant, of course, you'll need to drink something other than milk. Just be sure to avoid anything caffeinated, including most teas, as these will stimulate your body rather than relax it.*

### 2 Don't go to bed until you feel sleepy

*If you're like me, you'll know it's time because your mind wanders from the book you're reading. Television, by the way, is NOT recommended: it dulls the mind rather than relaxes it.*

### 3 Mentally review your day

*Before you lie down, go through the day's events. Many people find it helpful to actually make some notes on the day's highs and lows, and some do this in their dream journal. Not only does this simple exercise help clear the mind of the day's events, it also passes them to the unconscious for processing.*

### 4 Read your dream journal

*Going through your dream journal before you turn out the light is also a good way to encourage yourself to remember your dreams. The gentle reminder of your own particular dream themes seems to serve as stimulus for further work on those themes.*

### 5 Set an alarm

*If you set an alarm to go off a little earlier than you normally awaken, chances are quite good you will wake up in mid-dream, and thus remember the dream. As you may recall from Chapter 3, the longest REM sleep period is the last one, just before you wake up in the morning. This is when we have our longest and most complex dreams.*

# TECHNIQUES TO ENHANCE DREAMING

The power of suggestion should not be underestimated: simply suggesting to yourself before you go to sleep that you will remember your dreams is often enough for you to do precisely that. At the same time, a little meditation never hurt anyone, and some meditation that helps you to both sleep and dream can be just as simple. Try the following, adapted from *The Dream-Working Handbook* (see *Further Reading* at the end of this book), and see how it works for you:

**1 Deep breathing**

*Lie down, close your eyes, and breathe in and out deeply. Consciously follow your breath as it enters and exits your body.*

**2 Tensing and relaxing alternately**

*After a few minutes, tighten your toes as you breathe in, then relax them as you breathe out. Do the same with your feet, then your calves, knees, and upward, working your way to your head until every inch of your body has been tensed and then relaxed.*

**3 Dream mantra**

*Many find it helpful to recite a personal dream mantra before they fall asleep. The words of such a mantra should be natural to you, while at the same time have a calming, soothing, rhythmic effect. Some suggestions: Tonight I shall remember my dreams. My dreams and I are one. Dreams, be mine. Oh, my dreams, reveal myself to me.*

**4 Willing yourself to remember**

*Tell yourself that you will remember a dream in the morning. If you'd like, picture yourself waking up and writing that dream in your journal.*

*The most important thing you can do to prepare yourself to sleep and dream is to have a regular bedtime ritual. Whether it's brushing your teeth or wishing upon a star, keep your ritual consistent and your dream recall will be consistent as well.*

### Trivia...

K.I.S.S. Guide to Yoga author Shakta Khalsa says that her teacher encourages getting up at 4 a.m. for yoga and meditation. The yogis understand that this prime dream time is naturally an excellent time for meditation.

# Remembering and recording your dreams

*PART OF THE REASON it's so difficult to remember our dreams is that our long-term memories are disengaged when we dream. That's right: recent research has shown that before dreaming begins, norepinephrine and serotonin, the chemicals responsible for long-term memory, are suppressed.*

## Practice makes perfect

These facts make recording your dreams in a journal all the more important. As with anything, practice improves the skill, and it appears that if you make it a practice to remember and record a dream every morning on waking, you are far more likely to remember a dream to record.

*Recent studies indicate that B vitamins, especially vitamin B-6, enhance dream recall. As with any change in vitamin intake, be sure to check with your doctor before you do so.*

## Keep writing

Obviously, it's best to record as much of your dream as you can recall as soon as you wake up, but if you can't, write down what seem to be the most compelling and important details, and return to the dream as often as you're able during the day to capture more. Sometimes, a routine early morning activity will result in spontaneous dream recall. Fragments of dreams may occur to you during your morning exercises, while you're showering, or while you're walking the dog. For this reason, it's a good idea to keep pen and paper within easy reach no matter where you are.

■ **Dream recall** *may occur any time – while you're walking down a street on your way to work, or while you're brewing a cup of tea.*

# DREAM-CATCHING

If a dream seems just out of your grasp as you awaken, there are a number of things you can do to try to bring it back:

**1 Lie very still**

*Don't open your eyes. Gently ask yourself what you have been dreaming.*

**2 Let the mind take over**

*Try to keep the events of the coming day from intruding. Allow your mind to wander.*

**3 Think of those close to you**

*Think about the important people in your life. If they appear in "unreal" situations, chances are what you're seeing occurred in a dream.*

**4 Change your position**

*If you still can't recall your dream, slowly and without opening your eyes, change your position into your customary sleeping one. This is often enough to stimulate dream recall. Try it and see!*

**5 Write down whatever you recall**

*As soon as a dream fragment occurs to you, reach for your journal and write it down. The simple act of recording that first fragment often encourages further recollection. Write down anything and everything you recall, no matter how meaningless it may seem.*

*I find that giving every dream a title helps. Don't think about it too much, just name your dream. Some of my recent dream titles include "The Flood," "The Attic," "The Tea Party." You'll find that this shorthand will help you recall a dream with little effort.*

■ **What would you call this dream?** *Pastoral landscape, flowering wilderness, sleeping in the meadow . . . ? The artist, Magdolna Ban, calls it Lena's Dream.*

# Reviewing and interpreting a dream

*CAPTURING A DREAM is only the beginning, which is why the rest of this book is devoted to various ways of working with your dreams. Before you can begin that work, however, you'll want to establish a method of noting certain things about each dream.*

## A simple dream-review form

Methods of reviewing and interpreting dreams are as numerous as dream researchers and theorists. If you are someone who craves order, you may find it helpful to create a simple form. You might want to include questions such as these:

- Does the dream have any connection with something that happened the day before?
- Are the dream events possible or imaginary?
- Is the dream difficult to understand?
- Do I know the people in the dream?
- Are the people in the dream from my past or my present?
- Is there something I am particularly worried about?
- Do I play a prominent role in the dream?
- What are the symbols in the dream?
- Do I act or react in the dream?
- What is the dream's theme?

The first question is designed to establish the context of the dream. If you know what it's about, after all, interpretation is much easier. Say, for example, you had an argument with your spouse the day before, and then dream that you can't find him or her. Your interpretation of the dream might then be that you fear arguing with your spouse could lead to losing him or her.

■ **Lewis Carroll's** Alice-in-Wonderland *is a story that uses the bizarre characters and events that can appear in dreams to great literary effect.*

## Rating your dream

After you've established the context of your dream, you can use the remaining questions to help you rate it. To begin with, dreams can usually be categorized as either/or in a number of ways.

*a* **Subjective/objective:** In general, if a dream is difficult to understand, the dream events are imaginary, or the people unknown, the dream deals with a subjective issue that's important to you personally. Easy-to-understand, realistic dreams peopled with those you know are considered more objective dreams whose meaning has less personal resonance. Many dreams, of course, are both subjective and objective.

*b* **Compensatory/confirmatory:** When a dream doesn't seem to make sense to you, or if you act out of character, the dream is likely compensating for your usual behavior. When you can connect dream events to a waking concern, however, it is more likely a confirmatory dream, telling you that the path you're on is right for you.

*c* **Transitory/enduring:** When a dream deals with an enduring issue, it is often peopled with those from your past, or even people you don't know (actors from film and television fall into this latter category, as well as other celebrities). The more contemporary the dream people, places, and situations, on the other hand, the more likely the dream deals with a transitory issue.

*d* **Reactive/proactive:** If you passively go along with whatever happens in the dream without actively responding, or if you are an observer of the dream's action, the dream is considered to be reactive. However, when you take part in the dream action it is called a proactive dream.

■ **In a proactive dream** *you actively participate in the events taking place in your dream. This may be to change a situation, resist it, or move it along.*

Once you have determined if your dream is subjective or objective, compensatory or confirmatory, transitory or enduring, and reactive or proactive, you will achieve some sort of "dream rating."

*A subjective, confirmatory, transitory, proactive dream acts to confirm your current behavior in a waking situation. A subjective, compensatory, enduring, reactive dream, however, will likely deal with a larger, more subtle issue with which you have not yet come to grips.*

## Symbol and metaphor

Okay, let me say it up front: I hate the term "symbol." I find it reductive and limiting, and discourage my students from using it. Instead, I prefer the term "metaphor," which I consider more open-ended and all-encompassing. In other words, sure, water may "symbolize" emotion, but sometimes, it's just the place where a boat is floating.

That said, developing and understanding your own personal metaphors will help you interpret your dreams far more effectively than reductive dream dictionaries or symbol systems. But how do you discover what those personal metaphors are? The answer, not surprisingly, is in your dreams.

■ **Different objects or creatures** *in your dreams may have very obvious symbolic meanings but you should avoid this kind of crude interpretation.*

## JUST SAY "NO" TO DREAM DICTIONARIES

Because dream dictionaries tend to reduce everything to a universal symbol, they don't often help you interpret your own dreams. Instead, try creating a personal dream dictionary of your own metaphors. Here's an example. Where a dream dictionary might say that dreaming of a car means you will take a journey, your personal dream dictionary might include more than one car, each with its own special meaning. Your first car, that 1968 VW bug, might represent your carefree youth, while your father's Buick could stand for conventional thinking. Then there's that silver Alfa Romeo; you might think of that as your "dream car." If you looked in a dream dictionary after dreaming of any of these cars, you might be left wondering where you'll be going. Your personal dream dictionary will remind you that "wherever you go, you are there."

## Your personal metaphors

As you keep your dream journal, you'll naturally want to read back through your dreams to discern patterns and themes. It's in these patterns that you'll begin to notice your personal metaphors. Look at the examples in the box "Just say 'no' to dream dictionaries" on the previous page – each car has a meaning all its own. Different people can represent different aspects of yourself. Even though my father died 25 years ago, for example, he makes fairly regular appearances in my dreams. Recently, however, as I've approached the age he was when he died, our "dream" relationship has changed. Often, now, I represent the older and wiser me, while he represents the me who is "stuck in the past."

*Personal metaphors can take many forms: a certain person may stand for a certain attitude; a certain house in which you once lived may represent a feeling or emotion.*

You may find it helpful to organize your personal dream dictionary in some way, although it's certainly not a necessity. Some people use index cards, arranged alphabetically. Others simply keep related lists, such as the various cars above. Frankly, I haven't written down my own dream metaphors, but then, I have quite a good memory.

## Exploring the feelings in your dreams

While I've concentrated on dream imagery for most of this chapter, it's important to be aware of how you're feeling in your dreams, too. Feelings are one of the reasons dreams stay with us long after we awaken – even when we can't quite recall the dream's images. Some schools of psychology hold that feelings are what dreams are all about, whether they be unresolved, unexpressed, or simply unconscious.

Dream feelings are a lot like waking feelings: they can make us feel very good, and they can make us feel very bad. Sometimes, dream feelings seem to be the opposite of how we "should" be feeling; in that case, the dream was probably a compensatory one. When we're young and haven't yet learned how to deal with our feelings, what happens in dreams can be very confounding or frightening, as you may recall from some still-vivid dreams or nightmares of your own.

■ **Dream emotions** *often stay with us through the day; what we feel in our dreams is as important as what we see.*

## Recording the emotions

Dream emotions can be not only roller-coaster, but also confusing. For this reason, as you record your dreams, always note how you felt during the dream, as well as how you felt when you woke from it.

*Recording your dream feelings can help you understand the tone of your dream. If your brother is killed in a dream and you feel relieved, it doesn't mean you want your brother dead. Rather, it may indicate that you no longer need the aspect of yourself represented by your brother in the dream.*

And now, armed with all these notes about your dreams, you're ready to take the next step: using your dreams to discover yourself. We shall discover this in the next part of the book, *Dream Interpretation*.

# A simple summary

✓ Using a dream journal to record your dreams immediately upon waking will also help improve your dream recall.

✓ Stress, fatigue, medications, and alcohol can impair your ability to sleep and dream.

✓ Preparing for dream-sleep involves letting go of the day's stress and activities and establishing a regular bedtime routine.

✓ Meditating before sleep is a good way to encourage yourself to remember your dreams.

✓ Determining if your dream is subjective or objective, compensatory or confirmatory, transitory or enduring, and reactive or proactive will result in a sort of "dream rating."

✓ Developing and understanding your own personal metaphors will help you to interpret your dreams far more effectively than reductive dream dictionaries or symbol systems.

✓ Recording your dream feelings as well as your dream images can help you understand the tone of your dream.

# PART TWO

# Dream Interpretation

HOW DO YOU INTERPRET the people, images, places, actions, and feelings in your dreams?

# Chapter 5

# The People in Your Dreams

I F YOU WERE TO BE asked the single most important aspect of your dreams, chances are you'd answer, "people." Whether you agree with the theories of Fritz Perls, Carl Jung, or dream researcher Calvin Hall regarding the meaning of these people, or are quite simply curious to know just what all those friends, relatives, and strangers are doing in your dreams, your questions will begin to be answered here.

*In this chapter...*

✓ **You are your dreams**

✓ **Archetypes in your dreams**

✓ **Family members in your dreams**

✓ **Other people in your dreams**

# You are your dreams

*BY NOW, IT'S PROBABLY clear that, as long as people continue to dream, dream theorists will have varying theories about what dreams and their content mean. Still, it's possible to draw some broad conclusions from their various ideas, the first being that you are your dreams. To put this another way, your dreams have particular meaning for you, or, as Fritz Perls so succinctly said, dreams are "a message of yourself to yourself."*

■ **The people in your dreams** *may be "playing" themselves or may represent some aspects of you.*

It follows that the key to understanding your dreams is learning to decipher these messages. As I noted in Chapter 4, dream dictionaries are far too reductive for this purpose (*see also* p.69). Instead, you'll want to examine each dream and its cast of characters individually. Sometimes, for example, you are yourself. At other times, someone else is playing you. And, still other times, you are everyone in your dreams. How do you figure out, then, not only who's who, but who's you? And what does this all mean for you, the dreamer? Let's examine the people in your dreams in order to discover some possibilities.

## You as yourself

In most of your dreams, you are represented by your persona, a character archetype that your dreaming mind recognizes as yourself. Your ***dream persona*** may or may not resemble you physically, and may or may not behave as you would, but you will nonetheless "know" that this character is you.

Within the dreamscape, your persona will encounter situations and other characters, and will act and react accordingly. When you awaken, though, you are often left with no more than a feeling: "That was odd" or "How silly of me," or "Now I understand." Once you've recorded the dream in your dream journal, however, you can begin to explore the people in your dreams, including yourself, and move beyond initial reactions.

# I, ME, MYSELF . . . IN MY DREAMS

One way of looking at your dream persona is to ask whether or not you yourself would behave the way "you" did in your dream. Here's an example:

*I was driving along with some friends at night and we came to this stop light. There were a lot of people out and a lot of noise coming from here and there. The street looked a little unfamiliar and the noise was really loud. I stopped at this stop light and all of a sudden saw a friend who I rarely see riding in the car next to me. So I waved, and he was out of my sight. So I drove on and heard men yelling at each other very violently. I drove slowly by, not really knowing what was going on.*

*Then I saw the men wrestling on the ground with each other and the cops were telling everyone to keep on going; the man had a gun. Then a shot came right towards me. The bullet hit me on the side of my head and I felt the entire impact: the blood, the pain, and the adrenaline, but also sadness. That's when I woke up.*

The dreamer, a 22-year-old woman, noted that she had this dream after a week of "really no sleep at all." Plus, she added, "I was in a foreign place." When I asked her if she felt as if parts of her life were out of her control, she said that yes, she did sometimes feel that way, but added that she "kind of liked it that way" (ah, to be 22 again . . . ).

For our purposes here, the key questions to ask are whether the persona seen in the dream is the dreamer herself, and whether the dream persona behaves as the dreamer would. In this dream, the dreamer is driving the car, that is, is "in control" of her forward motion, when a shot hits her on the side of her head. She feels everything about the shot's impact, including "sadness." Coupled with her feeling that life is a bit out of control but that she likes it that way, these images suggest that she feels she is "in the driver's seat," while at the same time open to the unexpected that can come with the way she is living right now – even though she knows that not everything that comes will make her happy.

■ **Your dream persona** *may react in a way that seems very different from how your waking self would react to certain situations.*

## You as another

Sometimes, your own situation is represented by someone else in your dream.
To illustrate, here's a recent dream of my own:

> *Joanie and Rich (good friends of ours who live in southwest Colorado) have fallen in love with a house, but there are all sorts of complications. The seller is out of town, and they must deal with his sister, someone with whom both Joanie and Rich have not always had good business relations, and who lives in another, not so nice, part of town. There are also problems with the roof, and while a Propanel roof would be the obvious choice, they can't have one. Toward the end of the dream, it also occurs to me that they may also have trouble selling the house they've recently built.*

According to dream researcher Calvin Hall, whose work I'll explore more fully in Chapter 8, the other people in our dreams take on different roles for different situations. My good friend Joanie, for example, sometimes represents herself – that is, my good friend Joanie who lives in Colorado – but at other times she represents other aspects of herself and sometimes aspects of me. Keeping this in mind, when we discuss this dream we find:

(a) In this dream, Joanie and her husband Rich, who are freer with their money than we are, are not only themselves, but Bob and I as well. That's because Bob and I recently made an offer on a house with all sorts of problems, including a leaking roof (Joanie and Rich, who were visiting at the time, went to look at the house with us before we made the offer).

(b) The day before this dream, I had spoken at length to a local realtor about the house we'd made an offer on (our low bid was rejected), so it was clearly on my mind when I went to sleep.

(c) To my unconscious, Joanie and Rich played Bob and me in this dream because to my unconscious they apparently represent people who spend money more freely than we do, which in this case may not be wise – especially, it seems, because of the roof.

(d) In the dream, the most obvious solution to that problem (getting a Propanel roof) isn't possible because of my waking knowledge that Joanie and Rich's restrictive covenants don't allow Propanel roofs.

In the event, it's probably just as well our offer was rejected! Six months later, as I work on the final version of this book, that house still hasn't sold – for more reasons than its roof.

***In dream researcher Calvin Hall's view, the people in one's dreams assume more than one role, and can also represent the dreamer him- or herself.***

## You as everyone in your dreams

When is a house not a house? When it's you, the dreamer!

*Gestalt founder Fritz Perls, whom we first met in Chapter 2, asserted that every aspect of a dream represents the dreamer – not just the people, but everything: that house, those clouds, that ladder, and that stranger.*

To see how Gestalt dream therapy works, let's apply it to a dream sent to me by a male high school friend:

*I was alone in a swampy, vine-filled location. As I made my way through the swamp something very weird began to happen. The vines started to swell and forms began to appear. I wasn't frightened at all; in fact I was very curious. The forms were taking the shape of people, male and female. Soon, I was surrounded by all these figures, and I started to recognize them. They were people I knew, all of them. Friends, associates, relatives all forming before my eyes. They weren't talking, but they were alive and moving. Unfortunately, I woke before I could figure out what was going on.*

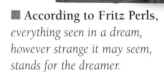

### The Gestalt interpretation

Who are these people? Had the dreamer recently seen *The Night of Living Dead*? (He says no.) According to Perls, the vine-creatures here are aspects of the dreamer himself.

■ **According to Fritz Perls,** *everything seen in a dream, however strange it may seem, stands for the dreamer.*

*a* The dreamer begins the dream alone, in a morass that practically all dream analysts would agree represents his unconscious.

*b* It's within his unconscious then, that the dream metamorphosis takes place. Various aspects of the dreamer "grow" from his unconscious, and the dreamer realizes that he "recognizes" and "knows" all of these aspects. As they aren't "talking" yet, however, they haven't yet reached the dreamer's conscious mind.

If the dreamer were to take this dream to a Gestalt therapy session, he would be asked to act out the dream, assuming all of the roles within it, including the vines and the vine-people. He might also be encouraged to question some of the dream characters and then answer them to determine what aspect(s) of himself they represent. Waking up "before (the dreamer) could figure out what was going on" is not an important issue for Gestalt dream therapists. By working with the dream while awake, the dreamer can discover its meaning.

# Archetypes in your dreams

*IN CHAPTER 2, I INTRODUCED YOU to Carl Jung's archetypes, aspects of the Jungian collective unconscious, which is itself a sort of universal storehouse of myth and idea shared by all of humanity. Jung defined seven major archetypes:*

- The persona
- The *anima* and the *animus*
- The trickster
- The wise old woman

- The divine child
- The shadow
- The wise old man

***The idea behind archetypal characters in dreams is that while dreams are profoundly personal, our personal experiences often touch on universal themes.***

By understanding how these mythological motifs operate, we can learn more about ourselves and our own particular situation. In other words, archetypes offer us another way of understanding the people in our dreams. You've already learned how the persona archetype can appear in your dreams. Now let's take a look at the other six archetypes and explore them in more detail.

## The divine child

According to Jung, the presence of an infant in a dream can be considered an archetypal representation of the dreamer's innocence or naiveté. The divine child archetype in its purest form is not just vulnerable, however; it represents the transforming power of pure self, "before the Fall," so to speak. To dream that you yourself are a baby does not necessarily mean you feel helpless, but rather are open to all possibilities.

■ **The infant Jesus** is, *of course, one of the most obvious examples of Jung's theory of the divine child; he is vulnerable, yet has the power to change the world for the better.*

Some Jungian therapists propose that dreams which include a divine child archetype can serve as reminders of how far we have strayed from our original ideals. The divine child can represent a time when ego was less important, and the self more fully integrated.

*In* Pregnancy & Dreams *(see* Further Reading *at the end of the book), Patricia Maybruck points out that in early stages of pregnancy, women often dream of themselves as infants. She suggests that this may be because they are not yet psychologically ready to visualize themselves caring for an infant of their own.*

## The *anima* and the *animus*

According to Carl Jung, ignoring our unconscious oppositions can lead to distorted perceptions and unrealistic expectations of others. Archetypally, the persona is considered the outward face of the self, while the inward face is represented by the *anima* (female) in males and the *animus* (male) in females.

One of the more obvious ways you might dream of your *anima* or *animus* is when your dream persona is of the opposite sex. But there are other ways your opposite reveals itself in your dreams as well. For example, you might find yourself in your spouse's closet – or wearing your spouse's clothes – or exhibiting opposite-sex physical traits, such as a woman growing a beard or a man growing longer hair.

### Why do we dream of our *anima*/*animus*?

Dreaming of your *anima* or *animus* can suggest a need to consciously acknowledge your own *anima* or *animus* qualities. For instance, for men, this might mean learning to express emotion, while for women, it might involve learning to assert oneself. For either sex, accepting the *anima/animus* is often about perceptions of self-control versus a willingness to accept possibility.

■ **Art and literature** *are filled with tragic couples who represent the* anima *and* animus. *The subliminal suggestion seems to be that our completion (our* anima *or* animus) *lies within ourselves.*

## The shadow

We have a natural inclination to assume that our shadow self is "bad" while our persona is "good," but this is not precisely the case. Rather, the shadow represents the side of ourselves that we try to keep hidden because we consider its instincts unappealing or unnatural. After all, Jung called the shadow the most "animal" of the archetypes.

*It's important to note that the opposition represented by the shadow is often an aspect the dreamer needs to incorporate in some way. In fact, when our persona and our shadow are working together, psychic wholeness can be the much-desired result.*

In dreams, the shadow can assume a variety of guises.

*a* **The pursuer or the bully:** Sometimes the shadow archetype leads the dreamer into a confusing maze and then disappears, or runs ahead of the dreamer, throwing obstacles in his or her path

*b* **The persona:** Dream shadows can also take the form of the persona, with the dreamer behaving in ways he or she never would in waking life

*c* **The intimate friend or relative:** A dream shadow may take the form of someone to whom the dreamer is close, such as a brother, sister, or good friend

*d* **Animals:** Dream shadows are even played by one's faithful pets, who may suddenly assume the frightening proportions of animals in a horror movie

■ **The silent observer** *in a dream may represent an aspect of the shadow self. According to Jung, it suggests an unconscious urge that has not yet reached consciousness.*

# The trickster

The trickster archetype is considered by some to be an aspect of the shadow. That's because this shape-shifting prankster can, like the shadow, be malicious or cruel. The difference, however, can be found in why one or the other archetype appears in a dream. The trickster makes an appearance only when the ego has backed itself into a corner; the shadow is with us always.

Like the shadow, the trickster represents our personal potential for transformation, but unlike the shadow, the trickster is a mocking presence, not a threatening one. When the trickster appears in a dream, the dreamer's emotions may include discomfort or embarrassment, but the fear often engendered when the shadow appears isn't likely to occur.

## When does the trickster appear?

The trickster archetype most often appears when we're uncertain about a new direction we're taking. It's quite possible, for example, that one of my brothers might appear in my dreams while my husband and I consider whether we want to make another offer on the house I dreamed about recently.

Or I might dream of a fiddler on the roof of that particular house. Either way, the dream archetype would be suggesting that I'm still undecided about whether to take this very big step. (That is, is it literally a step off the roof?)

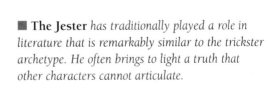

■ **The Jester** *has traditionally played a role in literature that is remarkably similar to the trickster archetype. He often brings to light a truth that other characters cannot articulate.*

*In my dreams, the trickster role is often assumed by one or both of my younger brothers, or sometimes by one of my stepbrothers. It seems that the clown aspect of the self and our unconscious feelings about our siblings are closely related.*

# WISE OLD MAN TELLS ALL!

When you awaken from a dream involving a wise old man archetype, you may feel as if you've acquired some special knowledge. For example, one woman dreamed that she came upon a large book, lying open on a stand in a dusty old library. When she dusted off the cover, she discovered the author's name was "Augustus," and when she opened the book, she found it full of answers to questions she'd never asked. She awoke from this dream feeling as if someone had indeed shown her "the answer" – even though she couldn't say precisely just what that "answer" was.

## The wise old man

If you found Obi-Wan Kenobi the most appealing character in the *Star Wars* saga, it may be because he represented what Jung called a mana personality, the most powerful representation of primal growth – and destruction. Obi-Wan is just one incarnation in a long line of wise old men, beginning with the Old Testament God and continuing on through Dante's Virgil and the wizard Merlin, to Dumbledore of the Harry Potter series, and *The Lord of the Rings*'s Gandalf.

Carl Jung himself often conversed with a wise old man named Philemon whom he first encountered in his dreams. Horned like a bull and winged like an angel, Philemon was characterized by Jung as an extremely learned old man who held four keys, each poised and ready to unlock a door. Like Philemon, wise old men can appear in your dreams to reveal the "keys" to your own unconscious. They may appear quite literally as guides, or they may be disguised as other strong male figures in your life, including your own father, an influential college professor, or your old pediatrician or veterinarian.

■ **Santa Claus is one** *of the many guises of the wise old man in literature and popular culture – the fatherly or grandfatherly figure who rewards you for good behavior and comes bearing gifts.*

## The wise old woman

Variously referred to as the great mother or the old crone, often disguised as a witch or a beggar, the wise old woman is as prevalent an archetype today as she was for the original readers of *Grimm's Fairy Tales*. In fact, more than once when I've worked on a character exercise with groups of fourth-graders, the resulting archetype was some variant of a 102-year-old, toothless, but wise bag lady who lived in a dumpster in New York City. The wise old woman appears in our dreams to guide or nurture – or to devour or possess. Many experts believe that this archetype is rooted in the real mother, the giver of life who is also jealous of our growth away from her.

■ **The witch is** *a good example of the negative aspects of the wise old woman – dominant, powerful, and threatening.*

# Wise old women through the ages

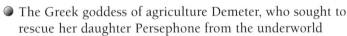

Mythological and literary wise women include:

- ● The Greek goddess of agriculture Demeter, who sought to rescue her daughter Persephone from the underworld
- ● Juliet's nurse in *Romeo and Juliet*, who helped the young lovers plan the elopement that was ultimately their demise
- ● The many variants of wicked stepmothers who pervade both *Grimm's Fairy Tales* and their Disney adaptations
- ● The Queen of Hearts in *Alice-in-Wonderland*

■ **Attis is the Egyptian Goddess** *of Fertility. Almost every culture in the world has a goddess of fertility or an "earth mother" type of deity.*

■ **Dream archetypes** *may be rooted in the dreamer's religio-cultural tradition. Images of cherubs and angels (representing the divine child and the wise old man or woman archetypes) might well occur in the dreams of a person with a Christian heritage. Shown here is* Paradise, *a wall painting by Domenico Veneziano and Jacopo Tintoretto.*

# Family members in your dreams

*WHEN FAMILY MEMBERS APPEAR in your dreams, they may be playing themselves, aspects of yourself, or even you. As I mentioned earlier in this chapter, by way of example, my brothers often assume the trickster role in my dreams, shaking me out of my complacency. The important people in your life can quite literally help to reveal yourself to you in your dreams.*

## The familiar faces

When your child appears in your dream, he or she is not always him- or herself, although that is often the case. Your child can also represent a more vulnerable you, or someone you consider younger and less wise.

If your parent or stepparent is in your dream, they may show that you are acquiring knowledge or understanding that you previously thought only they could have. By way of illustration, we can discuss the end of a dream my 22-year-old daughter Kaitlin recently related to me ("Bob" in her dream is my husband, Kaitlin's stepfather):

■ **There are some obvious archetypal roles** *for family members – father, uncle, or grandfather as wise old man; mother, aunt, or grandmother as wise old woman; sister, brother, or cousin as persona, shadow, trickster, anima, or animus; and infant or child as divine child or trickster.*

*I was on the subway again delivering the last package. Bob was on the train also. Somehow Bob got shot and then everything came back to myself at the beginning of the dream. I was in the same room again. All I could think was, "Now I have to tell my mother her husband is dead." So I brought my mother into the room and told her Bob was shot. She said, "No he's not, he's right . . . " Then I woke up.*

Kaitlin has just been accepted to art school (which is located next to a subway station), and will be moving from Virginia to San Francisco to attend. Kaitlin's decision to pursue art as a career is a big step for someone as practical as she is. Her parental examples are myself, who didn't begin writing full time until recently; her father, who continues to practice law full time while writing as a hobby; and Bob, her stepfather, who pursues his music on weekends. To me, this dream suggests that while those who don't pursue their artistic side (represented here by Bob) are "killed," those who do (represented here by me) will discover that it doesn't mean "death" after all.

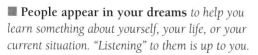

***Don't assume that just because two 22-year-old women have dreamed of someone getting shot, it's a common motif in the dreams of 22-year-old women. While Jung insisted there are no coincidences, I believe one should never say "never."***

# Other people in your dreams

*WHILE WE'LL BE EXPLORING other people in your dreams in more depth in Chapter 8 when we look at dream relationships, this is a good place to explore some of the more mysterious people who appear in your dreams, whether they are absolute strangers, actors or characters from books, or people you haven't thought about in years.*

■ **People appear in your dreams** *to help you learn something about yourself, your life, or your current situation. "Listening" to them is up to you.*

# "WHY DO I KEEP DREAMING ABOUT 'KATHERINE'?"

**Dreams** *often dredge up long-forgotten people from our past.*

A friend recently asked me this question, then proceeded to explain to me who "Katherine" was: a woman with whom she had gone to school and been friends with simply by proximity rather than any real connection. In fact, my friend characterized Katherine as rather plain and dull. Throughout her life, my friend said, Katherine seems to appear in her dreams whenever she is feeling stuck, even if she hasn't consciously realized it.

In our dreams, long-lost acquaintances often represent the very aspects of ourselves that they themselves represent to us. My friend saw Katherine as dull, but she sometimes sees herself this way as well, and when she is feeling stuck, along comes Katherine to show just how boring she sees herself! Katherine, in fact, tells her that if she doesn't occasionally try something new, she may end up just like Katherine.

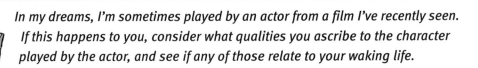

*In my dreams, I'm sometimes played by an actor from a film I've recently seen. If this happens to you, consider what qualities you ascribe to the character played by the actor, and see if any of those relate to your waking life.*

While it is easy to fit the people in your dreams into a "type," it's not always a fruitful thing to do. Dream characters are probably an amalgam of two or more types, or may take partially from many types, and may even slip through the categories! This makes analyzing them tougher, but more interesting.

**Even actors and actresses,** *people whom we do not know personally and yet "know" in terms of the characters they play, can play a significant role in our dreams.*

## Interpreting presences

In the end, who the people in our dreams represent can only be ascertained on a dream-by-dream basis. Still, as dream expert Gayle Delaney observes in her book *In Your Dreams* (see *Further Reading* at the end of this book), "If you created the dream image, you usually have enough information to interpret it." Asking the following questions about the dream characters can help you begin:

- Who is it? Does the character have a name?
- How would you describe this person?
- Is there something about this description that you like or dislike in yourself?
- Is there something about the way the person behaves in your dream that connects to a current situation in your waking life?
- How do you feel about this person in your waking life?
- How do you feel about this person in your dream?

*The people in your dreams most often are there to help you understand something about yourself. Let go of your assumptions about them, explore who they are within the dream, and you'll learn something important about yourself.*

# A simple summary

✔ In most of your dreams, you are represented by your persona, a character that your dreaming mind recognizes as yourself.

✔ One way of looking at your dream persona is to ask whether or not you yourself would behave the way "you" did in your dream.

✔ While dreams are profoundly personal, our personal experiences often touch on universal or archetypal themes.

✔ When family members appear in your dreams, they may be playing themselves, aspects of yourself, or even you.

✔ In our dreams, long-lost acquaintances often represent the very aspects of ourselves that they themselves represent to us.

✔ Who the people in our dreams represent can only be known on a dream-by-dream basis, by asking a series of questions about them.

# Chapter 6

# Symbol, Metaphor, and Imagery

W HILE STANDARD DREAM DICTIONARIES apply specific meanings to every dream symbol, contemporary dream analysts – and I – will tell you that the pictures in your dreams are as individual as you are. Comprised of everything within both your own memory and the collective unconscious, unafraid of puns, and using right-brain shorthand rather than left-brain logic, dream imagery contains many levels of meaning. So how do you proceed to unravel the symbol, metaphor, and imagery that crowd your dreams? You begin with a picture, a picture of a dream.

## In this chapter...

✔ **Picture your dreams**

✔ **Image and imagination**

✔ **Object and objectivity**

A LIGHT OF UNDERSTANDING WILL SHINE THROUGH THE MOST COMPLEX DREAM IMAGERY

# Picture your dreams

*YOU MAY RECALL that in Chapter 4 I suggested you draw a picture from your dream in your dream journal. If you haven't yet done that, take a moment to do so now, selecting a dream image that you feel carries some particular resonance for you. We're going to embark on a little dream journey using just such an image. In the sections that follow, I'm including a drawing of my own (although despite co-authoring a drawing book, I'm no artist), which we'll use as both illustration and roadmap on the way to dream interpretation.*

## Drawing and listing

This picture is an image from my "ladder to attic" dream I first mentioned in Chapter 3, in which my brothers are shaking a ladder as I try to carry boxes up to the attic. To begin interpreting what this dream might mean, let's make a simple list of each of the images that occur in the picture of the dream:

- Ladder to attic
- The box(es)
- The hole leading to the attic
- The attic (not visible)
- My brothers, below, shaking the ladder

Now take a look at your own dream sketch. The basic elements that constitute the dream are sure to leap out at you. Make a simple list of such images from your dream drawing. You may have more or fewer images on your list, depending on the detail of your dream and your drawing.

■ **If you can look at a picture** *and say what it means, you ought to be able to look at your own dream pictures and interpret them, according to dream researcher Calvin Hall.*

# INTERPRETING A DREAM IMAGE

There are a number of ways to examine your dream imagery for meaning, including Freudian free association, Jungian questioning of the image, and a Gestalt engagement with the image itself. Let's go through each image on my "ladder to attic" dream list to see how this works.

*My first assumption for any dream is that none of the images are merely what they appear to be. Nor do I stop at a singular meaning for each image.*

**a** **Ladder to attic:** Standard dream dictionaries suggest that climbing a ladder means prosperity and unstinted happiness. While it's tempting to stop right there, this clearly is not all that this particular ladder represents.

- **Freud** would tell me that the ladder is a phallic symbol, and the entrance to the attic the womb. I, the dreamer, would be seeking either to return to the comfort of the womb or to assume the male role in sex
- **Jung** would say that the ladder represents a path between my conscious and my unconscious. While Jungian theory would usually place the unconscious at a lower level (below the ladder), in this case it seems to be represented by the attic (since it's a hiding place) above the ladder. This may be because I personally view the unconscious as the "higher" mind
- **Gestalt therapy** would make me question the ladder: "Where are you going?" "To the attic." "Why?" "Because it is where I want to store these boxes." And so on
- **For me** the ladder represents a combination of many of these ideas: a way (or path) upward toward the attic

**b** **The box(es):** What's in those boxes?

- **Freud**, of course, would take the sexual view, that they contain my deepest, darkest sexual secrets
- **Jung** would have them holding ideas I prefer to keep in my unconscious
- **Gestalt therapy** would have me question them: "What are you?" "I am a box." "What do you contain?" "Things you cannot see." "Why can't I see you?" "Because I am inside a box"
- **For me** the boxes mean a combination of all these ideas: the boxes are containers for something I am not yet ready to "see" consciously

# INTERPRETING A DREAM IMAGE (CONT.)

**c** **The hole leading to the attic:** Here, the interpretations would go thus:

- **Freud** would see this hole as an entrance to a womb, as I've already suggested
- **Jung** might see it as a portal, or, more archetypally, the entrance to the underworld (even though this entrance is above, not below)
- **Gestalt therapy** may lead to questions such as: "Where do you lead?" "To yourself." "But I am I. How can you lead me to myself?" "Come in and see"
- **For me** the idea of this hole as the entrance point to my own unconscious is very appealing

**d** **The attic (not visible):** Rather than lead you once again through everyone else's ideas (I'm betting you've got the idea by now), I'll just give you my own interpretation of the attic.

- **For me** the attic is where I "store" ideas, memories, and thoughts that I'm not yet ready to use or acknowledge – it is my own unconscious mind

**e** **My brothers, below, shaking the ladder:** In Chapter 3, I mentioned that my brothers often assume trickster roles in my dreams, and their role here is no exception. While in this dream "I" would prefer to simply climb the ladder, deposit my box, and then descend to retrieve another, my brothers will not allow it to be so simple. Representatives of my childhood and of my younger unsure self, my brothers remind me of our sibling rivalry and our entire old family dynamic. In this dream, they're literally trying to "shake" me. Is it malicious? Is it something that needs to be done? In Chapter 3, I told you that I had a sudden revelation within this dream that I didn't need to be carrying these boxes up to the attic anyway; I could use what was in them in my work.

- **For me,** in this dream, my trickster brothers shake me out of my business-as-usual mode and help me to see that I can use these "secrets" in my work; that is, my writing

*Remember: you created your dream's meaning and you hold the key to unlocking it!*

## Steps to remember

Go carefully through each level of analysis in the box "Interpreting a dream image" and see if you can do the same with your own dream sketch.

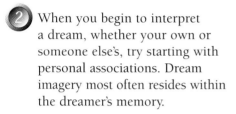 Go through each step with each image: Freudian, Jungian, or Gestalt (Perls's), and then your personal analysis.

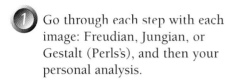 When you begin to interpret a dream, whether your own or someone else's, try starting with personal associations. Dream imagery most often resides within the dreamer's memory.

■ **Don't ignore dream images** *that you cannot "see" clearly – they may turn out to be the most significant ones.*

## Symbol and metaphor

Although I dislike the word "symbol" and everything it connotes, I thought it might be fun to wander through a dream dictionary from 1909 (Gustavus Hindman Miller's *The Dictionary of Dreams*), to see just how reductive symbolic systems can be:

- **Door:** To dream of entering a door denotes slander
- **Lagoon:** To dream of a lagoon denotes that you will be drawn into a whirlpool of doubt and confusion
- **Peaches:** Dreaming of seeing or eating peaches implies the sickness of children, disappointing returns in business, and failure to make anticipated visits of pleasure

I'm sorry; I'm laughing too hard to go on. Sometimes in a dream a lagoon is just a lagoon and a peach is just a peach. Still, I won't be surprised if I dream tonight of eating peaches next to a lagoon after passing through a door. After all, day residue is an important repository of dream material.

*Day residue refers to people, situations, or events of the day that appear in a different guise in that night's dreams.*

Having eliminated "symbol" from our collective vocabulary, we can now examine the concept of metaphor in more depth. While you may recall from grammar school that a simile is a comparison that uses "like" or "as" and a metaphor is any other comparison, a definition that allows metaphor to stand alone will be more useful here. A metaphor is a seemingly related idea or image standing for another. Shakespeare's adage "All the world's a stage" is an oft-cited example of a metaphor.

■ **Your dreams are likely** *to be made up of recent and distant memories. That day's events may feature alongside objects you were familiar with as a child.*

## Dream metaphor

Dream metaphor can take a variety of forms, including linguistic or literal puns, association, imagery, or an intriguing use of day residue combined with long-term memory. This is because dreaming is the time during which new information from the day is absorbed into our store of memory.

Dream researcher Kelly Bulkeley takes the concept of metaphor further in his pioneering book *The Wilderness of Dreams* (see *Further Reading* at the end of this book). He examines the concept of the "root metaphor," which he calls "the idea that all human thinking is fundamentally metaphorical in nature." Bulkeley asserts that by examining the metaphors in religion, art, and dreams we can begin to understand what has previously been unknowable.

**INTERNET**

**www.dreamresearch. ca/rem/symbols.html**

*At this site you'll find tools for developing your own methods of interpreting your dreams, rather than a reductive dream dictionary.*

*Linguistic puns aren't always the ones we use consciously. Even a simple word with multiple meanings may be used by the unconscious. You might dream that you are "passing" someone on the road when you're worried about "passing" a test.*

# Image and imagination

*YOUR MIND IS A STOREHOUSE of every image you've ever seen. You've probably had a sensation of déjà vu, in which something you know you've never seen before nonetheless looks very familiar. Sensations like déjà vu originate in your long-term memory, and, because this is also where dream imagery originates, you will sometimes awaken from a dream with a similar "long-lost" feeling.*

## Warehouse of images

In your dreams, the storehouse of both your imagination and the collective unconscious are available for images. Picturing this as a warehouse can help you to understand how many images there are. The more you work with your dreams, the more you'll discover your own "regular" imagery (mine seems to regularly include items hidden in boxes and car journeys). You'll also be better prepared when something out-of-the-ordinary appears.

## *PERSONAL MYTHOLOGY*

**Stop thinking of "myth" as something that is synonymous with "falsehood."**

So, what kind of mythology are we talking about in this context?

- Joseph Campbell's famous definition goes: "A myth is a public dream; a dream is a private myth"
- Myths and dreams utilize the same pool of metaphoric thought and language
- Myths reside in the collective unconscious, dreams originate in what David Feinstein calls "personal myths . . . a combination of images, emotions, and concepts, organized around a core theme that addresses at least one of the domains within which mythology traditionally functions"

Feinstein believes that accessing and understanding one's personal mythology may well be the difference between psychic health and psychic disorientation. Personal myths, he asserts, arise from four sources: biological, cultural, personal/historical, and transcendental. Dreams serve to process new information from these four areas into the personal myth that is already in place, or, when that is not possible, to work toward synthesizing a new personal mythology.

## An image list of your own

I've found that one of the most exciting aspects of exploring my dreams has been discovering my own particular dream metaphors. While I'm far too inefficient to have developed a written record of my more common imagery, I've nonetheless found that what appears in my dreams also appears in my fiction and poetry. Chances are, your personal image list will bear little resemblance to mine. That's why I feel comfortable sharing a few of these images and their significance with you:

■ **Do your dreams** *contain pastoral images even though you live in a city? Make a habit of listing all such out-of-the-way images to understand their significance.*

*a* **Complacent cows in a field:** As I grew up in an industrial city, I was startled when I realized how frequently this image appears in both my dreams and my writing. It appears so often in the latter, in fact, that it's now been added to my "automatic delete" list. When it appears in my dreams, it often signals a surface quiet masking turmoil beneath.

*b* **Lost around the corner from a familiar place:** Because I am one of those fortunate people with a strong internal compass, the few times I have been disoriented were accompanied by a real physical nausea. In my dreams, however, I sometimes turn a familiar corner and find myself in a completely unfamiliar place. You've probably guessed that these dreams occur when I'm about to try something new, including my frequent moves to new locations.

*When a dream image appears in a variety of ways throughout a dream, your unconscious is trying to let you know it's particularly important.*

*c* **Those boxes . . .** There they were last night, in fact. This time, they were in the trunk of someone else's car I'd been driving, and something in one of the boxes far back in the trunk was what I was looking for. "Boxes" seem to be where I hide things in my unconscious; sometimes I find what's in them, sometimes I search in vain.

After you've recorded some of your dreams, you'll see your own recurring imagery. While their meanings may change over time, chances are these images will always be significant for you. Make notes about your favorites (and others) and come back to them two, ten, or even twenty years later. What you discover may both surprise and delight you.

# Object and objectivity

*DREAM RESEARCHER GAYLE DELANEY suggests that whenever you begin to examine a dream image you should pretend that you come from Mars. While this may sound silly, it is actually quite a good way of gaining some objectivity about any dream object. Approaching dream imagery in this way means getting rid of predispositions and suppositions, and starting from scratch.*

## Questioning your assumptions

Try to describe something familiar as if it were something you'd never encountered, a toothbrush, for example. Your first response would be, "It's an implement used to brush teeth." A Martian, however, will question all of this. What's an implement? What are teeth? Why would you "brush" them? The more you work with your dream images, the more you'll discover about your own themes, ideas, psyche, and personal mythology.

*One way to gain objectivity about dream images is to use a dictionary. Looking up a word whose meaning you know can reveal associations that your unconscious mind may be using.*

## A simple summary

✓ Because you create your dream's meaning, you hold the key to unlocking it.

✓ Day residue is an important repository of dream material.

✓ Dream metaphor can take a variety of forms, including linguistic or literal puns, association, imagery, or an intriguing use of day residue plus long-term memory.

✓ Dreams sometimes give you a feeling of "déjà vu," as if you've encountered the image before, because dream images originate in your long-term memory.

✓ Your personal mythology both evolves from your dreams and works with them.

✓ To gain objectivity about a dream image, try describing the image as if you came from Mars.

# Chapter 7

# Actions, Feelings, and Landscapes

LIGHTS, CAMERA, ACTION . . . Actually, this film analogy is not a joke. It turns out that many of us have dreams in which the action unrolls as if we were watching a film. But while dream actions may often seem the stuff of fantasy, their access to our own storehouses of activities is where it all begins. Similarly, the emotions we feel in our dreams have their roots in our own experiences, and the landscapes where it all takes place can also be found within our memory banks. In fact, when it comes to dream actions, feelings, and landscapes, the big surprise may well be that there really are no surprises – once you discover the key to unlocking their secrets.

## In this chapter...

✓ **Dream actions**

✓ **Dream feelings**

✓ **Dream landscapes**

HOW DO YOU FEEL *IN* YOUR DREAM? HOW DO YOU FEEL *ABOUT* YOUR DREAM?

# Dream actions

WHAT HAPPENS IN *your dreams unfolds like a story, and is, quite literally, a story about yourself. Often, however, what you do and what everyone else in the dream does can seem confusing or even surreal. Examining a dream's **narrative** for connections to your own ongoing story is one way to begin to understand dream actions.*

> **DEFINITION**
>
> **Narrative** *is a term for the process of telling a story or series of events. A dream narrative, then, is your telling of a dream's story.*

## Diagramming dreams

While you may have never learned to diagram a sentence while you were in school, diagramming a dream is a good way to examine it. Essentially, it means marking the different elements in your dreams (by underlining them or highlighting them) so that they stand out. Using different markings for dream actions, feelings, and landscapes and then looking at each of them separately will help you make sense of the bigger picture your dream presents. Ultimately, you'll want to view your dream holistically, as one big picture. Still, examining it first by its parts can help you understand it.

## Tools for examining dream actions

Let's begin by examining dream actions:

1. If you've started recording your dreams in your dream journal, you've already taken the first step toward understanding dream actions.

2. Go back to your journal now and find a dream you'd like to examine further.

3. For this exercise, you'll want to either type this dream into your computer and then print out a hard copy, or write out a separate copy you won't mind marking up. As you'll be using this same page throughout this chapter, you may want to use a different-colored pen to note what we'll be discussing in each section.

■ **Recording your dreams** *in a journal is the first step toward understanding them.*

## Verbs in action

First, as you read through your dream, use one color to underline every verb or verb clause, to highlight the dream actions. I've simply underlined them in the following example. (You will be using the same manuscript to highlight other significant words.)

*I was <u>walking</u> through a forest. The trees <u>were crowded</u> together, but it <u>didn't seem</u> ominous, as sunlight <u>filtered</u> through from high above. Ahead in the distance, <u>I could see</u> a house in a clearing. <u>I walked</u> toward it, but <u>never seemed to get</u> any closer, but then all at once I <u>was standing</u> at its door.*

In this dream fragment, the persona is walking – in motion, in other words – through the dreamscape. The first action external to the persona is the trees: they are "crowded together." The next is the sunlight, "filtering," and the last external action here is a lack of action, the house that "never seemed to get any closer." The actions the persona performs in this fragment are walking, seeing, and standing, while the external actions are crowding, filtering, and that house that doesn't get any closer. Quick now, without knowing anything else about the dreamer, what might these actions suggest to you? Did you say that:

■ **Dream actions,** *studied separately from the dream objects, might provide valuable pointers to events in your waking life.*

**a** The dreamer is feeling closed in by her life, with hope (light) filtering in from far away?

**b** No matter how hard the dreamer tries (walks), she can't seem to get any closer to her goal?

Both of these assumptions are good ones, and are in fact quite close to what the dreamer ultimately discovered from her dream.

*Try to connect your dream actions to things happening in your life now. Even though the dream objects may be unfamiliar, when you separate the actions from them, what's going on may become clearer.*

# SAMPLE DREAM: THE TRIBE LIVES ON

Let's try applying the dream diagramming method to a longer dream, one with lots of action and excitement. The dreamer was in her late teens when she had this dream, but it remained so vivid that she was able to report it in detail almost 30 years later. I've underlined the verbs and verb clauses.

AN ACOMA PUEBLO SETTLEMENT, NEW MEXICO

*I am a member of a small pacifist Native American tribe that is constantly attacked by the Apaches. We live high on a hill which I knew nothing about at the time. Our tribe hires an Anglo (this term is used in the southwestern US to refer to all Caucasians) gunslinger because it cannot fend off the Apaches by itself. The gunslinger and our chief plan a surprise attack early one morning to mete out maximum damage (killing their chief) without directly endangering our entire tribe – the attackers could be anyone . . . not just us. There is a scene as the two men descend our hill, the camera pans to show the entire tribe . . . we're of every walk of life . . . men, women, children, farmers, wise men.*

*The attack is preempted through a leak and the whole Apache nation is waiting at the base. The sky goes black as our leader and the gunslinger are engulfed by thousands of angry killers. As we wait, we hear a pure, high-pitched note (I've never heard it in my waking life) and know our chief is dead. In the dream, I've been both the gunslinger and an observer. Now, I yell, "Someone better declare himself chief and get down there to retrieve the bodies." By the time someone does, the bodies have been desecrated, chopped, and disrespectfully covered in dirt. The new chief begins to dig out the bodies with his hands. As he unburies them, the dead chief and gunslinger turn into traditional wooden Christo santos (representations of Christ and saints common throughout the southwestern US).*

*The last scene begins with the smell of pine. We <u>are in a huge room</u> filled with white light. All of us are <u>dressed </u>in white buckskin, the maidens with their hair in ponytails. Drums <u>beat</u>, a plaintive mood of death and mourning <u>permeates</u> our motions and then <u>changes</u> to something proud, defiant. We <u>are not sad</u>. The life-sized santos are back to back on a wooden spool, its top and bottom wreathed in pine boughs. As we <u>sing</u>, they are <u>lifted up</u> by men of our tribe, lifted into brilliant, white light. Knowing the Apache <u>have violated</u> many unwritten Native American codes of ethics in this murder, I <u>stand</u> in the back of the room and <u>say</u>, "Woe to the Apache Nation, for they <u>have been cursed and damned</u>."*

## Analysis

The first thing you probably noticed about this dream is its archetypal, cinematic scale. Even though the dreamer insists that "at that point in my life, I was . . . uninterested in Native Americans or *santos*," the dream's access to the collective unconscious is evident. Still, let's start with the assumption that all dreams are personal, and examine the action words separately.

We should first determine what "tribe" the dreamer herself belonged to when she had this dream. As she was 17 at the time, let's assume her tribe is herself and her high school peers, while the constantly attacking "nation" that lives "below" their lofty perch is her tribe's parents and teachers. Can you see how we arrived at this conclusion?

When the tribe decides to take preemptive action, someone rats, and the nation down below quickly gets the upper hand, killing both the tribe's leader and their hired helper. This, too, is a metaphor for a fairly typical high school occurrence, where teens' independent forays are often aborted by well-meaning teachers and/or parents. As the dreamer notes, she's been both an observer and the gunslinger in this dream, but, as the latter is now dead, it's the observer persona who hollers, "Somebody better do something." Unfortunately, the dead haven't been accorded respect by the enemy, but this is quickly remedied by members of their own tribe. In fact, not only is a memorial service held, but the ritual ceremony allows the tribe's dead their rightful place in the cosmos, while the enemies will be damned forever.

If we read this dream on a purely personal level, we might say that the dreamer has felt threatened by those in positions of power, and that the dream reminds her that *she* is the one with ultimate control over her place in the world. If we choose to read it more archetypally (and in accordance with Alfred Adler's dream theories that dreams are about power issues), we would say that the dream is emblematic of the first political power struggle the dreamer has felt a part of. In it, we can see her initial feelings of powerlessness evolve into an understanding that it's not about one small battle, but the bigger picture.

# Dream feelings

*HOW WE FEEL WITHIN our dream is often as nonsensical as dream actions. Someone close to us may die and we feel elated; we may get what we want and yet feel angry and confused. While the emotional narratives of dreams run parallel to their action narratives, the two don't always line up as our more logical waking selves would like or expect. Learning to understand the feelings in our dreams can help us unravel our deeper feelings about waking issues and deal with them more effectively.*

## Tools for examining dream feelings

To examine your dream feelings, go back to the dream you copied at the beginning of the chapter. This time, you'll be marking emotions rather than actions. You can either use another color pen, or mark them in another way, such as with a wavy line or by circling them. Emotions can be divided into four basic areas – pleasure, pain, anger, and fear – and can often be found in the adjectives you use to describe your dream. I've used bold face to mark the emotions.

> *I was <u>walking</u> through a forest. The trees <u>were</u> **<u>crowded</u>** together, but it <u>didn't seem</u> **ominous**, as sunlight <u>filtered</u> through from high above. Ahead in the **distance**, I <u>could see</u> a house in a clearing. I <u>walked</u> toward it, but <u>never seemed to get</u> **any closer**, but then all at once I <u>was standing</u> at its door.*

## Simple steps to unraveling emotions

Once you've marked the emotions in your dream go through the following steps:

**1** See if there is one emotion that predominates.

**2** Note any reactions you have to the dream emotions as you read through the dream: do you feel angry when you read about being angry in the dream, for example?

■ **Just as in waking life**, *dream emotions are accompanied by physical signs of emotion. Tension means an increased heart rate; fear, rapid breathing; pleasure, relaxed muscles.*

3 Think about the day before you had the dream, or about something that is happening in your life that generates similar emotions, or where you haven't allowed yourself to feel the emotions that are present in the dream

4 Note if the emotions in the dream, separated from the action and landscape of the dream, tell you something about how you feel regarding that particular issue

*I've found that separating the emotional narrative of a dream from dream events helps me pinpoint emotions I may be avoiding in my waking life.*

## SAMPLE DREAM: MEN IN THE CLOUDS

The dreamer who sent me this dream noted that she had it when she was in first grade – in October 1923! I've boldfaced the emotions, including the emotion-laden words.

> *I dreamed I was **looking up** at the sky from the lawn of my house. I **felt apprehensive**. The air was **warm and humid**. The sun was setting behind **long, ropy** cloud formations. I thought to myself, **this is the way it will feel**. I became aware of innumerable lumps forming along the surfaces of the clouds. **Suddenly, there were little men with sledgehammers, pounding** the lumps until they **popped like balloons**. The clouds **thinned**, and **I was terrified**. I kept **whispering** to myself, they're **destroying** it all!*

The dreamer adds, "The activity of the men with the sledgehammers was connected to an article my father had read to me about the destruction wrought in World War I; this dream was the beginning of my childhood belief that the world would be destroyed from the air – a recurring nightmare, which I never told to anyone else."

### Analysis

While day residue is an important aspect of this dream, the first thing to do is to determine which of the four basic emotions is prevalent. For this dream, the prevalent emotion is fear. When we take into account what the dreamer tells us, it's obvious that learning about the destruction in the larger world, represented in the dream by the sky, was extremely frightening to an impressionable six-year-old.

*You decide what connotes emotion in your dream. If you mark phrases such as "long, ropy" in the above dream, it's fine. As with all dream interpretations, go with your instincts.*

# Dream landscapes

THE LAST AREA of your dreams we'll examine in this chapter is your dream landscapes. Whether comfortingly familiar or frighteningly strange, the places where our dreams unfold have much to tell us about ourselves.

## Representative dreamscapes

As in the previous "men in the clouds" dream, dream places can be both what they appear to be and representative of something other than themselves. Houses, for example, often represent the dreamer, while outdoor landscapes often characterize the larger world outside the dreamer.

*Don't make the mistake of assuming that in a dream your house is your house, your office is your office, or your car is your car. Dream locations are seldom what they appear to be.*

## Tools for examining dream landscapes

When you begin to examine your dream landscapes, it can be helpful to ask a number of questions about the places in your dreams. Some suggestions:

- What does the landscape look like?
- Have you ever been in a place like that?
- Does it remind you of anything?
- Have you ever been somewhere that *felt* like that?

■ **A landscape in your dream** *might represent an idea or a person. When interpreting the metaphors of your dream landscape, remember that nothing is what it seems.*

Go back to the dream you copied at the beginning of this chapter. Use yet another color pen or marking to note all the locations within the dream (I've used a highlighter). Answer the questions I've listed for this dream fragment; even though it's not your dream, the places in it are likely to resonate for you in some way. Do the same for your own dream.

*I was <u>walking</u> through a <mark>forest.</mark> The trees <u>were crowded</u> together, but it <u>didn't seem</u> ominous, as sunlight <u>filtered</u> through from high above. Ahead in the distance, I <u>could see</u> a <mark>house in the clearing.</mark> I <u>walked</u> toward it, but <u>never seemed to get</u> any closer, but then all at once I <u>was standing</u> at its <mark>door.</mark>*

# HOUSES OF DREAMS

Just like real houses, the houses in our dreams have many aspects, such as doors, windows, and rooms, as well as features like keyholes and faucets. Thinking about these features as metaphors can unlock many dream doors:

### 1 Windows

*Windows are openings and suggest the dreamer's need to either go out into the larger world outside or into the smaller world inside.*

### 3 Rooms

*Your mind has many levels of comprehension, and often uses this common metaphor for them in your dreams. Specific rooms have certain significances; for example, the kitchen may represent either a place for replenishing the self or a place where the family gathers.*

### 2 Doors

*Opening a door in a familiar place and finding a room one hadn't known existed suggests an untapped area of the dreamer's unconscious mind.*

### 4 Keys

*Keys unlock doors, as well as many other things that are "locked." Possessing them in a dream suggests that you yourself hold the answer you are seeking.*

## Sample dream: The canyon

Let's apply these questions to a longer sample dream. This one comes from the same dreamer as "men in the clouds." She notes that she had this dream in 1931. For this dream, I've boldfaced the landscapes and locations.

*I was standing on the **north rim of Palo Duro Canyon**, Texas. **The sky was lemon yellow and the air was full of dust. Looking east, I could see a denser cloud of dust. Two hundred feet below me,** emerging from the pall of dust, a panicked crowd came running toward the west, their eyes wild and mouths frozen in O's of terror. For a minute, I felt the fear that drove them. My heart began to pound and I couldn't swallow the cold lump in my throat. Then, I got hold of my fear. What is there to be afraid of? I have nothing to fear.*

■ **An opening,** *entrance, or hole in your dream landscape may represent the need to understand something that lies below the surface.*

**INTERNET**

members.tripod.com/ ~o45tu/sen.htm

*Can't get a handle on what a particular dream landscape or scenery means? This contemporary dream landscape dictionary can give you linguistic clues toward understanding the metaphors of your own dream places.*

*Instantly, I was at the **bottom of the canyon with its many layers of red and white and gray strata.** There were **cave-like entrances in the wall.** I walked confidently inside, where the **ceilings were like those in Carlsbad Caverns.** A man sat on a high stool with a ledger on his lap. He looked at me, and ran his finger down the names in the book, then beckoned to someone. I found myself being escorted to a **passageway with small oval openings, each fitted with a gate of bars.** I knelt down and crawled backward through the open gate, and the bars closed behind me. I lay quietly in a **sand-floored alcove just large enough to hold me** and went to sleep.*

*When I wakened, I found the bars removed, so I crawled out and went to find the man with the book. He looked at me and nodded, checked something in the book and said, "You may go out now." I walked out into **the canyon** again. **The air was clear, and the sky was deep blue. Across the shallow water of the creek, tall cottonwoods grew along the opposite bank,** and under them were people of all ages, laughing and eating picnic lunches, calling to the children who ran and played in the water. The peace and calmness were as real as the earlier panic.*

## Analysis

The dreamer grew up near Palo Duro Canyon, so the location of the dream was familiar to her. So, while this dreamscape is on its surface familiar, deeper down, it metaphorically represents something the dreamer is trying to understand.

*Remember, dream landscapes, whether familiar or unfamiliar, both* **are** *and* **are not** *themselves.*

Inside this dream canyon are "cave-like entrances," "passageway(s) with small oval openings," and "alcove(s)." The dreamer enters one such opening willingly – and falls asleep. Could this hidden world be her own secret world of dreams? This interpretation becomes more likely when the sleeping dreamer awakens and discovers the threatening world newly cleansed, with "peace and calmness." This dream reminds the dreamer that she can find the answers to her waking problems by simply falling asleep and dreaming about them, something she's done many, many times in her 86 years!

# A simple summary

✔ Examining a dream's narrative for connections to your own ongoing story is one way to begin understanding dream actions.

✔ Try to connect your dream actions to things that are happening in your life now.

✔ Learning to understand the feelings in our dreams can help us unravel our deeper feelings about waking issues and deal with them more effectively.

✔ Emotions can be divided into four basic areas: pleasure, pain, anger, and fear. For any dream, note the prevalent emotion, which can often be found in the adjectives you use to describe the dream.

✔ Separating the emotional narrative of a dream from dream events can help you to pinpoint emotions you may be avoiding in your waking life.

✔ Whether comfortingly familiar or frighteningly strange, the places where our dreams unfold have much to tell us about ourselves.

✔ Asking questions of your dream landscapes can help you uncover their metaphoric meanings.

# Chapter 8

# What's in a Dream?

DREAM RESEARCHER CALVIN HALL asserted that what's in our dreams isn't nearly so mysterious as we think. In the early 1950s, Hall and his associates implemented an unprecedented number of dream studies, focusing on and categorizing the content of dreams. Hall's studies were so basic and logical that everyone from Freudian analysts to New Age dreamers find something they continue to utilize today. In this chapter, I'll discuss Calvin Hall's ideas, and examine what's behind some of our more disturbing dreams, including those age-old bogies, nightmares.

## In this chapter...

✓ **Calvin Hall and content analysis**

✓ **Up close and personal**

✓ **Disturbing dreams**

NIGHTMARES ARE SAID TO REFLECT UNRESOLVED WAKING PROBLEMS

# Calvin Hall and content analysis

*THE CONSENSUS AMONG dream researchers regarding Calvin Hall's theories is striking: nearly all agree that Hall's no-nonsense analysis of dream content was both logical and fundamental. Because Hall's work focused on the content of dreams, it is called content analysis.*

## Hall's research and findings

Hall conducted his exhaustive research (largely with student volunteers) on dream content in the mid-1950s. His basic thesis was that dreams embodied thoughts and hence were a *cognitive process*. Hall's original questionnaire asked respondents to "Write down your dream in as complete detail as you are able to." Hall and his research assistants then analyzed each dream's content and tabulated the results. The most frequent location in dreams, for example, was a house or a building (24 percent). As for the people in dreams, Hall discovered the following:

> **DEFINITION**
>
> **Cognitive process** *is a fancy term for thinking. By calling dreaming a cognitive process, Calvin Hall was suggesting that dreaming is, quite simply, another way of processing thought.*

- For 15 percent, the dreamer was the only character
- For 43 percent, the other characters were strangers
- For 37 percent, the characters were friends or acquaintances
- For 19 percent, the others in the dreams were family members, relatives, or in-laws

■ **A house** – *whether unfamiliar or one's own home – is a common dream image.*

Based on these findings, Hall concluded that dream content could be categorized into one of five principal areas of life:

**(1)** Concepts of self

**(2)** Concepts of other people

**(3)** Concepts of the world

**(4)** Concepts of impulses, prohibitions, and penalties

**(5)** Concepts of problems and conflicts

## So, what are dreams?

According to Hall, "Dreams . . . provide us with maps of regions which are inaccessible in waking consciousness." For this reason, he believed that dreams are the best way of discovering personal thoughts and how they explain behavior.

*"A dream is a personal document," wrote Hall, "a letter to oneself." In his view, dreams are not a way in which we hide things from ourselves, but rather a way of revealing them.*

Hall further posited that dream content concerned itself with five major conflicts:

1. The child's struggle to understand him- or herself and his or her parents

2. The conflict between freedom and security

3. The conflict between one's male and female aspects

4. The conflict between one's "animal nature" and societal expectations

5. The struggle to understand life and death

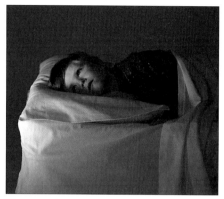

■ **According to Calvin Hall,** *children often dream of themselves as victims of attack by adults, animals, or monsters.*

What's most striking about Hall's theories (besides their methodical nature) is their opposition to Freud's contention that we hide everything from ourselves. Hall believed that in the rare event we do keep things from ourselves, our dreams will reveal them.

## *THE FOUR SIMPLE RULES*

Hall believed that it doesn't take special training to understand our dreams, merely an understanding of our own imagery. He proposed four simple rules for interpretation:

- A dream creates a picture of one's particular reality
- Everything in a dream comes from the dreamer's own mind
- We each have multiple conceptions of ourselves and our worlds
- Dreams occur in series and should be interpreted that way

# Up close and personal

IF DREAMS REFLECT *reality, it follows that "up close and personal" dreams reflect what's closest to our hearts at a particular time. However, when we dream about relationships, they often involve strangers or casual acquaintances and seem to have no connection with our waking life. Then there are dreams about body matters – walking around naked in public, urination, or defecation. Because the locations in these dreams are often familiar, their bizarre aspects make them quite disturbing, and, because of this, they are most often the dreams we remember upon awakening.*

■ **Even if your dream** *setting is familiar, it may be populated by strangers.*

## Dream relationships

Let's use Hall's rules for dream interpretation on a sample dream to see how this works. (Incidentally, this dreamer points out that she has never been married.)

*There was a Christmas tree up in the place I lived with my husband. The place seemed more like a large department store than a house. For some reason, my husband was agitated (though not at me). All of a sudden, he, I, and the tree are outside in the back yard (which looked like my real back yard). It's summer weather – sunny, green grass, etc.*

*The tree had been a real one, but now it's artificial. My husband pushes it over. I'm concerned about the ornaments on the tree, but I check and none are broken. My husband has disappeared. I right the tree. Then I go farther out into the yard. I turn around – suddenly it's night, very dark except for city lights in the distance as if I'm looking at Chicago or Boston from the water. I know I am quite far – a mile or two – away from my house, and I'm standing in very shallow (about 1 inch deep) water. I run back to my house, in shallow water all the way, then search the house – which really looks like a department store now – for people, finding my mother and my husband.*

## Analysis

Let's begin with the people in this dream: the dream persona, the dream husband, and, at the very end, the dreamer's mother. Carl Jung's rule of thumb for dream characters applies here. When people we see regularly appear in our dreams, they usually represent some aspect of ourselves; those we don't see often, and strangers, are the ones who likely represent the people in our life.

**1** We can safely assume that in this dream the dream persona represents the dreamer. Next, applying Jung's rule of thumb, the dreamer's mother here probably represents some aspect of the dreamer herself rather than her actual mother, while the dream husband, who doesn't exist in waking life, represents someone – or something – who is in her life. Knowing the dreamer and her job situation, I'd bet that bad-tempered "husband" represents her job, while the "mother" in the house represents the dreamer's sense of security.

**2** Next, as you may recall from Chapter 6, your dream houses often represent you, the dreamer. The house in this dream "seemed more like a large department store" to the dreamer, who in fact leads a many-faceted life. One of her primary job responsibilities as manager of a small office is dealing with the public over the phone. (She's also very good at "righting trees" after others' temper tantrums, even when her initial perception of the tree as "real" turns out to be false.)

**3** During the summer, when she had this dream, people were signing up for the organization's fall conference. Helping people select from the conference's many options probably makes her feel like she's running a department store at times. The fact that people are signing up for a fall conference in summer may also help explain the dream's confused seasons.

**4** Lastly, the shallow water she must wade through to get back to her dream house may well be the emotions of others she must deal with for her job security.

■ **Your mother's appearance** in *your dream may represent your own attitudes, traits you like or dislike in yourself, or even your relationship with someone else.*

## Body matters

In *Let Your Body Interpret Your Dreams* (see *Further Reading* at the end of this book), respected psychologist Eugene T. Gendlin, PhD, notes that if defecation appears in dreams, we should remember that it is "natural stuff," "organic bodily matter, left over from digestion." Trying to clean it up, Gendlin goes on, may be something you think needs to be done, when in reality, "it can heal something."

Everyone has dreams involving what we consider the less pleasant aspects of having a body, including urinating and defecating. The fact that we consider these aspects less pleasant is quite telling when it comes to our dreams. Without becoming Freudian and suggesting that toilet training is at the root of all such dreams, it's nonetheless safe to say that in our society, there is some shame associated with processes of elimination. So we tend to them behind closed doors, as quietly as possible.

■ **If parents handle** *a child's toilet training insensitively, the child may develop a permanent sense of shame about bodily functions, according to Freud.*

*Dream analyst Jeremy Taylor believes bathroom dreams are metaphors for the "'digested' emotional and physical material that nourishes and sustains us" and must be "brought out" regularly for us to be physically – and psychologically – healthy.*

It follows that if we don't bring out the digested matter in our waking life, of course it will come out in our dreams. Therefore:

*a* When you dream that a toilet you are using lacks privacy, you may actually be expressing a fear of exposure or ridicule

*b* Dreams that reveal a lack of control over these natural physical acts may suggest that you are concerned with expressing things in public you think are better left private, or that you think may show you actually do lack restraint

*Don't be reductive when talking about dream images. You must examine your dream images within the context of their particular dream.*

# A SIMPLE GUIDE TO NUDITY IN DREAMS

### (a) The reductive explanation: Dream Encyclopedias

*"Being naked in a dream suggests . . . being vulnerable to how others see one, feeling ashamed of being found out . . . It also suggests being unencumbered and uninhibited." Are you as confused by that analysis as I am? It's one of many reasons I tend to dislike reductive symbolic dream systems.*

### (b) A more inclusive explanation

*My answer is that naked dreams reveal both vulnerability and lack of inhibition (which go hand in hand), and a whole lot more besides. Writers, for example, often report naked dreams just as they begin a new project; after all, the best writing requires an openness that must transcend fear of exposure.*

### (c) What experts say

*Dream researcher Gayle Delaney feels that a dream of nudity in public means that you are working through your feelings of vulnerability. According to Jeremy Taylor, clothes represent the persona of the dreamer, so, when you are naked, you're allowing more of your true self to show through. Yet other experts suggest that you ask yourself if you are afraid of being seen for what you really are.*

### (d) What it is not

*Interestingly, no dream researcher suggests that dream nudity has anything to do with sex!*

### (e) Covering up your nakedness

*Some dreamers resort to extreme measures to cover up their nakedness, disguising themselves or trying to hide in unusual places. Dream analysts suggest that these dreamers may be avoiding some issue in their waking lives, or trying to make excuses for something that's best faced up to.*

### (f) Nothing to be afraid of

*Many dreamers discover that even though they are naked in public, no one else seems to notice, and as a result, they realize their own fears are groundless.*

# Disturbing dreams

*BEING CHASED OR ATTACKED, losing or forgetting things, and other nightmarish occurrences in dreams can leave the dreamer with a lingering uneasiness for days after the dream has occurred. We've already looked briefly at why dreams of bodily elimination may make us uncomfortable, but what about dreams of being lost, chased, or attacked?*

## When and why

Why do we have disturbing dreams? Do we have them at specific points in our life? What are they telling us about our waking lives? Dreams that disturb us reflect unresolved issues both great and small. Sometimes they occur because we've experienced a major trauma, such as the death of a loved one, a personal illness, or an accident of some sort. But disturbing dreams can also occur when our lives seem to be going fairly smoothly, and when this occurs, you'll want to examine the dream pictures more closely. Do remember, the pictures in your dreams come from your own mind.

■ **Being chased** *may be the most common disturbing dream for both adults and children.*

## Being chased or attacked

It has been found that while adults are usually chased by an unknown male, for children the pursuer is more likely to be an animal or fantasy figure.

*Dream analyst Jeremy Taylor suggests that dreams of being chased or attacked are at their most basic level archetypal dreams, a living out of a timeless drama that goes back to our days as cave-people.*

Such dreams are very often accompanied by strong emotions, including fear, anxiety, despair, disappointment, or resignation. Taylor believes that when we have dreams of being chased or attacked, we are likely dealing with deep-seated lifetime issues that relate to our fundamental concepts about ourselves and our worlds.

# FROZEN IN PLACE

As you may recall from Chapter 3, one of the physiological effects of REM sleep is a freezing of voluntary muscular activity. Still, this is little comfort when you're unable to move in your dreams. Dream researchers are nearly certain that external paralysis is connected to in-dream paralysis. Perhaps, some suggest, it acts as a stopper when we might otherwise actually harm someone if we mimicked the dream motion, such as hitting or kicking, or we might harm ourselves if we actually got up and ran. But that doesn't explain why it's so hard to make one's foot move to that dream brake in that runaway car, or why it's so hard to put one foot in front of the other along that dream pathway.

*Being frozen in dreams may well indicate that in waking life, too, we feel as if we can't get something under control or make any forward motion. As always, let the dream's context be your guide.*

Did you experience what Dr. Ann Faraday, author of *Dream Power*, calls an "aha!" when you read the words "our fundamental concepts"? If you did, it's because we're back to one of Calvin Hall's basic theories: that all dreams deal with these concepts. Frightening dreams are no exception. They help us incorporate experiences into our personal storehouses of memory. Dreams of being attacked or chased may be scary because the real-life experiences they reflect are disturbing as well. Understanding the basis of such dreams is often just a first step; healing can take time.

*Since we often awaken from frightening dreams with the dream emotions and their bodily indicators – rapid heartbeat or erratic breathing – still in place, we remember these dreams more often than run-of-the-mill ones.*

## Lost in the funhouse

When we forget or lose things in our dreams, it's not really any fun at all, yet one of the most common dream themes is losing one's purse or wallet. Most dream analysts agree that on a basic metaphoric level, these items represent our identity, and losing them in dreams can indicate that our self-concept is threatened in some way.

One dreamer, for example, reported that she dreamed she was having lunch with some friends at a new restaurant she'd been wanting to try. When it was time to leave, however, she discovered that she'd lost her purse. Her friends tried to help her find it, but it was nowhere to be found. "Maybe you left it home," one friend said. At this, the dreamer became very angry, and then awoke.

### Analysis

Less than a year before she'd had this dream, the dreamer's husband had died suddenly. Because she is of the generation of women who married and had children while their husbands went off to work, his death was, of course, a fundamental blow to her identity. Even though she had begun to make a new life without him in the year since he'd died – represented in the dream by going out with her friends – her fear of making her way without him still remained at a fundamental level. This dream clearly reflects that fear.

## Nightmares

Everyone has nightmares, because everyone's life has its ups and downs. While dream researchers aren't certain what causes nightmares, they do have a number of ideas. Some factors that may increase the odds of having a nightmare include:

- Major life trauma, such as death or illness
- Any life stress, such as job change, marital difficulties, pregnancy, moving house, worries about money
- Certain drugs and medications (or withdrawal from them)
- Learning to deal with fears (especially in children's nightmares)

## Why nightmares occur

Like all dreams, nightmares usually occur to help the dreamer deal with waking issues – even if it doesn't seem that way at the time (although research has indicated that creative and emotionally open and trusting people sometimes have nightmares that are not connected to waking issues). Further, nightmares often deal with transitory issues, and cease to occur once the matter has been resolved.

Children's nightmares, for instance, usually decrease and then disappear over time, as they learn to understand the fears that precipitated them. Similarly, nightmares can help an adult deal with the issues in his or her waking life by presenting a difficult situation in a new light.

■ **In medieval times,** *nightmares were thought to be visitations by demons. Henry Fuseli's painting,* The Nightmare, *plays upon this idea.*

## The positive side

You can deal with your nightmares yourself, or ask for help.

1. Interestingly, not everyone finds nightmares disturbing. Many find them interesting rather than distressing, or consider them evidence of their own creativity. This suggests that how we ultimately regard our dreams, even the more frightening ones, is an important aspect of our approach to what's in them as well.

2. When nightmares don't decrease or lose their effect over time, do not hesitate to consult a therapist. Therapists are trained to help you work through difficult times, and seeking their help is sometimes the best thing you can do for yourself.

**INTERNET**

www.asdreams.org/
nightma.htm

*The Association for the Society of Dreams (ASD) provides a web page that answers "Common Questions About Nightmares." You can also link to the ASD homepage from this site.*

# *A simple summary*

✓ Dream researcher Calvin Hall believed that dreams are the best way of discovering personal thoughts and explaining behavior.

✓ In Hall's view, dreams are not a way in which we hide things from ourselves, but rather a way of revealing them. Hall believed that it doesn't take special training to understand our dreams, merely an understanding of our own imagery.

✓ Dream analyst Jeremy Taylor suggests that bathroom dreams may be metaphors for the

"'digested' emotional and physical material that nourishes and sustains us."

✓ Dreams that disturb us reflect unresolved issues both great and small.

✓ Nightmares can help dreamers deal with their waking issues by presenting a difficult situation in a new light.

✓ How we ultimately regard our dreams, even the frightening ones, is an important aspect of our approach to what's in them.

# Chapter 9

# Life is But a Dream

DREAMS CAN HELP YOU understand and deal with larger, life-changing events, and recent research has focused on a number of these areas. For example, physical changes, such as those found during pregnancy, show up in our dreams, as do those that occur during illness. At the same time, our dreams may be about various rites of passage, such as weddings, confirmations, and funerals: dreams can help us integrate these transitions into our consciousness as well. In this chapter, I'll look at the ways our lives are in our dreams – and the way our dreams can help us live our lives.

## In this chapter...

✔ **Pregnancy and birth**

✔ **Dreams through the life span**

✔ **In sickness and in health**

✔ **Ritual and ceremony**

✔ **Death is a fact of life**

EVERY MILESTONE OF LIFE CAN BE A DREAMY OCCASION

# Pregnancy and birth

WHEN IT COMES *to the relationship between pregnancy and dreams, Patricia Maybruck, PhD, literally wrote the book. First published in 1989,* Pregnancy & Dreams *examines how dreams reflect both the physical and psychological changes a woman undergoes during pregnancy and birth, and the unique qualities of pregnant women's dreams.*

## Dreaming in pregnancy

Patricia Maybruck notes that animal dreams are an integral aspect of pregnancy. Small animals such as kittens, puppies, fish, and lizards often represent your fetus early in your pregnancy, while whales and elephants, as well as dinosaurs, lions, tigers, and bears, will show up when you're further along.

*"Both times I was pregnant, I dreamed of whales and elephants", a good friend remarked after I told her I was working on dreaming in pregnancy.*

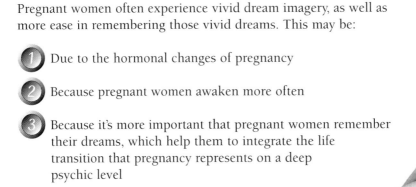

Pregnant women often experience vivid dream imagery, as well as more ease in remembering those vivid dreams. This may be:

1. Due to the hormonal changes of pregnancy

2. Because pregnant women awaken more often

3. Because it's more important that pregnant women remember their dreams, which help them to integrate the life transition that pregnancy represents on a deep psychic level

This transition – the cycle of birth and death from generation to generation – is reflected in pregnant women's dreams of their mothers or of mother figures. In the later stages of pregnancy, especially in the third-trimester, women often appear in their own dreams as someone large. For instance, a woman saw herself as Mother Nature.

■ **Having negative dreams** *when pregnant? Patricia Maybruck says that more than 70 percent of the dreams reported by pregnant women produced anxiety, far more than those of the general population.*

# BEARING LIFE, BEARING DREAMS

What's perhaps most striking about the dreams of pregnant women is how much their dream imagery has in common. Not only do various animals appear, there are other recurring images, including plants, vehicles, and different family members in a variety of roles. Some examples:

| Image/Idea | First Trimester | Second Trimester | Third Trimester |
|---|---|---|---|
| You | Your mother<br>Bicycle | Your recent self<br>Car or boat | Someone else<br>(often a large woman)<br>Train or truck |
| Your baby | Seeds or small plants<br>Kittens, puppies<br>Babies | Flowers and shrubs<br>Fish, lizards<br>Yourself as a child | Jungles, orchards<br>Large dogs, whales<br>Your other children |
| Your womb | Small rooms | Intricate caverns | Large buildings |

■ **Pregnant women** *who already have children sometimes dream of predatory animals attacking smaller animals. Such dreams may represent concern about the older children's jealousy of the new baby.*

*Dreaming of a deformed baby does not mean that your own child will be deformed. Such dreams seem to be one of the mind's ways of coping with the natural fears associated with pregnancy.*

## Anxiety in pregnancy

Maybruck believes that pregnancy often compounds the already high stress levels of contemporary women. She cites aspects such as the superwoman syndrome and the career-versus-motherhood conflict, but adds that natural fears about pregnancy and childbirth have always existed – and likely always will. According to Maybruck, no matter what a woman's age, financial status, education level, race, religion, or career, her anxiety-laden dreams almost always relate to one or more of these fears:

- Will my baby be healthy?
- Will I be a good parent?
- What if I lose my spouse?
- Will I have a difficult delivery?
- What if I lose emotional or physical control?
- What if I don't have enough money?

# EXPECTANT ANXIETY

A study conducted by Dr. Myra Leifer in 1980 found that the physical and psychological changes that accompany pregnancy can lead to anxiety, which in turn can result in negative dream imagery, even in the most confident of women.

Patricia Maybruck suggests a five-step program to help alleviate the anxiety such dreams can create. These activities are very enriching at the best of times, and will be even more beneficial in the context of a stressful pregnancy.

- Keep a dream diary
- Interpret your dreams
- Understand your emotions
- Learn to recognize your personal dream imagery
- Control your dreams

**1** **Exercising**

*While exercising is essential for your health, it is doubly useful for an anxious mother-to-be since it releases feel-good hormones into the body. Most experts recommend yoga as a safe and relaxing exercise option. Yoga will also encourage you to develop breath- and mind-control that is conducive to dream control (see Chapters 10 and 11).*

## Negative to positive

When you consider how life-changing pregnancy is – both during pregnancy and after the baby is born – it's easy to see that the dreams of pregnant women reflect that transition rather than forecast any real difficulties. In fact, in Maybruck's studies, there were no instances where such dream fears turned out to be true.

*Patricia Maybruck counsels understanding as much about pregnancy and childbirth as you can, and ultimately discovering how to turn your negative dream images into positive ones.*

Turning negative dreams to positive is not as impossible as it sounds. I'll discuss this idea in more depth in Chapters 10 and 11.

### ② Massaging

*Day-time stress and anxious dreams at night will be allayed by a good massage. Massage soothes your muscles, stimulates your nerve ends, and produces a much-needed feeling of calm and well-being. Consult a massage expert and then do it yourself at home, with your partner's help if possible.*

### ③ Sharing your feelings

*If you join a pregnancy-exercise class, you will have the additional benefit of being able to talk to women going through similar emotions. Many women find that simply voicing the fears that their anxiety dreams illustrate helps alleviate their worries about their pregnancies.*

# Dreams through the life span

*JUST AS PREGNANCY signals the transition to parenthood, other stages of life bring other transitions and the dreams that accompany them. It goes without saying that each individual's experience with a particular transition is unique; nonetheless there are certain parallels to be found, especially when it comes to our dreams. In Chapter 8, for example, I mentioned that as young children begin to comprehend and explore their own autonomy, they'll have more frequent nightmares. There are many other examples of how dreams change throughout our lives – through adolescence, middle age, and old age.*

■ **Anxiety-producing dreams** *often occur at a transitional stage of our life, such as stress-prone middle age.*

1 **Birth:** It may surprise you to see birth on this list, but studies have found that some recurrent dreams may be connected to difficult birth experiences. In an example cited by Robert L. Van de Castle, PhD, a woman's dreams of difficulty in breathing were ultimately traced to the fact that her umbilical cord had been wrapped around her neck during her birth. Another case Van de Castle relates concerns a woman who was born by Caesarean section, and whose dreams involved images such as being paralyzed on her back on a high table.

*My daughter was born in 1979, her umbilical cord wrapped around her neck. When I asked her, she said she had choking dreams "all the time!" But since we talked about the birth/dream connection, she no longer has these dreams.*

2 **Adolescence:** The dreams of young teens are often disturbing and difficult, reflecting this frequently uneasy time of life. Ambiguity seems to be a recurring theme here, with settings that may be hard to name, characters (including the persona) exhibiting anger or dissociation, and themes of alienation and discomfort. Robert L. Van de Castle notes that girls' dreams at this age are not as troubled as boys', although the reasons for this difference are unclear.

3 **Middle age:** By the time we reach middle age, our dream themes and patterns are well established, even if we aren't consciously aware of them. The transitions we encounter in our 40s and 50s may include the deteriorating health or even the death of one or both parents, children leaving home, divorce, or career change: Our dreams will work at helping us resolve these issues. Understanding your own particular personal dream imagery can help make these changes easier to integrate into your own life.

*Empty or unfamiliar house dreams, or dreams in which we discover an unfamiliar place beyond a door in a familiar room, are most common during times of personal or career change.*

 **Active senior citizens** *report more lively and interactive dreams than those who stay at home or in nursing homes. That's because dreams reflect our lives: the more active we are, the more active our dreams.*

4 **Old age:** Two of the more common dream themes of seniors are those of loss and scarcity. Researchers have also found that the settings in seniors' dreams are often unfamiliar, and there may be fewer characters than in the dreamer's younger years. In addition, older dreamers frequently report dreams where they are frustrated or disrupted as they try to do things, or where others try to stop them from doing what they want. It's clear that for this age group, anxieties about everything from money to health find their way into dreams.

# In sickness and in health

*THE ROLE OF DREAMS in illness and recovery has been the subject of a number of recent studies, and in Chapter 14, I'll discuss healing dreams in more detail. In this section, we'll focus on the body/mind/dream connection.*

## A human whole

Many contemporary dream researchers like to say that there is no real line between the conscious and unconscious; rather, we are *holistic* beings, with our bodies and minds working together. Dreams, it follows, are part of this interconnectedness, and so don't just alert our minds to what's going on with our bodies, but also help our bodies heal.

**DEFINITION**

**Holistic** *means all-of-a-piece. We, and everything in the world, are part of an interconnected whole.*

As sensors in touch with our holistic selves, dreams "know" when something is not quite right with our bodies, just as they "know" when something is disturbing us mentally. Many dream experts believe that dreams can help us avoid potential health problems, as well as heal ourselves when we are ill. Dream expert Patricia Garfield, for example, realized that before she broke her wrist in 1988, she'd had at least two dreams that warned her it might happen. Further, although her injury was initially diagnosed as a sprain, a dream told her that her wrist was broken, which an X-ray then confirmed. As she slowly recovered from her injury (which had been complicated by the misdiagnosis), she noticed that her dreams were reflecting her trauma. Garfield noted seven stages common to dreams of illness and recovery:

- Forewarning dreams
- Diagnostic dreams
- Crisis dreams
- Post-crisis dreams
- Healing dreams
- Convalescent dreams
- Wellness dreams

■ **Dreams** *can aid the healing process after illness or injury, in much the same way as meditation and exercise.*

# THE MIND-BODY-DREAM CONNECTION

Eugene T. Gendlin, PhD, took the mind/body/dream connection that Patricia Garfield delineates one step further. In *Let Your Body Interpret Your Dreams*, Gendlin describes the physical sensation we have when we "know" something's right: "Suppose you have forgotten (something). You know there was something, but not what it was. You have an odd, unclear sense of this forgotten task . . . When at last you do remember, there is a physically felt relief . . .." Gendlin believes we can use this same sensation to help us "know" when we are right about our dream interpretation. To facilitate this process, he developed a series of 16 questions designed to discover what the dream is "saying."

**The first 3 questions: Associations with the dream**

- What comes to you when you think about this dream?
- Are there feelings associated with this dream?
- Is there a connection to something that happened yesterday?

**The second 3 questions: The dream's particular drama**

- What about the dream location resonates for you?
- What's intriguing about the dream's story?
- What's interesting about its characters?

**The third 3 questions: The dream characters**

- What part of you is each character?
- How would you be that person?
- Can the dream continue in waking life?

**The fourth 3 questions: Decoding the dream**

- What personal symbols reside in the dream?
- Can you make any body-related analogies?
- Does the dream contradict what you know to be true?

**The last 4 questions: Exploring the dream as a vehicle for personal development**

- Does the dream connect to your childhood?
- Is it related to personal growth?
- Is it about your sexuality?
- Is there a spiritual aspect to the dream?

# Ritual and ceremony

*THE MORNING OF my grad school graduation, I dreamed I overslept and missed the ceremony, angering the classmates who'd selected me to present our class gift to the college. An anxiety dream like this one is very common, but that doesn't make dreams like this any easier to wake up to.*

## Why the anxiety?

If rituals and ceremonies are designed to help us through life transitions, why do they so often produce anxiety dreams? Part of the reason is that while rituals were originally designed as celebrations of transition, they've evolved into events with meanings of their own, meanings that are often quite separate from the transition they're meant to celebrate. Whether a graduation, a wedding, a religious rite of passage, or a funeral, rituals come with an enormous amount of stress.

## Runaway brides and grooms

No modern ritual is quite so stressful (or as expensive) as a wedding, which is probably why a recurring theme in these dreams is forgetting to show up on one's wedding day. Others include forgetting the ring or one's lines, the dress or tuxedo not being ready, or being stood up at the altar.

■ **Research has shown that** *up to three months before the wedding day, 40 percent of the bride's and groom's dreams will relate directly to anxieties about the ceremony itself.*

## Wedding anxiety dreams

In *Dreams That Can Change Your Life* (see *Further Reading*), Alan B. Siegel, PhD, divides wedding anxiety dreams into categories:

- Conflicts over wedding details
- Tension with family and in-laws
- Performance anxiety
- Fears of intimacy and commitment
- Fears of losing freedom
- Fears of repeating mistakes of parents
- Anxieties about change in identity, both literal (name change) and figurative

Because books assure us that our wedding is supposed to be the happiest day of our life, we may worry when we fail to live up to that picture-perfect image. While fairy tales promise "happily ever after," they never tell us just what that entails. The truth is that it's perfectly normal to be less than happy about such an enormous change, and this is what our dreams are trying to tell us.

### Trivia...

*When a ritual or ceremony appears in your dream, even though there's nothing like that going on in your life, Jungian theory holds that the dream originated in the collective unconscious. Dreaming of a wedding when you (or someone close to you) are not going to get married could represent a union within the self of the* anima *and the* animus, *while a funeral might suggest the end of a certain period in one's life.*

## Dream ceremonies/life ceremonies

Like all dream imagery, dream ceremonies are not necessarily what they seem to be. Some might represent endorsement of the status quo; others may suggest the need for major change. In order to determine which your dream ceremony might represent, two questions to consider are:

 What's going on in your life?

 Why do you think you had this particular dream at this particular time?

Here's an example. Shortly before my father died after a brief illness, I had this dream:

> *I was flying over some sort of event at a bleacher-lined field in a park in Buffalo, which is where I grew up. As I flew over (I was wearing a flowing white dress I owned at the time), I realized that it was a funeral, not a sporting event, but that everyone there (the bleachers were full) seemed to be having a good time anyway. Curious, but not wanting to disturb the festivities, I landed in a discrete tree branch and watched. At some point, I knew it was my father's funeral, but this did not upset me. In fact, I was pleased that it "had gone so well."*

And that is the feeling I awoke with. The ceremony in this dream served to help me come to terms with my father's imminent death. The fact that I could fly – and that I chose to perch in a tree to watch – reminded me that my life would go on without him.

# Death is a fact of life

*AS THE DREAM in the previous section illustrates, realizing that death is a fact of life can help us deal with the death of someone close to us. Another angle is presented in the lovely dream that follows, reported by a woman who had recently turned 80:*

> *I found myself giving a big party – one of my long-time delights. I had invited everyone I knew. The party was in full swing. The sound of laughter and conversation had reached B-flat, which I had always called the party pitch. First, I became aware that almost all of the guests were dead, though they were eating and drinking and making merry just like always. Then, I realized that they were gradually disappearing. I went to the huge window at the end of the room and looked out on the enormous clear sunset. There were my guests, sailing out into the sky with their arms outstretched and their ankles touching neatly behind them – happy, eager, full of energy. For a moment, I was daunted by the sense of loss and fear. Then, I thought, I can do that. I began to feel joy and anticipation. I stretched out my arms and, rising on my toes, I pushed myself gently and confidently into the freedom of the air, joining the skyful of tiny figures, which were moving faster and faster into the expanding sunset.*

I love this dream! I cried the first time I read it, both because of the lovely imagery and the dreamer's "joy and anticipation." What's most important about it, however, is its acceptance of its own metaphor: a recognition that as she ages the dreamer's friends are dying, and that someday she will as well.

■ **Coming to terms** *with death can be symbolized in your dreams by some other action, such as "flying away." An actual dream of dying, on the other hand, could indicate some transition in your life.*

## Death in dreams

Just as dreams of ceremonies aren't necessarily about transitions, dreams of death aren't necessarily about dying.

*Death dreams aren't always about death; often they're about transformation. And dreams about death don't always have death in them. Finally, death in dreams is often not the negative experience we've been raised to think it is.*

Major change often requires the "death" of an old way. You might need to quit your old job in order to start a new one or you may need to quit smoking for your health. Such change can be frightening, which is why many of us avoid it. When it's necessary for our growth, however, our dreams may begin to insist we pay attention, and that's when death dreams may occur. A man with a drinking problem, for example, dreamed he shot himself in the head. When he examined the imagery, he realized that his drinking was like shooting himself in the head, and attended his first Alcoholics Anonymous meeting.

# A simple summary

✔ The hormonal changes of pregnancy often translate into vivid dream imagery and make it easier to remember.

✔ The dreams of pregnant women share common imagery, including plants, animals, vehicles, and various family members.

✔ Dreams change as we pass through our lives. Understanding our personal dream imagery can help make life changes easier to integrate.

✔ Dreams can not only alert our minds to what's going on with our bodies but can also help our bodies heal.

✔ It's perfectly normal to be nervous about getting married, which is what wedding anxiety dreams are trying to tell us.

✔ Like all dream imagery, dream ceremonies are not necessarily what they seem to be.

✔ Death dreams aren't always about death; sometimes, they're about transformation.

# Part Three

# Dream Techniques

Here, you'll learn about types of dreaming and how they can help you enhance your life.

# Chapter 10

# What is Lucid Dreaming?

LUCID DREAMING is the awareness that you are in a dream. Dream researchers like Stephen LaBerge offer both dramatic evidence and step-by-step exercises toward developing your own lucid dreaming abilities, making this potentially life-changing aspect of dreams accessible to anyone who's interested in learning. Lucid dreaming is so intriguing that I'll be devoting two chapters to the subject: this first one will explain just what it is and illustrate some of its benefits, while the next chapter will show you how you too can learn to fly through your dreams.

## In this chapter...

✔ "I must be dreaming . . ."

✔ Benefits of lucid dreaming

✔ How to write your own dream scripts

IMAGINE THE EXHILARATION OF CONTROLLING YOUR DREAMS!

# "I must be dreaming..."

*"HOW CAN YOU KNOW you're unconscious when you're unconscious?"* dream researcher Jayne Gackenbach asks about the paradox of **lucid dreaming**. Paradoxical as this kind of dreaming may seem, however, dreamers as early as Aristotle have noted the ability to dream lucidly. Today, lucid dreamers are discovering there is no limit to their own potential within their dreams. Lucid dreamers may work to develop self-confidence, practice their brushstrokes, or perfect their tennis serves, to name a few possibilities.

> **DEFINITION**
>
> **Lucid dreaming** *means being aware that you are dreaming while you are dreaming.*

## A lucid dreaming chronology

The study of lucid dreaming is a fairly recent aspect of dream research.

- **Early 20th century:** The term was probably coined by Dutch psychiatrist Frederik Willems van Eeden, a prolific lucid dreamer.

- **1968:** The first contemporary book on the subject was written by Celia E. Green in the United Kingdom.

- **1960s and early 1970s:** Scientists first began to look seriously at lucid dreams when Keith Hearne, PhD, also in the United Kingdom, began reporting his findings.

■ **Lucid dreaming** *can be a useful tool for practicing your game, or rehearsing any day-to-day situation.*

Others who have extensively studied lucid dreaming are Patricia Garfield, PhD, who has explored the benefits of creative visualization; Jayne Gackenbach, PhD, who is interested in lucid dreamers themselves; and the acknowledged leader in the field, Stephen LaBerge, PhD, whose doctoral research in the 1970s confirmed that lucid dreaming can be taught, and who developed methods for observing lucid dreamers in the laboratory.

*It has been found that at least half of all adults have at least one lucid dream during their lifetime. As many as one-quarter have one lucid dream a month!*

## Spontaneous lucid dreams

While LaBerge and others have developed methods for incubating lucid dreams (which I'll explore in depth in the next chapter), many have reported spontaneous lucid dreams in which they realized they were dreaming while they were dreaming, without even trying. One of my own dreams, as fantastic as it sounds, is actually a fairly typical spontaneous lucid dream scenario:

> *I was having my usual trouble getting my foot to move onto the brake of a runaway vehicle when I thought, "Wait a second. I'm dreaming." Immediately, the car (and its mechanical difficulty) was gone, and I was instead flying to my dream destination.*

## The moment of realization

Nearly all lucid dreamers report a dramatic change in their perception at the moment of realization. Such changes include:

(a) Knowledge that one can fly, almost always followed by flying

(b) Ability to manipulate dream events

(c) Change in or disappearance of perceived threat or danger

(d) Willingness to confront perceived threats

(e) Increased self-awareness and self-confidence

(f) Awakening (I'll discuss how to avoid this in the next chapter)

■ **A remarkable clarity** *of scents, tastes, sights, sound, and touch will come to you at the moment you realize that you are dreaming, in your dream.*

Stephen LaBerge suggests a number of preliminary steps that can be taken to increase the incidence of lucid dreams. We'll explore each of them individually in the following sections. (Interestingly, LaBerge has also devised tools for enhancing lucid dreaming, such as a NovaDreamer – a sleep mask that sends out signals to the sleeper during the REM period, to "remind him" that he is dreaming.)

*Stephen LaBerge's books include* Lucid Dreaming *(1986),* Exploring the World of Lucid Dreaming *(1990), and* A Course in Lucid Dreaming *(1995). An excellent book on lucid dreaming is LaBerge's and Gackenbach's collection of essays,* Conscious Mind, Sleeping Brain *(1988).*

## Improving dream recall

While there are those who have reported spontaneous lucid dreams, the vast majority of us need to learn how to develop this skill. The good news is that it is very learnable.

1. The first step is to be able to recall at least one dream every single night. Not only will this help you recognize your own particular dream metaphors, it will help you learn to recognize that you are dreaming as well

2. The single best way to improve your dream recall is to keep a dream journal, as I discussed in detail in Chapter 4

3. LaBerge suggests setting an alarm at intervals throughout the night to capture still more of your dreams. After all, the more dreams you can recall, the easier it will be for you to recognize them from within the dream itself

*If you don't easily recall your normal dreams, you may have lucid dreams and not remember them!*

## Improving lucid dreaming skills

Pinch yourself. Did you feel that? While the pinch test was the long-accepted way of discovering if one was dreaming, it turns out that it's not the most reliable: dreamers who pinched themselves in their dreams felt the pinch in the same way you just did. So how do you ascertain if you are dreaming? This question is not so foolish as it sounds. Many things happen throughout the day that are unusual in some way – haven't you sometimes glimpsed something out of the corner of your eye, which is gone by the time you shift your glance? To encourage lucid dreaming, you should:

1. **Ask yourself, "Am I dreaming?" every time something unusual occurs**: Test whether you are awake or dreaming quite specifically and methodically. Stephen LaBerge suggests looking at the time on a digital watch or clock and then immediately checking it again: in a dream, the time will change. Or, you can look at some writing and then look at it again: this, too, will change if you are dreaming.

2. **Ask yourself, "Am I dreaming?" even when nothing out-of-the-ordinary occurs**: That's because by asking yourself if you're dreaming while you're awake, you will also learn to ask yourself if you're dreaming when you're asleep. When you perform tests of your dream state such as those suggested above when you are dreaming, you may then become aware you are dreaming within the dream.

**INTERNET**

**www.lucidity.com**

*This is the web site of the Lucidity Institute, founded by Stephen LaBerge. It offers a detailed introduction to lucid dreaming, excerpts from Dr LaBerge's books and articles, FAQs, links, and more.*

## Dream signals and dreamsigns

**Dream signals** and **dreamsigns** are two more aspects of your dreams that can help you develop your lucid dreaming ability. Discovering your dream signals is as close as your dream journal. Once you've recorded at least a dozen dreams, you can go back through them to find objects and images that seem to recur. Dream signals can be:

- Places, such as cars or houses
- Animals, whether exotic or domestic
- People, either those you know or certain types, such as "doctors"

Anything else that occurs frequently in your dreams can be a dream signal for you. The only limit is your imagination, which, of course, has no limits.

*My own dream signals are easy to note: cars, stairways, and those darned boxes I'm always moving from place to place. You'll find yours equally easy to identify, once you've recorded a number of dreams in your journal.*

## Using dreamsigns

Dreamsigns are equally intriguing. Some common ones are:

- Flying
- The appearance of someone who has died, though we often don't remember they are dead

Our usual "rational" response within a dream when a dreamsign occurs is to explain away the anomaly: "I can fly because I bought these wings." Using dreamsigns to become lucid means that instead of explaining away or ignoring the dreamsign within the dream, you will use the dreamsign as a signal to let yourself know you are dreaming: "I can fly because I am dreaming." "My late father is here because I am dreaming." In the next chapter, you'll learn specific ways in which you can do this.

■ **The appearance** *of something fantastic in your dream is an "in-dream sign" that you are dreaming.*

# Benefits of lucid dreaming

*NOW THAT YOU UNDERSTAND what lucid dreaming is, you can probably imagine some of its potential benefits. While a good many lucid dreamers use lucid dreaming as a vehicle for adventure and fantasy fulfillment, it's also possible to utilize lucid dreams as tools for improving your waking life. Because you can control the dream situation, lucid dreams give you the opportunity to (a) creatively visualize situations, (b) solve problems, and (c) confront your dream demons.*

## Creative visualization

Creative visualization is a way of seeing something in your mind's eye in order to work with it before it actually occurs. Creative visualization and dreams seem to go hand in hand. That's because, as a highly visual medium, dreams can help you "see" things before they actually occur.

■ **Most lucid dreamers** *report flying dreams and many can actively induce such dreams, enjoying unparalleled feelings of freedom, power, and pleasure.*

## It's simple!

The interesting thing is that you don't have to be in a "creative" field of work to use lucid dreaming creatively. You can also benefit from it in your day-to-day life, even in what may seem to you more mundane activities. In fact, if you have ever imagined and re-imagined a future event, you've already used creative visualization at its most basic level.

While picturing something in a nonlucid dream can help you solve problems, particularly if you've begun exploring what your own dream metaphors may mean, lucid dreaming offers you the opportunity to:

● Decide what problem you want to work on
● Picture it within a lucid dream
● Work with it until you get it right

# CREATIVE DREAMING

A well-known creative dreaming story is that of the poet Samuel Taylor Coleridge (1772–1834), whose poem *Kubla Khan* (you probably read this one in school) came to him during an opium-induced dream. The story goes that after taking some opium, the poet fell asleep as he read the words "here the Kubla Khan commanded a palace to be built." He awoke several hours later with the poem *Kubla Khan* ready in his mind. As Coleridge was interrupted while recording the poem, however, he considered it forever unfinished.

■ **Samuel Coleridge's dream** *gave birth to lines like "And 'mid these dancing rocks at once and ever / It flung up momently the sacred river . . ."*

Don't lose heart – you need not be a famous poet or an opium-taker to have creative dreams! Examples of people who used creative dreaming to solve problems abound:

*a*    Students who solved complicated math problems in their sleep

*b*    Project managers who developed work schedules while dreaming

*c*    Writers whose stories wrote themselves in their dreams

*d*    People who worked through relationship issues while asleep

You'll find much more on creative dreaming in Chapters 12 and 13.

## Facing your fears

We're all afraid of something. Most of us, in fact, are afraid of many things: even for adults, the world can be a scary place. We may be afraid that something will happen to our spouses, or our children – or to ourselves. Many people are afraid to venture out after dark; others are afraid of heights, of flying, or of crowds.

Lucid dreaming offers the unique opportunity to face our fears within our dreams. Let's say, for example, that like many people, you're afraid of making a presentation at a meeting. If you know that you *must* make a presentation, and if you've learned how to dream lucidly, you can "rehearse" making the presentation in your dreams until you get it right. Stephen LaBerge calls turning negatives into positives "rehearsing for success." He notes that "because the activity of the brain during a dreamed activity is the same as during a real event, neuronal patterns of activation required for a skill . . . can be established in the dream state in preparation for performance in the waking world."

■ **You can actually "practice"** *public speaking in a lucid dream and eventually overcome your nervousness.*

## *LUCID DREAMING – FOR AND AGAINST*

Not all dream researchers believe that lucid dreaming is a good idea. If dreams are messages from the unconscious, they say, tampering with them via lucid dreaming may hinder self-understanding. Stephen LaBerge's response is that:

*a* "Dreams are not messages, but models of the world"

*b* "Dreams . . . are more like clues into the inner workings of our minds. The conscious and critical awareness that accompanies lucid dreams allows dreamers to thoughtfully interpret their dreams while they happen"

*Lucid dreams don't inhibit self-understanding, they enhance it.*

## Confronting dream demons

Those who have recurring nightmares know the feeling: "Oh no. Not again!"

*Recognizing that a dream demon is one that you've encountered before is actually a big step toward lucid dreaming, because it's a recognition of something that occurred only within a dream.*

Nightmares, as we discussed earlier, are dreams filled with terror and anxiety which the dreamer *seems* unable to resolve within the dream. I emphasize the word "seems," because lucid dreamers have discovered that it is possible to resolve a nightmare when they are aware they are dreaming. Here's an example in which the dreamer confronted her "shadow" – precisely what she needed to do.

*I was sitting at my desk when I felt that sensation again. I knew there was something behind me, and, as usual, I felt as if I'd forgotten how to breathe. I could actually feel a dark shadow moving across me. Then I remembered: I was dreaming! Immediately, I could breathe again, and the shadow receded, but I knew the presence was still there behind me. I turned slowly in my chair and there it was, this black shadow. I wasn't frightened. "Who are you?" I asked it. "What do you want?" "You know who I am," it said, and I did: it was my fear that my writing wasn't any good, that sitting here at my desk was a waste of time. As soon as I knew that, the shadow became light and sparkly and then dissolved into fairy dust. It sounds so silly and trite, but that's what happened.*

*There's often the temptation, when empowered by lucidity in a nightmare, to destroy the dream demon because you can. But it's far better to learn why the demon comes to you so that you may confront and understand your fear.*

■ **A pursuer** *in a dream could indicate the "shadow" – the Jungian archetype that represents an aspect of ourselves that we do not wish to confront.*

■ **A nightmare** *depicts a terrifying situation, such as being caught in a fierce storm, from which there appears to be no way out. However, if you practice lucid dreaming, you can actually dream your way out of a nightmare. Shown above is* Torre de Belem, *a painting by J.T. Serres.*

# How to write your own dream scripts

*ONCE YOU'VE BEGUN to practice lucid dreaming, you can learn to "write" your own dream scripts. By this I mean you can decide either beforehand or within the dream to alter the dream's course, shift to another character's point of view, or change the dream's location.*

## The good news – it's possible!

The idea of controlling your dreams may sound odd, but with practice you can do it:

*a)* The first step, of course, is to believe that you *can* do it.

*b)* In *Exploring the World of Lucid Dreaming* (see *Further Reading* at the end of the book), Stephen LaBerge cites dream pioneer Alan Worsley's approach: Think of the dream as something on television. Just as you can with a television, you can change the channel, adjust the brightness, and fiddle with the volume. You can even hook your dream TV up to a VCR or disk player and change the film.

*c)* In a lucid dream, you don't need to stop at what you can ordinarily do with a television, either. You could imagine that you can smell the roses in the garden on-screen or taste the soufflé that the chef is taking from the oven, or feel the waves tickling your toes as you walk along a beach at sunset.

■ **Unlike in an** *ordinary dream in which you can only "see" things, in a lucid dream you can actually feel the waves, smell the sand, and enjoy the breeze.*

Another way of writing your own dream script is to decide before you fall asleep that there is something you would like to explore from a number of different angles. For example, you might be thinking about asking your boss for a raise. In a lucid dream, you would ask your boss in a number of different ways. You would then see how he or she reacts.

By now, you're probably eager to find out how you can become a lucid dreamer. For that, let's turn to Chapter 11.

■ **You can "be" your boss** *in your dream. Lucid dreamers say that such dream scripts help them prepare for real-life encounters and inspire confidence at the same time.*

## *A simple summary*

✔ Lucid dreaming is the state of dreaming while being aware that you are dreaming. What you do within a lucid dream is limited only by your imagination.

✔ Some ways to improve your ability to have lucid dreams are improving dream recall; asking yourself if you are dreaming when you are awake; and noting your dream signals and dreamsigns.

✔ Benefits of lucid dreaming include solving problems and creatively visualizing potential situations.

✔ By lucidly confronting your dream demons, you can learn to face your fears.

✔ With practice, you can actually learn to "write" the scripts for your own dreams.

## Chapter 11

# Becoming a Lucid Dreamer

I N THIS CHAPTER, you'll learn various ways to recognize within a dream that you're dreaming; how to get the most out of a dream once you're lucid; and how to work with dream content to enhance both your dreams and your life. I'll also explore aspects such as false awakening, something that seems to occur far more often in lucid dreams; and show how you can use your "near-misses" to add to your dream signal and dreamsign inventories – and your self-understanding.

## In this chapter...

✓ **Creating a lucid dream-sleep environment**

✓ **Incubating lucid dreams**

✓ **Recognizing lucid dreams**

✓ **Dream control**

LUCID DREAMING IS MUCH MORE THAN JUST A FLIGHT OF FANCY

# Creating a lucid dream-sleep environment

*BECAUSE MOST LUCID DREAMS occur in the longest period of REM sleep just before dawn, the single best way to encourage lucid dreams may be simply to sleep longer.*

## Rearranging your sleep pattern

Lucid dream researcher Stephen LaBerge goes one step further, suggesting in *Exploring the World of Lucid Dreaming* that you rearrange your sleep time:

**1** If you normally sleep from midnight to 6:00 a.m., get up at 4:00 a.m.

**2** Stay awake for two hours, doing whatever you need to do.

**3** Go back to bed and catch up on your remaining sleep from 6:00 a.m. to 8:00 a.m.

*It's important to relax! If you push yourself to have a lucid dream, your efforts may have the opposite effect.*

## Why rearrange?

During the two hours of delayed sleep you will have much more REM time than you would have had sleeping at the usual time – and you will enjoy an increased likelihood of lucid dreaming, with no time lost to sleep.

## What if you can't?

Of course, not everyone has the luxury of rearranging their sleep time. If you don't, try going to bed a little earlier than you normally do so that you can allow for a two-hour, middle-of-the-night awakening by sleeping a little later. This simple step can give you the extra REM time that you need for your first lucid dream.

■ **Do something** *you enjoy, like reading or writing, in your two hours of wakefulness.*

# Incubating lucid dreams

*INCUBATING LUCID DREAMS means taking the material you collected in preparation for lucid dreaming and putting it to work. Do you recall how, in Chapter 10, you took three critical steps toward this end? These steps were: 1) cataloging your dream signals; 2) inventorying your dreamsigns; and 3) asking yourself if you are dreaming.*

■ **If you are** *writing your dreams in your journal and have begun to identify your dream signals and dreamsigns, you are ready to take the next step toward becoming a lucid dreamer.*

## Reality tests

Now, you're going to teach yourself to use this material while you are dreaming, by creating your own "reality tests." This means that instead of allowing yourself to explain away dream anomalies rationally within a dream, any time a dream signal or dreamsign appears, it will serve to remind you that you are dreaming.

But how do you train yourself to do this? The answer is that you will learn to activate a critical-reflective attitude toward your state of consciousness. Simply put, you'll ask yourself the critical question "Am I dreaming?" throughout the day, until asking that question becomes second nature; that is, reflective. The more automatically you ask yourself "Am I dreaming?" when you are awake, the more likely you are to ask yourself this question when you are dreaming.

*Learn to ask yourself "Am I dreaming?" when you go to bed and are getting ready to fall asleep or if you wake up during the night.*

## Check your perception

It's important when you ask the question "Am I dreaming?" that you don't automatically answer, "Of course not." This may seem foolish now, but you'll find that the way you answer when you're awake makes a big difference when you begin to ask this question when you're dreaming. Rather than simply say no, you should instead come up with a consistent way of checking to see if you are awake or asleep. You might, for example:

**ⓐ** Check the time on a digital clock or watch and then immediately check it again. Has the time changed?

**ⓑ** Read something, look away, then read it again. Is it the same?

**ⓒ** Look at someone else, then look at him a moment later. Is he wearing the same thing? Is he still the same person (or animal)? Has he moved in some way that would not be physically possible in the waking world?

**ⓓ** Pick a fixed object that cannot move, study it, and then look at it again. Has it moved, altered, or even disappeared?

*In dreams, I've seen the time on my nightstand digital clock read 4:48 and then immediately 11:17. I've read handwritten directions on a 3 x 5 card and had them turn into a cash register receipt when I looked again.*

You will find that the key to discerning if you are awake or dreaming is consistency. If you're often in a car in your dreams ask yourself if you're dreaming whenever you're driving (or a passenger), then check your car clock and check it again. Do this every time you're in your car, and eventually you will do the same in your dream car, only to realize that the time has changed dramatically from one glance to the next. This can then serve as your signal in the dream that you are dreaming.

■ *If you often dream of cars, then you should ask yourself the "Am I dreaming?" question whenever you sit in a car during your waking day.*

# Recognizing lucid dreams

*STEPHEN LABERGE DEVELOPED Mnemonic Induction of Lucid Dreams (MILD) as a dream induction method after realizing that he himself was less likely to have a lucid dream when he tried too hard. MILD combines the external mnemonic devices you already use to remember things like phone numbers and grocery lists and the brain's goal-seeking system into a consistent method for recognizing within a dream that you are dreaming.*

## It's all in the mind

Like any mnemonic system, however, MILD is an acquired skill. If you're not good at remembering things when you're awake, you're not very likely to remember them when you're asleep. LaBerge suggests working to improve your waking memory before using this system to try to trigger lucid dreaming.

*Give yourself a list of unrelated items to remember every morning and then recall the list every evening until you can do so easily.*

## MNEMONIC INDUCTION OF LUCID DREAMS (MILD)

Once you know you can remember things easily when you're awake, you're ready to trigger your brain to remember to let you know when you're dreaming. MILD involves five simple steps:

1. Resolve to wake up and remember a dream during every REM sleep period.

2. Each time you awaken, recall as much as you can of the dream.

3. Remind yourself to remember your dream the next time you're dreaming.

4. Visualize yourself lucid in the dream you have just had. A good way to do this is to pick a dreamsign and tell yourself the next time you see that dreamsign, you'll become lucid in the dream.

5. Sleep, and dream.

## Wake Induced Lucid Dreaming (WILD)

While similar to MILD in some ways, Wake Induced Lucid Dreaming (WILD), as its name suggests, begins while you're awake rather than when you're asleep. You may recall from Chapter 3 that just before you fall asleep you enter a period of nearly hallucinogenic imagery, called hypnogogic dreaming. You can now learn to move from this state to a state of lucid dreaming.

***Using meditation techniques, WILD teaches you how to focus on hypnogogic imagery so that you may "ride" it into the dream state.***

### Calm and relax your mind and body

Use whatever meditation technique works best for you. One popular choice is progressive relaxation: This involves consciously tensing and then releasing small parts of your body one step at a time. To practice progressive relaxation, follow these steps:

1. Begin with your toes, tensing and releasing them one at a time, then tense and release the arch of each foot, then the heel, ankle, and so on.

2. Work your way up your legs and your trunk and then down each arm.

3. Relax your neck, then work through the muscles of your face, all the way to the top of your head.

Once you have finished, you will move quickly into the hypnogogic state.

### Observe the images that form before your eyes

Try to follow the images without thought or judgment, observing them passively without attempting to control them. Gradually, these images will evolve into scenes, which will in turn move into dreams.

### Enter your dream as a detached viewer

This is the hardest part, as you will want to do this as a passive observer rather than active participant. One way to enter a dream from the waking state is to focus on one object in a way similar to Tibetan and Buddhist meditation. Meditations like these require both concentration and training, but learning to "carry" an object from wakefulness to a lucid dream can be well worth the effort.

■ **Buddhist meditation** *techniques involve concentrating on an object, such as a prayer wheel (shown here), until it becomes part of your "non-conscious" state.*

## The DreamLight

Developed by Stephen LaBerge and engineer Darrel Dixon in the mid-1980s, the DreamLight is a mechanically induced way of alerting a dreamer to the fact that he or she is dreaming. Using mask-mounted sensors to indicate when REM sleep begins, the DreamLight then flashes a light to signal the dreamer that it's dreamtime. The DreamLight has proved to be a very effective way of inducing lucid dreaming.

■ **If you use** *a DreamLight mask to aid lucid dreaming, the light it flashes into your eyes may get incorporated in the narrative of your dream.*

## Now I see light

The main difference between light-induced dreams and spontaneous lucid dreams seems to be the light itself. One of the interesting side effects of using the DreamLight to induce lucid dreaming has been the ways dreamers incorporate the light itself into the dream.

*Usually, while the dreamer sleeps, external stimuli are often incorporated into the dream itself as dream imagery.*

- The dreamers may recognize the light for what it is
- They may see it as an image within the dream
- They may see it as being outside the dream
- They may see it imposed on the dream, like a veil or pattern
- They may sense it rather than see it

# Dream control

*DREAMS, PARTICULARLY lucid dreams, are every bit as vivid as waking life. And, just as with waking life, how much you can influence what happens is very much up to you. Think of dream control as a chain of cause and effect where the effect is yet to be determined, and you begin to understand the potential of where you can go in your lucid dreams.*

**INTERNET**

www.sawka.com/spirit
watch/tableof.htm

*This web site provides papers on a variety of lucid dreaming and dream control topics by a who's who of dream experts.*

## Cause and effect

In their article "Testing the Limits of Dream Control" (available at the lucidity.com web site), Lynne Levitan and Stephen LaBerge conclude that "dreams can be directed, but still do their own thing." In other words, while lucid dreamers can indeed influence dream causes, they have little control over the effects. At least, not yet . . .

## Pushing the frontiers

Lucid dream pioneer Alan Worsley has documented his attempts to control various tasks within his dreams. He discovered that it was easy to move through dream walls, make dream sounds, and fly close to the ground, while it was harder to read more than a few words, turn on a light in a darkened room, or fly far above the ground.

■ **Moving through objects** *is one of the feats you can achieve while lucid dreaming.*

## False awakening

Have you ever dreamed your alarm has gone off, you've gotten out of bed, shuffled to the bathroom, brushed your teeth, and then gone into the kitchen to start your coffee, only to suddenly awaken and find that you're still in bed? The dream where your day began without you is called a *false awakening*.

While fairly common in regular dreams, false awakenings seem to be an even more frequent occurrence in lucid dreams. Beginning lucid dreamers in particular report false awakenings, because the impetus for these events seems to be the knowledge that one is dreaming. Because false awakening seems to occur far more often in lucid dreaming, you should learn to recognize its signals.

## DON'T WAKE UP!

One of the most difficult things about lucid dreaming is staying asleep. You may be so excited to discover your awareness that you're dreaming that you wake up. Stephen LaBerge has found that the best technique for maintaining your lucidity is spinning yourself around within your lucid dream. Apparently, the spinning movement within the dream keeps the dreamer dreaming.

Some dream spinners report that they have the sensation of hitting their arm on their bed while spinning, which then leads to a false awakening. You can likely avoid this snag if you remember to perform your "Am I dreaming?" reality check if it seems you've awakened after spinning to stay in a dream.

■ **The sensation of** *spinning within a lucid dream helps you continue dreaming.*

## "Near-misses"

Shortly before I began writing this chapter, I had the following dream:

*I am in my Explorer on the approach from the Robert Moses Parkway to the North Grand Island Bridge (in Niagara Falls, near where I grew up). I've always thought this was a poorly engineered ramp, and I've dreamed it many times before. In the dream, I think, "Oh no, not this dream again. I'm so tired of this dream." Then, in the dream, I realize that it's a dream, and then I think I wake up – but I'm still on the ramp.*

*As I start to wind up the long approach to the bridge, I realize I can't see the road in front of me and I know what that means. Sure enough, off the ramp and into the water my car and I go. "Not again," I think, but the Explorer is already sinking. I know it's real this time, and I'm very angry that after dreaming this so many times I've gone and done it anyway. I'm already having difficulty breathing when I realize that this car has power windows and that even though it's sinking, I'll be able to press the button and get out. As I reach to do so, I wake up for real. I'm furious with both myself and the dream: Haven't I learned anything?*

### Analysis

Being lucid in a dream doesn't always mean the nightmare is going to end, as this dream illustrates. In fact, a number of elements concerning lucid dreaming come into play here, so let's discuss them one at a time.

1. **I realize I'm dreaming and think I wake up:** The dreamsign that I'm on the Grand Island Bridge in my Explorer should have been a giveaway, because I live in New Mexico; also, when I visit my family, I drive a rental car. I've now added "in Western New York" to my dreamsign inventory.

2. **I can't see the road in front of me:** Here's another dreamsign. I may be short, but I can almost always see the road in front of me. Instead of recognizing this dreamsign in the dream, however, I get angrier. Anger, in fact, is the primary emotion in this dream, and, realizing that it's also appeared in many others, I've added it to my dream signal inventory, too.

■ **In a lucid dream** *you can experience normal and dreamlike situations simultaneously.*

**I realize a way to change the usual outcome of the dream:** I'm on the verge of lucidity again at the moment I realize that I don't have to drown because my car has power windows, and, as often happens to even experienced lucid dreamers, I at once wake up when this occurs, for real this time. I am left, however, with the primary dream emotion of anger, as well as a feeling of "Why haven't I learned anything?"

In fact, I've learned a great deal from this dream. And this time, I've written it all down. Not only have I added a number of important dream signals and dreamsigns to my personal inventories, I've recognized that, while I think I'm being more honest with myself emotionally, I still have a tendency to substitute the wrong emotion – in this case, anger – for fear.

*As you work with your own efforts at lucid dreaming, nightmarish "near-miss" dreams will help add to your dream signal and dreamsign inventories, while, at the same time, help you explore the larger theme of the dream.*

## A simple summary

✓ The single best way to encourage lucid dreams may be simply to sleep longer.

✓ Instead of allowing yourself to explain away dream anomalies rationally, any time a dream signal or dreamsign appears, letting it serve to remind you that you are dreaming will help you incubate lucid dreams.

✓ Ask yourself "Am I dreaming?" throughout the day and you will teach yourself to ask the same question in your dreams as well.

✓ Mnemonic systems like MILD and WILD and devices like the DreamLight can help induce lucid dreaming.

✓ Because false awakening seems to occur far more often in lucid dreaming, you should learn to recognize its signals.

✓ You can use your "near-misses" to add to your dream signal and dreamsign inventories and explore the larger theme of the dream.

# Chapter 12

# The Stuff of Dreams

T HE STUFF OF DREAMS has been fodder for the creative imagination for as long as humans have been creating. Dreams have helped writers write their books; visual artists have depicted their dreams in painting, sculpture, and film; musicians have heard their next composition in their dreams; scientists have discovered simple answers to complicated questions while asleep; and everyday creative dreamers have learned how to use their dreams to solve problems from the mundane to the profound.

*In this chapter...*

✓ **Literary dreams and dreamers**

✓ **Dreamy art**

✓ **Celluloid dreams**

✓ **Dream solutions**

✓ **Everyday creative dreamers**

# Literary dreams and dreamers

ONE OF THE BEST-KNOWN *literary dreamers is Robert Louis Stevenson, who credited little people he called "Brownies" for his finest work, including the psychological masterwork* Dr. Jekyll and Mr. Hyde. *According to Stevenson, he would begin to work on a book and then set it aside. Then, while he was asleep, his Brownies would set to work and continue to write the story for him. He'd capture their work upon awakening.*

■ **Mary Shelley dreamed** *of the creature that became Frankenstein's monster, after being challenged to write a horror story. Shown above is a scene from the film* Bride of Frankenstein.

## Dreaming up stories

Stevenson isn't the only literary dreamer, of course. Another well-known story is that of the poet Samuel Taylor Coleridge, whose poem *Kubla Khan* came to him in an opium-induced dream (see *p.143*).

Edgar Allan Poe is another writer who used his dream imagery in his work. To cite one example, Poe reported that his poem "The Lady Ligeia" was inspired by a woman he met in a dream whose eyes were "far larger than the ordinary eyes of our race." In fact, there are probably few creative writers who have not turned to dreams for inspiration at one time or another. Among those who have noted their success with creative dreams are Jack Kerouac, Katherine Mansfield, Robert Penn Warren, Graham Greene, Charlotte Brontë, and Franz Kafka (and me!).

*One night in 1816, Mary Shelley, her husband – the poet Shelley – and a group of friends were telling ghost stories when Lord Byron challenged them to write a horror story. That night, Mary Shelley dreamed of the creature that would become Frankenstein's monster.*

# Dreamy art

*SALVADOR DALI'S dreamscapes may be the most familiar "dreamy" art, but visual artists have been exploring dreams for millennia. Dream imagery has been found in relics from both Ancient Egypt and Ancient China, to name but two civilizations.*

## Colors in the night

More recent examples can be found in the work of 19th-century French painter Henri Rousseau, whose famous painting *The Dream* (see p.24) depicts a young woman sleeping in the forest, surrounded by the passive animals and lush foliage of her own dream. The artist Jasper Johns achieved his first success after dreaming about painting an American flag.

■ *The Scream* (1893) *by Edvard Munch (1863–1944) depicts the pervasive fear that defines a nightmare.*

Johns's contemporary, Salvador Dali, noted that his fascination with dreams began after he'd read Sigmund Freud's *Interpretation of Dreams*. Surrealist artists like Dali frequently mined their dreams for artistic inspiration, resulting in such familiar but disturbing canvases as the 1928 *Depths Unspoken* by Yves Tanguy and Edvard Munch's *The Scream*.

## Trivia...

*In a* New Yorker *article, alternative cartoonist Daniel Clowes says, "Authentic art comes mainly from an individual's unconscious, from stray memories, and fears and wishes – and particularly, dreams."*

Dreams have made their presence felt in fields such as pottery and jewelry-making as well. Native American artists in particular seem to take advantage of their dreams: An award-winning Native American jeweler, for example, first tried his trade after dreaming that his late mother gave him jewelry tools and said that he would "become a famous Indian" if he used them.

*Dreams have found their way into visual media such as sculpture, including French artist Jean Depre's Pieta.*

# Celluloid dreams

*WITH ITS VISUAL imagery, ability to "magically" change character and scene, and capacity to effortlessly move backward and forward in time, film is a natural medium for the expression of dreams. Several famous directors have taken advantage of this.*

## Picture this

- **Federico Fellini's** films, such as *La Strada*, *La Dolce Vita*, and *8½*, are full of surrealist dream imagery. "My films are not for understanding but for seeing!" Fellini said.

- **Ingmar Bergman**, director of *The Seventh Seal*, *Persona*, *Cries and Whispers*, and *Fanny and Alexander*, made films in which dreams form as crucial a motif as death and religion.

■ **Director Orson Welles** *said of his picturization of Franz Kafka's novel* The Trial *– "I attempted to make a picture like a dream I have had . . . I move from architecture to architecture in my dream."*

- **Robert Altman**, director of *A Wedding*, *Nashville*, *MASH*, and *Gosford Park*, made films in which the frames seem to spill over with dream-like imagery.

■ **Federico Fellini's films** *are said to be full of Jungian imagery – like fire, earth, and water.*

## MUSIC AND DREAMS

The last movements of *The Messiah* came to George Frideric Handel in a dream; Richard Wagner dreamed much of the theme of his opera *Tristan und Isolde*; and Guiseppe Tartini dreamed he handed his violin to the devil who then played the melody that became *The Devil's Sonata*.

Musical dreams aren't limited to scores, however; lyrics and librettos have been "found" in dreams as well. About 10 years ago, my husband Bob, a guitarist, walked about for weeks playing a lovely sequence of notes, until I was literally hearing them in my sleep. One morning, I awoke with three complete verses that seemed meant for the melody. I at once wrote them down, and the collaboration became "The Strength of What You Know" – to my mind, the best song on Bob's CD.

■ **Paul McCartney** *heard a haunting melody in his dream, confirmed that none of the other Beatles had heard it before, and wrote it down. It became the tune for the song "Yesterday."*

# Dream solutions

*YOU MAY RECALL FROM Chapter 1 how the dreams of René Descartes influenced the development of his philosophical theory of dualism. While this theory that separated mind and body may ultimately prove to be flawed, many other dream solutions Descartes found proved more lasting.*

## Math and dreams

Among Descartes's dream discoveries was the marriage of geometry and algebra, "Cartesian coordinates," which make it possible to represent quantitative relationships geometrically. Then, in the 20th century, a survey by Edmond Maillet revealed that many mathematicians had discovered solutions to problems in their dreams. And, in 1948, an Indian mathematician reported in a *Scientific American* article that he solved problems in his dreams with the help of a Hindu goddess.

## Science and dreams

Science, too, has profited from dreams. Well-documented cases include:

**1** **Frederick Banting:** This Canadian physician made an important discovery in a dream. While searching for the cause of diabetes, Banting woke up one night and wrote: "Tie up the duct of the pancreas of a dog. Wait for a few weeks until it shrivels up. Then cut it out, wash it out and filter the precipitation." This experiment resulted in the isolation of insulin, still used today to treat diabetes.

**2** **Dmitri Mendeleyev:** In the mid-19th century, Mendeleyev had been trying to find a way to organize the chemical elements. In a dream, he saw a table which became the Periodic Table of the Elements that probably hung in your science classroom when you were in school. According to Mendeleyev, in his dream table "all the elements fell into place as required."

**3** **Friedrich von Kekule:** Another scientific discovery that resulted from a dream was that of Friedrich A. von Kekule, who had been working to explain the structure of the benzene molecule. During a nap, von Kekule had a dream in which atoms danced before him, then began forming various shapes and designs. After a time, some rows of atoms twisted around each other, and then one of these "snakes" grabbed hold of its tail and began whirling. He awoke at once to create a model representing what he'd seen, ultimately revolutionizing organic chemistry.

MODEL OF BENZENE
MOLECULE

*Following his dream discovery, Friedrich von Kekule told the audience of an 1890 scientific convention, "Let us learn to dream, gentlemen, and then we may perhaps find the truth."*

## Mothers of invention

If "necessity is the mother of invention," dreams may well be the godparents – or the midwives. Like scientists, inventors have found that some of their best ideas came to them while they were dreaming.

**1** One example is a Bell Labs engineer named Parkinson, who in 1940 was working on an instrument to improve telephone transmission. In Parkinson's dream, a fellow antiaircraft carrier gunner showed him that Parkinson's device, located at the open end of his gun, made his gun consistently accurate in shooting down enemy aircraft. The all-electric gun director that Parkinson designed as a result of this dream ultimately evolved into the M-9 analog computer.

② Another dream invention came to Elias Howe, who was struggling with the design of a machine that would lock stitches in place as it sewed. One night, Howe had a nightmare: Cannibals were going to boil him alive.

Sitting in a big pot as he prepared to boil, Howe became distracted by the cannibals' spears, which had eye-shaped holes at their tips. When Howe awoke, he realized that placing the threading hole near the point of the machine's needle was the very detail he was missing to perfect what would become the sewing machine.

Other inventions and ideas that have found their "missing links" in dreams are the model of the atom, lead shot, a synthetic language, and the key to unlocking an ancient inscription from Babylonian finger rings.

■ **The sewing machine** *owes its origins to the nightmare imagery of inventor Elias Howe.*

*In 1789, Ernst Chladni awoke from a dream with an image of an unusually shaped instrument to create the special sound he'd been seeking. This image became the euphonium, a more melodious version of the tuba.*

# LET THERE BE LIGHT . . .

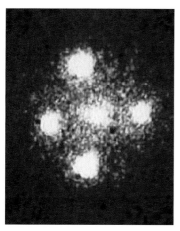

A DEPICTION OF EINSTEIN'S THEORY THAT GRAVITY BENDS LIGHT

Perhaps the most famous scientific dreamer was Albert Einstein. According to an interview with newsman Edwin Newman, even as an adolescent Einstein toyed with the idea of relativity, but because he was flunking math, his family encouraged him to be a plumber. During this time, he had a dream in which his sled raced faster and faster down a hill. In the dream, Einstein realized that he was approaching the speed of light, and with this realization looked up and saw that the stars were, as Newman noted, "being refracted into a spectra of colors that Einstein had never seen before . . . He understood that in some way he was looking at the most important meaning in his life."

# Everyday creative dreamers

*YOU DON'T HAVE TO WANT to build a better mousetrap to be a creative dreamer. If you've got an everyday problem to solve, **creative dreaming** can help you, too. It's important that you do not think of creative dreaming as something limited to "creative" fields. In fact, creativity is in evidence everywhere – even in your personal relationships.*

> **DEFINITION**
>
> **Creative dreaming** *is a way of using dreams to work with unresolved issues from our waking lives.*

## CREATIVE DREAMING – IT'S SIMPLE!

How can you use creative dreaming in your everyday life? Here are some examples of people who have done just that.

- *a* A highly successful lawyer rehearses her closing arguments in her dreams

- *b* A surgeon "performs" his surgeries in his dreams the night before, one step at a time

- *c* Parents use dreams to help them discover innovative approaches for working with their developmentally disabled child

- *d* A business executive's dreams help her steer her company in a new and profitable direction

- *e* A construction manager discovers a more efficient way of utilizing his employees and equipment in a dream

- *f* A woman who believed she was in a dead-end situation dreams a simple way out of it

■ **Job applicants** *have successfully practiced for interviews in dreams.*

## The dream game

Last, but certainly not least, athletes have long known how effective dream "practice" can be. In an example from the early 1960s, golfer Jack Nicklaus dreamed his way out of a slump. As Nicklaus described it to a newspaper reporter, one night he dreamed he was holding his golf club differently: "When I came to the course (the next) morning, I tried it the way I did it in my dream and it worked." In *Creative Dreaming*, Patricia Garfield reports that a student improved her tennis after "practicing" in her dream.

By now, you're probably eager to learn how you can become a creative dreamer. For that, let's turn to the next chapter, *Creative Dreams*.

**INTERNET**

**www.dreamgate.com/ dream/articles_rcw/ ed2-2inc.htm**

*Learn more about everyday creative dreaming in this article by Association for the Study of Dreams (ASD) member Richard Wilkerson.*

# *A simple summary*

✔ Writers whose dreams have helped them in their work include Robert Louis Stevenson, Samuel Taylor Coleridge, Mary Shelley, Jack Kerouac, Katherine Mansfield, Robert Penn Warren, Graham Greene, Charlotte Brontë, and Franz Kafka.

✔ Ancient artists, contemporary surrealist painters, Native American sculptors and jewelers, and filmmakers like Fellini, Altman, and Welles have all incorporated dream imagery into their work.

✔ Much music, from Wagnerian opera to the hits of the Beatles, has originated in dreams.

✔ The periodic table, the structure of the benzene molecule, and the isolation of insulin all came to their discoverers in dreams.

✔ Elias Howe's model of the sewing machine became finalized after he dreamed of its needle design.

✔ Everyday creative dreamers use their dreams to help them perform their jobs more skillfully, as well as to improve their relationships.

## Chapter 13

# Creative Dreams

CREATIVE DREAMING means using the expanded consciousness available to you when you are asleep to help you look at things from a different angle. Dreams offer us the opportunity to see everything from problems to projects in new ways, and, because we spend at least a third of our lives sleeping, creative dreaming can help us use that time effectively. Here, you'll learn exactly what creative dreaming is, and how you can become a creative dreamer yourself.

*In this chapter...*

✓ **What is creative dreaming?**

✓ **The benefits of creative dreaming**

✓ **Incubating creative dreams**

DREAMS CAN GIVE YOU A WHOLE NEW PERSPECTIVE ON THINGS

# What is creative dreaming?

*USING YOUR POTENTIAL for creative dreaming means employing your dreams to help you with your waking life. Patricia Garfield, PhD, who wrote the book* Creative Dreaming *(see Further Reading at the end of this book) in 1974, calls this concept "setting up a relationship" between dreams and waking life. Garfield's premise, revolutionary in 1974 but far more accepted today, is that we can use our dreams to actively work with problems, ideas, and questions.*

## To be human is to be creative

Garfield discovered that not only can our dreams help us with problems, we can use them to solve problems that have confounded us when we're awake. But before we begin to explore creative dreaming, let's take a moment to look at creativity itself. Do you think creativity is the province of a talented few? Not so. Creativity is a natural part of being human: the ability to take what we already know and apply it to new situations and ideas in novel ways.

■ **Discussing a problem** *with others is one of the ways in which you accumulate "solution-oriented" information. This is the first stage of any creative process.*

## The creative process

What does the creative process involve? The 19th-century German scientist Hermann Helmholtz was the first to divide the creative process into three stages:

**1** **Information gathering:** This stage is where we research the problem, think about potential solutions, brainstorm with others, and review possible options. It is often at the end of this stage that we say we will "sleep on" something – because we haven't yet arrived at a solution.

**2** **Incubation:** In the incubation stage, we seem to give up. In reality, we've done what I call "sending it over to right brain"; that is, we set our unconscious mind to work on the problem. Many who have reported important discoveries note that at this stage they had either decided to take a nap or went to bed for the night, only to awaken with an "aha!" – and the solution to the problem.

**3** **Illumination:** As you probably suspected, that "aha!" is the illumination stage. You may have experienced this sensation yourself when you've misplaced something: just when you give up looking for it, you often "remember" where it is. It's likely that this happens because you set the item down at a moment when your more imagistic right brain was dominant.

*Maybe you've seen the illumination stage illustrated in cartoons as a light bulb going on above a character's head. The sensation is indeed very similar to this graphic depiction.*

■ **The light bulb** *used to signify that a cartoon character has an idea is akin to the "aha!" you experience when you arrive at the solution to a problem.*

## Getting creative

Creativity researchers have discovered that creative people share certain characteristics. The good news is that these qualities are learnable. What traits are common to creative people?

*a* **Receptivity to experience:** Creative people are open to experience of all kinds

*b* **Evaluating skills:** They have a strongly developed inner critic/evaluator

*c* **Moving beyond:** They move easily beyond "acceptable parameters"

At the heart of these three traits is an ability to accept and at the same time *not* accept things at face value. This seeming contradiction involves:

- The ability to listen to others without judging while also processing what one is hearing
- The ability to read and evaluate information critically but open-mindedly
- A well-developed sense of gut feeling
- Perhaps most importantly, the ability to think "outside the box"

# *OUTSIDE THE BOX*

Here's a simple way of testing and developing your own creativity:

**1** **Consider a simple cardboard box**

*I won't even give you dimensions to this box, because it's a magic box that can morph into any size necessary.*

**2** **Consider its uses**

*Without giving it any thought, list ten potential uses to which you can put the box on a piece of paper.*

So what did you do with your box? I'm sure your ideas are creative and show an ability to think "outside the box." Now, all you need to do is apply the same skill to your dreams.

■ **Imagine the uses** *to which you can put a box: Will you turn it into a house? Cut it open and use it to cross a puddle? Line it with blankets for your cat?*

# The benefits of creative dreaming

*YOU CAN USE CREATIVE dreaming to solve problems, overcome blocks, or expand your artistic vision. The possibilities are limited, quite literally, only by your imagination. As dream consultant/author Gayle Delaney, PhD, points out, dreams help us "to understand ourselves better and to solve emotional and interpersonal problems."*

## So how do dreams help?

- They help you see things from different perspectives
- They help you notice information you may have missed
- They help you see if your own prejudices are obstructing the best solution

**Dreams can help you "see" solutions; what they won't do is make your decisions for you.**

## Solving dilemmas and blocks

I believe that the greatest potential of creative dreaming lies in using its problem-solving abilities to break through seemingly insurmountable dilemmas and blocks. Whether you are an editor laying out a book, a physician grappling with a complicated diagnosis, or a designer setting a room to its best advantage, creative dreaming helps you "see" your problem in new ways.

## *BRAIN TWISTERS*

An early 1990s study by psychiatrist Morton Schatzman explored how people solve problems in their dreams. Schatzman assigned "brain twisters" to be solved while students were asleep. One such problem asked the students to complete the sequence OTTFF. Seven students dreamed the correct answer, SSEN (six, seven, eight, nine; the first five letters stand for one, two, three, four, and five). In another question, students were asked what single English word is represented by the letters HIJKLMNO. The answer is "water"; that is, "H-to-O" (boo-hiss!). One student said he dreamed he was swimming, but couldn't come up with the answer.

## Spontaneous creative dreaming

One way of using dreams to solve problems is through what dream experts call *spontaneous creative dreaming*. It is very likely that you have already had your own spontaneous creative dreams without realizing that this phenomenon had a name. In its simplest form, you may have found something that had been misplaced, as mentioned earlier in this chapter. Or a problem may have been preying on your mind and you may have awoken with a solution to it, without having consciously incubated a dream to do so.

■ **Dreams help us** *to synthesize a variety of information on a daily basis. They're a natural place for us to work with scattered information until it fits in with our bigger picture.*

> **DEFINITION**
>
> **Spontaneous creative dreaming** *occurs without conscious dream incubation to solve a problem. In this type of creative dreaming, dream solutions occur even though the dreamer has not actively sought them.*

### A poem that wrote itself

I myself experienced spontaneous creative dreaming toward the end of writing a novel, when I awoke one morning with a three-stanza poem. I quickly wrote it down, as I was struck by both the poem's voice and its layers of meaning. As I was eating breakfast that morning, I realized that "I" hadn't written the poem at all. At that point in the novel, several characters were planning a memorial service, and the character who'd recently died in my novel was the one who'd "written" the poem. I knew at once that the poem would be read at her memorial service, and the last chapter of the novel fell into place as soon as I sat down to write it.

### Expanding your artistic vision

I hadn't consciously told myself I needed a solution to the dilemma posed by my last chapter when I had this dream. It occurred spontaneously because the book was on my mind. This is an instance of how you can deal with a "creative" problem by expanding your artistic vision in your dreams.

*As a learning aid, creative dreaming has been used for improving mastery of a foreign language or the ability to "count" cards during games such as bridge by incubating dreams.*

# Dreams and art

The fantastic visions of dreams are a fertile field for new creative ideas. Psychologist Fariba Bogzarin, for example, has been using her own and students' dreams as stepping stones toward her own artistic compositions for a number of years. Bogzarin believes that "our nightly journeys to the world of dreams offer a unique path to the discovery of our creative potential." The literary and art movement of the 1920s and 30s, Surrealism, was based on this concept. Surrealism explored the direct expression of the unconscious as revealed in dreams, unobscured by rational thought.

*Psychologist Fariba Bogzarin notes that, "Before surrealism, art was the representation of our waking world; at the height of surrealism and after, much of it became the representation of our dream world."*

## How dreams become art

Bogzarin believes that dreams manifest themselves through art in several ways. These include:

1. Translation of dream reality (Bogzarin calls this the "invisible") to waking reality (the "visible")

2. Integration of the invisible with the visible

3. Reproduction of dream scenes with no ties to waking reality. This is art at its most surrealistic

■ **Artist Odilon Redon** *(1840–1916) created paintings that were dominated by dreams. His imagery was fantastic, macabre, and often disturbing. Shown here is Redon's* The Cyclops.

# Incubating creative dreams

*CHANCES ARE, YOU'RE already dreaming creatively. That's because dreams are inherently helping us solve problems every night via spontaneous creative dreaming. Beyond spontaneous dreams, however, are incubated dreams – dreams that you actively seek to fulfill a purpose, such as healing or advice. You can elicit dreams to work on specific issues.*

## Bedtime rituals and creative dreaming

What do you do before you go to bed? Do you usually go to bed at the same time every night? Do you generally follow the same routine? If the answer to these last two questions is yes, you've taken two important steps toward incubating creative dreaming. Routine seems to be an important aspect of this process. Just as performing rote tasks enables us to think more creatively while we are awake, following a regular routine before bed fosters creative dreaming when we are asleep.

## Adding to your bedtime routine

When you want to incubate a creative dream, you'll add a few more steps to your nightly bedtime ritual (see the box "Preparing to be creative" opposite). Chances are, you'll find the result so fruitful that those steps will become part of your regular routine.

**INTERNET**

www.shpm.com/qa/
qadream/qadream
45.html

*Richard Wilkerson, who writes the Cyberphile column for the Association for the Study of Dreams newsletter, answers questions about creative dreaming at this link.*

■ **Regular bedtime habits,** *such as reading before bedtime and retiring at the same time every night, are a prerequisite for incubating creative dreams.*

# PREPARING TO BE CREATIVE

Dream literature offers a variety of approaches for incubating creative dreams. While each step-by-step approach varies slightly from the next, there are a number of steps they have in common, which I've consolidated into the following four points:

### 1 Be prepared

*Don't try to incubate a dream when you've had a tiring day at work, have overindulged, or know you must awaken early the next morning for one reason or another. The field for creative dreams seems to be a good night's sleep, as well as the time to record the dream in the morning.*

### 2 Get prepared

*Phrase the problem you would like to solve in the form of a question. A well-phrased question might be, "How can I make my project work?" or "What would be a good way for me to accomplish such-and-such?" You may also prepare some notes about the day you want to incubate your dream so as to pinpoint the day residue that appears in your dream. Reviewing in your mind the steps you've taken toward solving your problem thus far is also a good idea.*

### 3 Prepare for bed

*Write down your question just before you turn off the light and lie down. This act seems to focus your mind on your question at this fruitful moment just before falling asleep. Don't attempt to direct your thoughts at this time, except to keep them focused on things relating to the question itself.*

### 4 Remember your dream

*The key to benefitting from a creative dream is, not surprisingly, remembering and recording the dream as soon as you awaken. If you are concerned about remembering your dream, you may want to use one or more of the dream recall suggestions outlined in Chapter 4.*

■ **The uses of creative dreaming** *are vast and boundless. With a little practice you may interpret the meaning of a dream to answer your questions.*

## A dreamer gets creative

A woman felt she was at an impasse with her writing. Several projects seemed to demand her attention, but none enough so that she was actively working on it. Feeling negative about her work both in general and in particular, she asked for a dream telling her where she should go next with her writing. When the dreamer awoke, she felt as if her question had been answered. This is what she dreamed:

*My roommate and I are in our apartment (I don't live in an apartment, nor do I have a roommate) when G., an old boyfriend I haven't seen in years, and a crony of his show up. While my roommate and I are in another room, G. and his buddy take a number of things from the apartment and leave. My roommate and I return and see that lots of things are missing. But it's not until I realize my purse is among the missing items that I become furious.*

*I rush outside and reach the getaway car, which G.'s friend is having trouble starting, and tell G. he may think he can steal my things, but he can't have the contents of my purse. I tell him exactly what I think of him, too, which is how he's made so little of his life that he must steal others', and then, chastised and humbled, he gives me back the contents of my purse, one item at a time.*

### Analysis

Here's the dreamer's take on her dream: "I knew at once that G. represented my old, negative attitudes, while my purse represented my own creativity. G.'s 'stealing' of my purse meant that I was letting negative thinking get in the way, instead of just allowing myself to write and see what happened. In the dream, I storm out after the thief and tell him exactly what I think of him and his attempt to take away what's mine. (They can't seem to start that car full of my negative energy anyway.) I came away from this dream knowing that I was spending too much time brooding about my writing and no time actually writing, which was what I really needed to do."

## It's simple!

If creative dreaming sounds simple, that's because it truly is. The only impediments seem to be if you're too tired or if you try too hard. Other than those two roadblocks, incubating a creative dream is usually as simple as falling asleep.

*While many creative dreams are lucid, it's not necessary for the dream to be lucid to help you solve a problem.*

Remember all those creative dreamers in Chapter 12, and then go ahead and enjoy some creative dreaming of your own.

## A simple summary

✓ Using your potential for creative dreaming means employing your dreams to help you with your waking life.

✓ The creative process can be divided into three stages: information gathering, incubation, and illumination.

✓ Highly creative people are open to experience, have a strongly developed inner critic/evaluator, and move easily beyond "acceptable parameters."

✓ You can use creative dreaming to solve problems, overcome blocks, or expand your artistic vision. The possibilities are limited only by your imagination.

✓ By following a few simple steps, creative dreams can be incubated to solve specific problems.

# Chapter 14

# Healing Dreams

I T WAS ONLY NATURAL that as dream researchers began exploring the potentials of lucid dreaming and creative dreaming, a resurgence of interest in the ancient practice of healing dreams would emerge as well. The literal meaning of "heal" is "to make whole," and healing dreams are a part of the larger picture of holistic health and trying to live in harmony with our surroundings. Practicing such dreaming covers the gamut of both physical and emotional well-being, from giving early warning signs to ways of adjusting our lives to optimize our health.

## In this chapter...

✓ **What are healing dreams?**

✓ **The benefits of healing dreams**

✓ **Incubating healing dreams**

LET YOUR DREAMS LEAD YOU TO A SEA OF WELL-BEING

# What are healing dreams?

*AS YOU MAY RECALL from Chapter 3, one of the functions of sleep is to effect a sort of daily routine maintenance on your body. This means that if you've worked (or worked out) particularly hard on a given day, your delta sleep that night will be deeper as a result. Or, if you're under emotional stress or gave your brain a workout during the day, your time in REM sleep will increase that night to help you maintain a healthy emotional balance.*

## The mind/body connection

*Healing dreams* are a part of the mind and body's way of optimizing your holistic health. Just as sleep heals your body and mind, your dreams utilize mental imagery that can help you change or adjust your behavior, habits, and lifestyle to keep you healthy.

The potential of healing dreams has been recognized since ancient times, when dreams were used for both diagnosis and healing. Ancient Egyptians and Greeks, among others, believed that dreams could provide cures for everything from simple ailments to seemingly incurable conditions, and dream incubation was commonly practiced at temples dedicated to dream gods and goddesses (see p.18). Great temples, such as one located in ancient Memphis dedicated to the Egyptian god of healing Imhotep, were manned by dreamwork-trained priests.

> **DEFINITION**
>
> **Healing dreams** *are a way of staying in touch with your physical and mental states of being. Paying attention to dream imagery can alert you to early health warnings, help you discover ways to maintain and improve your health, and even suggest lifestyle changes to keep you healthy.*

■ **Ancient Greeks** *practiced dream incubation – usually in temples dedicated to their various gods – to cure illnesses. Pictured above is a Greco-Roman sarcophagus featuring the Greek god of sleep, Hypnos.*

In the late 20th century, a resurgence of interest in holistic health led quite naturally to a renewed exploration of the potential of dreams in the healing process. As dream researcher Patricia Garfield notes in her book *The Healing Power of Dreams* (see *Further Reading* at the end of this book), "Your dreams can help keep you healthy, warn you when you are at risk, diagnose incipient physical problems, support you during physical crises, forecast your recuperation, suggest treatment, heal your body, and signal your return to wellness."

## DREAM HEALTH WARNINGS

Dreams that forecast health problems are called prodromal dreams. Often, these occur before there are any physical symptoms. Learning to pay attention to your own early warning system (without becoming overly alarmed) can tell you when things may not be quite right either physically or mentally.

### Common elements

Carl Jung believed that dreams in which horses were injured were often prodromal, while more recent studies have shown that dreams of traumatic separation or of being lost or displaced (for women), and of death or injury (for men), are sometimes warnings of health problems. Dream researcher Robert C. Smith notes that the difference in dream subject matter may be attributable to the fact that, when confronted, men are more aggressive than women, who tend to respond to difficulties more interpersonally.

### Specific areas

Other prodromal dreams may pinpoint the area of distress. For some time I had dreams in which I would choke and forget how to breathe, and from which I would awaken gasping for breath. When I was diagnosed with Graves Disease, a thyroid disorder, some years ago, these dreams ceased almost immediately.

■ **If you learn** *to understand your dream imagery, you will recognize any unusual elements that may signal a physical or mental change.*

*Don't assume that a traumatic dream signifies there's something wrong with your health. Make sense of your dream in its context.*

## Learning to recognize healing dreams

As I described in the box "Dream heath warnings" (*see* p.187), I used to have dreams in which I would choke and forget how to breathe, but as soon as I was diagnosed with a thyroid disorder the dreams ceased almost immediately.

So how do you decide whether a dream of choking is a warning about possible illness in your throat area, as in my dream above, or possibly connected to birth trauma, as you may recall from my daughter's recurring dreams in Chapter 9? (My daughter was born with her umbilical cord wrapped around her neck and had choking dreams, as she said, "all the time!" The dreams ceased once we discussed the birth/dream connection.)

*The key to learning to recognize your own healing dream imagery is being familiar with your own particular dreamsigns and dream signals.*

Have you started making a list of your dreamsigns (impossible occurrences in a dream that can alert you to the fact that you are dreaming) and dream signals (your personal dream metaphors – people, animals, or objects that occur repeatedly in your dreams) as discussed in Chapter 10? If you have a dream featuring unusual imagery, very different from your usual dreamsigns and dream signals, ask yourself if the dream may be prodromal. See the box "The key pointers" on pp.190–91 for the various indicators of prodromal dreams.

## *THE DREAM SIGNAL CHANGES*

Let's say that ordinarily when you dream about your cat it is a pleasant experience. One night, as usual, you dream that you see your cat on the kitchen counter. When you call her, however, she turns, then leaps out at you, claws extended, striking you in your abdomen, and leaving long bleeding gashes. While you may awaken horrified, does it make sense to regard your poor cat warily for the next several days?

*a* A traumatic dream like this could suggest a number of possible health problems, from a simple upset stomach to a more serious intestinal disorder

*b* Of course, a dream like this could also be the result of something emotionally disturbing that happened the previous day, so it's important to take such things into account. Sometimes, for example, seeing your sweet little kitty with a mouse in her mouth is enough to generate a disturbing dream such as this one

■ **The sky is the limit** *when it comes to using dream techniques.*

# THE KEY POINTERS

Have you been having disturbing dreams lately? You can do a step-by-step analysis of your disturbing dream to decide whether it is prodromal:

**1 Note any disturbing event**

*Did something disturbing happen the day before you had the dream? If so, that may be the cause of the disturbing dream rather than something related to your health.*

**2 Note the dream signs and signals**

*Did a dreamsign or signal change dramatically in a way it hasn't before? Examples might be your sweet little kitty cat suddenly turning feral (see box "The dream signal changes" on p.188), or being unable to find someone you care about. Dreamsign changes are often disturbing, but are not necessarily dream health warnings.*

**3 Did the dream wake you up?**

*While this isn't necessarily the sign of a prodromal dream, either, when the imagery of a dream is disturbing enough to awaken you it is often worth examining more closely.*

**4 The overriding emotion**

*What overriding emotion did you awaken with? Determining whether you awoke frightened, angry, lonely, or depressed can help you decide if the dream is prodromal or a reflection of something that's occurring in your life.*

*Just as our dreams address our fears and hopes about our interactions with others and the larger world, they can also help us understand how we feel about ourselves and our bodies.*

### 5 Why were you disturbed?

*What specifically was disquieting about the dream? Review the images and emotions that led you to conclude the dream was disturbing. What made you fearful? What upset you or made you uneasy? What angered you? Why?*

### 6 Are the images recurring?

*Have you had dreams with similar (or the same) images? When the same image recurs in a dream or in more than one dream, we are literally trying to get ourselves to pay attention.*

### 7 Pinpoint the origin

*If the images are similar, did they begin recently? Try to pinpoint when the disturbing dreams began, and what the circumstances were when they did so.*

### 8 Different imagery, similar feeling

*Dream studies have shown that if our dreams can't get a message across to us with one image, they'll keep trying using other images until we "get it." Dreams that leave you with similar sensations, however vague, are trying to get you to sit up and listen.*

### 9 Pay attention to the words

*Pay attention to the words you use in analyzing the dream. In What Your Dreams Can Teach You,* Alex Lukeman *relates a dream in which his kitchen drain was "blocked by a coffee filter." Noting the meanings of "block" and "filter," he interpreted this dream as a warning to curtail his coffee drinking.*

■ **The mind is** *as important as the body in healing and may even take the lead in the body's healing process.*

# The benefits of healing dreams

*HEALING DREAMS serve a number of purposes beyond prodromal dreams. Not only can they help us heal our bodies, they can also help with emotional healing from loss, disappointment, grief, and other life-changing situations.*

## The healing process

In *The Healing Power of Dreams*, Patricia Garfield divided the healing process of dream metaphor into 7 stages:

■ **Dream images** *of injured animals may help you diagnose your health problem.*

1. **Forewarning dreams:** The imagery of these prodromal dreams can warn us that something is wrong. Examples include being unable to stop, being unable to move, getting caught in a storm, or a collapse or breakdown.

2. **Diagnostic dreams:** Correctly interpreted, these dreams can pinpoint the problem itself. Imagery may include fire, water, injured animals or dead plants, or damaged buildings or equipment. Dreaming of a car that can't get up a hill, for example, could point to physical and mental exhaustion.

3. **Crisis dreams:** At this stage, dream imagery is often violent and frightening. Images may include polluted air or water, invasive insects, accidents involving blood, or even physical violence.

■ **Ominous images,** *such as accidents, being attacked, or pollution, may signal a crisis in your physical or emotional state.*

**4** **Post-crisis dreams:** Even after the worst is past, dream imagery often continues to deal with the losses incurred by the illness. For this reason, post-crisis dreams may include images of dead animals or people, theft, assault, injury, or medical procedures.

**5** **Healing dreams:** When healing dreams begin, the crisis has passed. Imagery in these dreams may include lush surroundings, children playing, puppies and kittens, and other positive and soothing images.

**6** **Convalescent dreams:** In convalescent dreams, there's a renewed optimism, signaled by the acquisition of new things, or dreams of babies and ceremonies.

**7** **Wellness dreams:** When we are once again healthy and functioning well in our dreams, we have also healed in our bodies.

**INTERNET**

www.avcweb.com/
dreams/colour-in-
dreams.htm

*This web site provides a Color Healing Chart and various suggestions for examining possible meanings for the colors in your dreams. Read it for fun or print it out for future reference!*

■ **Pleasant dream images** *after an illness may suggest that your body is well on its way to good health.*

## Physical healing

Using our dreams to heal our bodies begins with an awareness of the connection between mind and body and an acknowledgment that our dreams can help us heal. Many dream experts cite stories of **spontaneous healing** in which people have healed themselves in their dreams literally overnight.

> **DEFINITION**
>
> **Spontaneous healing**
> *involves using the mind to heal the body.*

Jayne Gackenbach outlines a University of Texas Southwestern Medical School study whose subjects were instructed to dream that their cancer-killing cells were increasing. While these levels normally decrease during sleep, those who achieved lucidity during this experiment did increase them in their dreams. As Dr Dennis Jaffe and Dr David Bresler have noted, "Mental imagery mobilizes the latent, inner powers of the person, which have immense potential to aid in the healing process and in the promotion of health." If this is the case, as we learn more and more about dreams and healing, harnessing the mental imagery of our dreams to promote physical well-being may well be the next frontier of dreams.

## CASES OF SPONTANEOUS HEALING

■ **Actual injuries** *have been known to heal with the help of lucid dreaming.*

E. W. Kellogg, a lucid dream researcher, notes that some reports of spontaneous healing indicate that the dreamers noted a "warm, buzzing, electric" sensation, which healed them in their sleep.

This has been corroborated at least in part by an anecdotal case cited by Jayne Gackenbach, in which a construction worker healed his arm via a lucid dream: "I recall a man in my dream state twisting and poking around on my elbow," the man said, "and it hurt." The dream figure told him he was healing him, however, and when the man awoke, his arm felt as if it had gone to sleep. When it "woke up," it no longer hurt at all.

Both Stephen LaBerge in *Exploring the World of Lucid Dreaming* and intuitive consultant Rosemary Ellen Guiley in *Dreamwork for the Soul* cite this story of spontaneous healing: "My findings are that healing is possible in lucid dreams. I had a lump in my breast which I took apart inside my body in a lucid dream. It was a beautiful, geodesic cathedral-like structure! A week later the lump was gone."

■ **Dreams** *can provide a beacon of light in troubled times and guide us toward emotional health.*

# Emotional healing

Holistic health includes our emotional health as well as our physical well-being. When we're worried about something, our dreams will work to help us understand and resolve our worry. Here's one vivid example from a young woman in college who'd been having nightmares nearly every night for several weeks:

*I'm at a presentation in a small meeting room. Plush chairs are lined in 10 to 15 rows with an aisle between them. The carpeting is sea green, as are the walls. In the front of the room is a flower-adorned altar. Incense burns, and a sitar drones.*

*A guru is giving a lecture. I sit in the back, half listening. When I focus on the teacher again, I realize he's looking right at me and around me. I know he's reading my aura and feel violated, stiffening against his search. His quizzical expression is not what I expect. Neither is his voice, a combination of a Brooklyn cabdriver and an old Yiddish speaker. "What's the matter?" he asks. "You got somethin' to hide?" I look at him closely. He's a cross between an East Indian ascetic and Baba Ram Das (the American guru of the late 60s). "No," I say, still bristling. He smiles, nods his head. "Good. Because you're doin' just fine, just fine."*

## How dreams heal

As this narrative illustrates, our dreams can help us see that we're emotionally in much better shape than we realize. Another way that dreams can help us heal emotionally is by helping us make decisions to facilitate that healing. One example is cited by psychologist Alan Siegel, PhD, in his book *Dreams That Can Change Your Life* (see *Further Reading*), in which a woman with breast cancer is trying to decide whether to join a cancer support group. During a dream, she asks herself, "Why am I doing this alone?" The woman realizes on waking that joining the support group is precisely what she needs to help herself heal both emotionally and physically.

# Incubating healing dreams

*AN OFT-CITED STUDY by Dr Carl Simonton discovered that when patients with advanced cancer used healing imagery along with their chemotherapy and radiation, they survived twice as long. More recently, research at Stanford University has documented a relationship between dream imagery and physiological response. As researchers and scientists learn more about the mind/body connection, more studies exploring the potential of dreams for healing will surely be done.*

## Harnessing your dream

In the meantime, you can experiment with harnessing the power of your dreams to heal yourself. To begin, you can use one of the methods outlined in Chapter 11 to incubate lucid dreams, but you do not necessarily need to be lucid for a healing dream to help you. What is important is to recall the dream in the morning, so you will want to prepare yourself for sleep as suggested in Chapter 13 by making some notes and asking yourself what you wish to discover in your dream.

Let's say you'd like to find out why you keep waking up with shoulder pain. Just before you fall asleep, ask yourself what the source of your shoulder pain is. Then, when you awaken, immediately record your dream. If it doesn't seem to relate to your shoulder pain, try again the next night. As you've learned, persistence and perseverance are important aspects of working with dreams and their imagery.

■ **Harness your dream** *potential and take the leap toward a healthier you.*

## Diagnosing the dream

As with other dream benefits, you must work at understanding healing dreams.

*If you've begun recording your dreams and have noted your own recurring imagery, dreamsigns, and dream signals, you've already taken some important steps toward reading the messages of your healing dreams.*

Alex Lukeman, author of *What Your Dreams Can Teach You*, believes that, "If you take the trouble to learn to . . . read your own dreams with reasonable accuracy, you may be able to take steps to avoid potential health problems." Further, Lukeman continues, "If you are ill, you may be able to accurately monitor the real course of your illness and the effect of whatever treatment you are receiving."

*Can we truly heal ourselves in our dreams? More and more evidence suggests that "mind over matter" is far more than just a truism. My best suggestion is to try it for yourself and see.*

## A simple summary

✔ Healing dreams are a way of staying in touch with your physical and mental states of being.

✔ Paying attention to dream imagery can alert you to early health warnings, help you discover ways to optimize your health, and even suggest lifestyle changes to keep you healthy.

✔ Prodromal dreams forecast health problems, often before there are any physical symptoms.

✔ A traumatic dream does not necessarily mean there is something wrong with your health, but may signal a change in the state of your physical or mental health.

✔ Spontaneous healing involves using your mind to heal your body.

✔ You can work with dreams and their imagery to deal with health problems, both physical and mental.

# Chapter 15

# Spiritual Dreaming

Y EARS AGO, my mother attended a class where participants were asked to close their eyes and visualize their own guardian angel. My mother, to her surprise, immediately pictured her younger self. Ever logical, she took this to mean that she was her own best guide. My mother's guardian angel experience illustrates one of the many possibilities of spiritual dreaming: guidance by a higher power. Discovering the spiritual forces at work in your dreams can help you make your way through a world that isn't always easy to navigate.

## In this chapter...

✓ **What is spiritual dreaming?**

✓ **You and your chakras**

✓ **The benefits of spiritual dreaming**

✓ **Guides, masters, guardians, and angels**

LOOK FOR GUIDANCE AND YOU'RE SURE TO FIND IT

# What is spiritual dreaming?

**Spiritual dreaming** *can be as simple as a dream that provides you with a new understanding of something, or a more profound encounter. Such a dream may leave you with a sense of higher powers beyond your waking knowledge that changes your understanding of yourself and the world in some way.*

*INCUBATED OR spontaneous, easy to understand or mysterious, fundamental or ineffable,* **spiritual dreaming** *involves guidance from within yourself or without. Much depends on the dreamer. In fact, what separates spiritual dreams from their ordinary cousins is the dreamer's sense of their spirituality.*

## At its most basic . . .

At its most basic, spiritual dreaming is a way of making sense of the world through means not always available to us in waking life. As dream expert Jeremy Taylor points out, "Dreams always come to bring us to a deeper experience of the Divine." When we experience spiritual dreams, they can help us work toward understanding both our own unconscious experiences and the larger world of which we are a part.

■ **The images of spiritual dreams** *are often accompanied by a sensation of transcendental "knowing," and may remain with those who dream them for their entire lives.*

## ... and most profound

For as long as humans have been reviewing their dreams, a connection between the dream and spirituality has been assumed.

1 Historical figures from Genghis Khan to George Patton have reported dreams that served as impetus toward divinely inspired action

2 Islam began its ascent after Mohammed had a prophetic spiritual dream that led him to conquer Mecca

You don't have to be a figure "chosen by history" to have spiritual dreams. Whether you rely on your own inner compass (like many westerners, on some version of a Biblical God), or, like many of my friends, on a guiding spirit, intuition, or sense, discovering the spiritual forces at work in your dreams can help you make your way through a world where the path isn't always clear.

*The more spiritual a dream, the larger its themes: spiritual dreams often move beyond the personal into the collective psyche of humanity.*

■ **The more interested** *you are in greater spiritual understanding, the more likely you are to have spiritual dreams.*

# WITHIN YOU, WITHOUT YOU

In September 2001, an article in the *Perth Post*, Western Australia, related the story of an aboriginal elder who was working to reclaim a coastal bay for his tribe. The elder, Robert Bropho, told a reporter that everything from the hill and rocks to the wind and water at Freshwater Bay contained aboriginal spiritual dreaming. "It's on the dreaming track which starts in Fremantle and joins nations all over Australia," Mr. Bropho is quoted as saying. "My dreaming and my people's spiritual dreaming is still here. There are no limitations on our culture. It's here, there and everywhere. It's above us and below us and all around us in the wind and sand and birds and water – that's our spiritual dreaming."

# You and your chakras

AN IMPORTANT ASPECT of spiritual dreaming are the **chakras**. According to Eastern medicine, the body is divided into seven major chakras (as well as many minor ones), which interact with our bodies and minds to maintain our holistic health. When your chakras are functioning well, you will feel healthy and whole.

**DEFINITION**

*The seven **chakras** are the body's energy centers, each located at a major nerve plexus.*

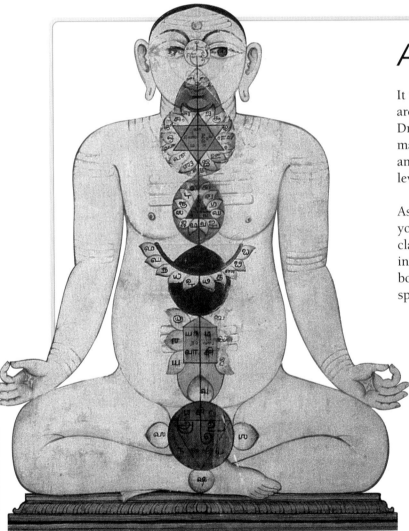

## A CHAKRA CHART

It is said that chakra dysfunctions are often signaled first in dreams. Dreams involving chakra energy may be healing, spiritual, or both, and often signal a move to a new level of understanding.

As you study the following chart, you'll see the simple logic and clarity of the chakra system and its interconnection with your physical body and your state of mental and spiritual well-being.

■ **This 1850 painting** *from Southern India depicts six of the seven chakras positioned along the spinal column. The seventh is on top of the skull.*

## Meet your chakras

Your chakras are divided into the "lower" chakras, which are concerned with your physical health, and the "higher" chakras, which deal with your spiritual and psychic well-being. At any given time, each of us has one or two chakras where much of our energy is focused.

Each chakra is associated with a color as well as with areas of your life. If you are "heart-centered," for example, your energy is concentrated in your green fourth chakra, while if you are focused on communication, you will have a blue – fifth chakra – concentration. Over the course of your lifetime, your chakra focus will periodically shift. Spiritual dreams may alert you to these shifts, or cause you to seek such a shift of focus yourself.

| Chakra | Location | Function | Color | Areas of Association |
|---|---|---|---|---|
| First | Base of spine | Life force | Red | Survival, physical health, sensation, vitality |
| Second | Pubic bone | Sexual energy | Orange | Reproduction, emotions, creativity, imagination |
| Third | Navel | Digestion | Yellow | Identity, judgment, strength, perseverance |
| Fourth | Heart | Circulation | Green | Love, kindness, compassion, giving |
| Fifth | Throat | Communication | Blue | Speech, interpersonal relations, giving and taking |
| Sixth | Forehead center | "Third eye" | Indigo | Thinking, seeing, intuition, worldview |
| Seventh | Top of skull | Spirituality | Violet-white | Integration of self and spirit |

*The eighth chakra is called the aura. This refers to the energy field that surrounds you and at the same time penetrates your body. Think of it as a sort of protective shield that also helps you interact with the larger world.*

# A SIMPLE GUIDE TO CHAKRA-CENTERED DREAMS

Balanced chakras are an important aspect of holistic health, and dreams are one way our minds communicate chakra imbalances to us. While we are dreaming, there's a continuous balancing of our physical energy, while at the same time our chakras monitor and inform us about our spiritual well-being. Chakra-centered dreams can not only pinpoint areas of physical, mental, or spiritual discomfort, they often suggest ways of healing as well.

### 1 First chakra dreams

**Imagery:** *Earth images; vehicles such as bicycles; animals associated with movement, such as horses.*

*A balanced first chakra represents your personal grounding and health, and dreams relating to the first chakra can indicate whether you are feeling unbalanced or physically unwell.*

### 2 Second chakra dreams

**Imagery:** *Water images, including creatures like fish and crustaceans; houses, and more specifically, bedrooms.*

*A balanced second chakra is connected to your emotional center, your sexuality, and your creativity, and second chakra dreams can show discomfort or difficulty in these areas.*

### 3 Third chakra dreams

**Imagery:** *Fire, as light or as a destructive force; wild animals like lions or tigers; alchemical or transformational processes.*

*This is the chakra of your personal power and centeredness, and your sense of identity. Third chakra dreams are said to reveal your feelings of powerlessness or inadequacy.*

*Don't assume that a dream that involves fire indicates powerlessness, or one that involves water means sexual dysfunction. Chakra dreams usually contain a cluster of suggestive imagery rather than just one.*

### 6 Sixth chakra dreams

**Imagery:** *Vision and seeing in their largest sense, as in "all-seeing" and "all-knowing;" play of light and dark; unusual visual imagery.*

*With their sensations of loss of self or of merging with something greater than the self, sixth chakra dreams are believed by many to be the highest possible chakra level for most people.*

### 4 Fourth chakra dreams

**Imagery:** *Air imagery – birds and airplanes, wind and storms, or breath and breathing; light-footed animals, like deer; flying.*

*This chakra repesents your capacity to move beyond emotions to a higher spiritual level. Fourth chakra dreams may indicate self-centeredness or a difficulty in sharing or giving.*

### 5 Fifth chakra dreams

**Imagery:** *Sounds, whether delicate or ponderous; female spirits; light sleek vehicles; high airy buildings.*

*Because this is the chakra of expression and communication, fifth chakra dreams can indicate difficulties in communicating your ideas and emotions, or in accepting what others seek to offer you.*

### 7 Seventh chakra dreams

**Imagery:** *Hard to describe since these dreams are extremely rare and there are no written reports of what they involve.*

*They are the province of mystical union such as that experienced by Jesus, Buddha, and Mohammed. As Ole Vedfelt says in The Dimensions of Dreams, "Experiences in this chakra are fundamentally ineffable."*

# The benefits of spiritual dreaming

*A RECENTLY WIDOWED friend told me the following: "After my husband of many years, Don, died last year, several of my children kept seeing and talking to him in their dreams. Even his god-daughter, who hasn't seen Don in years, called to tell me she dreamed of him, and said a psychic described Don as being 'just behind her shoulder, to help her.' When my dearest friend wrote to tell me she saw Don, too, I felt terribly left out. What was wrong with me, that he wasn't appearing in my dreams?"*

**INTERNET**

http://oz.sannyas.net/
quotes/chakra10.htm

*For a more esoteric approach to chakras and dreams, try this web site, where you'll find a detailed analysis of dreams and their chakra connections.*

## A dream appearance

My friend then continued: "While in Hawaii with my daughter and her husband, I was invited to participate in a group session with several couples and about seven singles, mostly women, ranging from 40 to 70. These people met weekly to describe the state of their lives: fears, disappointments, successes, hopes, and dreams. I shocked myself by explaining that I had come to Hawaii to heal, and felt the tears forming in my eyes.

That night I dreamed more clearly than I have in years. There was a very bright light in a doorway perhaps 30 feet away from me. Silhouetted in the door was Don, his form unmistakable. Before I could speak, he said clearly: 'Eileen, you're going to be fine.' Then he turned and walked into the light."

*Until you've expressed your need to heal, to yourself and others, you may not have the dream necessary for healing.*

My friend says that she is convinced that her husband, Don, appeared in dreams to the others because they were experiencing problems and really needed him to comfort them. While she missed him every day, she was going on with her life, creating the new person she wanted to become.

*Spiritual dreaming has the capacity to help us deal with emotional trauma in our lives through a connection with a universe that is much larger than our personal grief.*

# GAINING THE ESSENCE OF SPIRITUALITY

Louis M. Savary, STD, PhD, an expert on Judeo-Christian dreamwork, notes that, "In spirituality, the dream is the gift; dreamwork is what we do with it." Spiritual dreaming can help you through both personal and collective problems, including:

- Improving physical, mental, and spiritual health
- Creating a sense of connection with others
- Understanding the interconnection between thought, feeling, and action
- Gaining a knowledge of the true nature of self
- Acting on spiritual principles
- Practicing gratitude and grace
- Living in harmony with the universe

*Dreams and dreamwork can help us achieve higher levels of consciousness and learn how to "channel the energy and insights of the dream into daily life," says dream researcher Louis M. Savary.*

■ **Spiritual dreaming** *does not entail a withdrawal from the world. You can use it to bring enhanced meaning to your life, work, and hobbies.*

# Guides, masters, guardians, and angels

*MANY WHO HAVE HAD spiritual dreams have noted the presence of others who have helped them within their dreams. Such helpful beings can include spirit guides, dream masters, guardian angels, or even animal guides. Their common goal, however, is to assist the dreamer through his or her spiritual crisis or transition.*

**Spirit guides:** The guises of spirit guides are limited only by your imagination. That's because a spirit guide is any dream manifestation that advises you or guides you toward spiritual understanding. One example is the Baba Ram Das figure who appeared in Chapter 14 and who told the dreamer, "You're doin' just fine, just fine."

**Dream masters:** According to esoteric beliefs, dream masters can be living masters, archetypal or fanciful figures, or masters who have died and appear in the dreams of those who need guidance. Intuitive consultant Rosemary Ellen Guiley cites the ***ascended master*** Babaji, who has appeared in the dreams of many who had never heard of him to assist in their spiritual transitions.

**Guardian angels:** Because Judaism, Christianity, and Islam rely on a single all-powerful God, intermediaries are necessary dream messengers. Angels have served this role since Biblical times, often assuming human proportions to make them more accessible and understandable to earthly beings. Guardian angels may appear in dreams in protective guise, or may herald warnings or predictions. In the past 20 years, angels and the metaphoric guidance they represent have enjoyed a resurgence of popularity (remember the class my mother took, mentioned in the introduction to this chapter?).

■ **Angels have acted** *as dream messengers from God throughout history. This Pre-Raphaelite stained glass window shows a herald angel.*

**Animal guides:** Like guardian angels, animal guides have enjoyed a recent renaissance. Animal guides can help the dreamer realize his or her untapped potential.

- Mythical magic animals can guide the dreamer to his or her own spirituality
- Shamanistic power animals let a dreamer draw power from them
- Metaphoric animals represent potential creativity

While spiritual dreaming is an ancient tradition, it's only recently that western societies have begun to rediscover its potential. Since spiritual dreaming can help us translate our potential into possibility and awareness into action, it can be an important tool for positive change in our turbulent times.

■ **Animals represent humans** *at their most primal, and as a result, animal guides that appear in dreams often characterize raw energy.*

# A simple summary

✔ At its most basic, spiritual dreaming is a way of making sense of the world through means not always available to us in waking life.

✔ The more interested you are in greater spiritual understanding, the more likely you are to have spiritual dreams.

✔ Dreams involving chakra energy may be healing, spiritual, or both, and can also signal a transition to a new level of understanding.

✔ Spiritual dreams can help us deal with emotional trauma in our lives through a connection with a universe much larger than our personal grief.

✔ The common goal of spirit guides, dream masters, guardian angels, and animal guides is to assist the dreamer through a spiritual crisis or transition.

# Chapter 16

# Psychic Dreaming

THE REALM OF PSYCHIC or psi dreams – also called anomalous or New Age, precognitive or intuitive dreams – remains a largely unexplored frontier. Whether or not they are a manifestation of extrasensory perception (ESP), or merely a trick of the mind, has not been determined. For many, however, there's far more to such dreams than day residue and current events. Learning to use esoteric dream tools such as your psychic intuition, the Tarot, and numerology to explore your dreams can take you to realms you've literally never dreamed of.

## In this chapter...

✓ **Parapsychology and dreams**

✓ **Past, present, future**

✓ **Esoteric dream tools**

# Parapsychology and dreams

*HAVE YOU EVER awoken from a dream certain that what it contained was knowledge you couldn't possibly have obtained through ordinary means? Or, have you ever had a dream that later proved prescient? Among their many possibilities, **psychic dreams** are those that seem to herald future events or make connections with other people, times, or places while we are asleep. A dream of an event that hasn't yet happened, communication with someone else within mutual dreams, even "seeing" into another's mind – all these phenomena, and more, are the realm of psychic dreams.*

**DEFINITION**

**Psychic dreams**, *also sometimes called psi dreams, anomalous dreams, or New Age dreams, may be clairvoyant, prescient, telepathic, or precognitive. Their common thread is that they seem to contain information not available to us by ordinary means.*

■ **When popular art** *wants to get away from the "normal," it takes recourse to dreams. In the science fiction film* Total Recall, *dreams are implanted in people's minds.*

## Anomalous or psychic?

Parapsychology is the branch of psychology that studies psychic phenomena, which includes clairvoyance, telepathy, extrasensory perception, and precognitive dreams. Perhaps because so much about dreaming remains unknown, dream theorists are far more open than many other scientists and researchers to parapsychological phenomena. In fact, dreams may well be the doorway between our everyday world and the world psychic dreams reveal.

Dream researchers are careful to eliminate all other possible explanations for anomalous dreams before calling them psychic. Psychology professor Montague Ullman, MD, for example, notes that daily events that find their way into dreams are often those which connect in some way with unresolved emotional issues. It is possible that some dreams labeled as psychic may, on further examination, be metaphorically attempting to help us resolve those issues. So how do you determine if your dream is a complicated metaphor or a psychic connection? One way to begin this analysis is by examining the nature of time.

# Past, present, future

*DON'T WORRY — we're not going to delve into Einstein's theory of relativity here, except to note that one of its tenets is that time is far more fluid than we experience it as being when we are awake. While in everyday life the possibility of manipulating time seems absurd, in dreams time assumes a far more amorphous quality, one that many believe may be far closer to time's true nature.*

## Dream/time

Even awake, you have most likely experienced two different kinds of time, even if you've never really distinguished between them before.

***Dreams occur in kairos, and dream time does not follow the logic of chronos.***

 **Chronos** or clock-time: time measured in seconds, minutes, hours, and days

**Kairos** or what is called "holy time": the nature of which is expressed in expressions such as "Time flies," and "The hours just dragged by." Chances are, something that happened last week seems to you as if it occurred a very long time ago, while something that happened years ago is still very fresh in your mind. The sense of time that makes events feel this way is what kairos is all about

■ **In dreams,** *time takes on a different quality: dead people appear alive, we appear as our child-selves, and future events are presented as if they have already occurred.*

# Dreams of the future

Not all dreams of the future are prescient. In fact, many prove to have their roots in unconscious cues. When you can't connect the dream material to any recent events, however, it may well be anomalous. It's dreams like these that make headlines – and make us wonder if dreams are indeed a way to understand our psychic potential.

## Precognitive dreams

Two weeks before he was assassinated, 19th-century US President Abraham Lincoln dreamed that a body lay in state in the Capitol, surrounded by weeping people. When he approached one of the people in his dream to ask who had died, he was told, "The President. He's been assassinated." This true story is one of many recorded *precognitive dreams*. Often concerned with disasters, whether natural, manmade, or accidental, precognitive dreams at their most fundamental appear to forecast things that haven't yet happened.

> **DEFINITION**
>
> **Precognitive dreams** *share the common element of occurring before the event they feature.*

Dream books are full of examples of precognitive dreams. One often-cited story is of a Welsh schoolgirl who told her mother, "I dreamed I went to school and there was no school there. Something black had come down all over it." The little girl added that she wasn't afraid to die, "because I shall be there with Peter and June." Two days later, her school was buried beneath a pile of coal slag, killing 144 people – including the little girl who'd had the dream and her friends, Peter and June.

## Disasters foretold

More than half of the instances of precognitive dreams noted by various researchers involve some kind of disaster or death. Dream expert Jon Tolaas speculates that this "may be simply (because) dreams involving death, accidents, and illness are more impressive." But, Tolaas continues, "the high incidence might reflect the possible biological function of telepathy as a preverbal emergency channel."

■ **The majority of** *precognitive dreams herald a disaster, accident, or death.*

■ **An interesting finding** *about psychic dreams is that they are far more likely to occur when the weather is calm, and the air is still and free from electrical storms.*

## Making connections: clairvoyance, telepathy, and ESP

While precognitive dreams are the most often-recorded type of psychic dreams, many other categories of dreams are also considered anomalous. These include:

- **Telepathy:** connection to another person's mind
- **Clairvoyance:** a sense of events outside one's self
- **Extrasensory perception (ESP or sixth sense):** knowledge obtained beyond the standard five senses

*Expert Jon Tolaas says that dream sensing (incorporating subtle external stimuli into dreams) and fine cueing (unconsciously registering verbal and nonverbal clues) should be eliminated before a dream is labeled psychic.*

One of the most highly regarded controlled experiments in dream research history is concerned with these phenomena. Conducted by Montague Ullman and Stanley Krippner at the Maimonides Medical Center Dream Laboratory at Brooklyn College in the 1960s, this study involved dream "agents" who sent telepathic messages regarding target images to dreamers whose REM periods were being monitored by third parties. No one but the agents knew which target image would be selected, and the dreamers were awakened immediately after each REM period and asked to record their dreams.

The results of this study were striking: Similarities between target images and dreamed images were much greater than could be attributed to mere chance (the dreamers "scored" 68 percent of the time). Interestingly, some agents were better than others, and some teams scored much higher as well, which seems to validate the hypothesis that some people are more "tuned in" to their sixth sense.

## Psychic dream signals

Dream researcher Rosemary Ellen Guiley notes that psychic dreams, or "psi dreams" as she calls them, share certain signals that separate them from other "normal" dreams, including:

- The presence of someone who is deceased, often a close relative or friend of the dreamer
- Intense emotions, both during and after the dream
- A strong sense of the importance of the dream's message
- Vivid details

Guiley calls these signals "psi signatures." She adds that it's important to "always look for the simplest explanation in a dream first. Most dreams are not *psi* dreams."

**INTERNET**

www.dreamgate.com/
dream/library/idx_psi.
htm

*This all-encompassing site provides links to a variety of web sites and articles about psychic dreaming.*

## Boarding the astral plane and other OBEs

OBE is an acronym for out-of-body experience. Dreamers who have experienced this phenomenon share it with many who have had near-death experiences (NDEs). Recorded OBEs are remarkably similar. Here's one example:

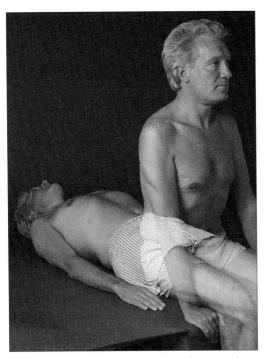

■ **Are out-of-body** *experiences "real" or are they part of your dream?*

*When I realized I was dreaming, I decided to try leaving my body, and as soon as I thought that, I was hovering above my sleeping self. There I was, and there was my husband next to me, snoring away as usual! I thought I'd wander around the house a bit, just to test this, and off I went, into the kitchen, and then the living room. Next I decided to go outside and at once I was in the back yard, floating above the garden and seeing the perennials from a very different angle. I knew I could go even further, but decided this was enough for one night and was at once back in my sleeping body.*

Many different names have been given to the entity that "travels" outside the body, including astral body, etheric body, soul body, and dream body. And OBEs themselves have been variously called astral projection, dream travel, and boarding the spiritual plane. Some argue that the experience is itself a dream, a thesis that's been neither proved nor disproved thus far.

# Esoteric dream tools

*NO DISCUSSION OF psychic dreaming would be complete without an examination of the connection between dreams and the esoteric arts, which include, among others, astrology, palmistry, the Tarot, numerology, and psychic intuition. Learning to use these esoteric dream tools can take you to realms you've literally never dreamed of.*

## How "scientific" are these tools?

While practices such as astrology or palmistry are not *exact* sciences, there is growing research and documentation taking place in these fields. Experts in these areas are very positive about the results they can show, while at the same time being sensibly cautious when opening up these horizons for lay persons. Most astrology or palmistry practitioners would tell you, for example, that they are not in the business of making exact predictions but of pointing out general trends and probabilities via your sun sign, birth chart, or the lines of your hand. So keep an open mind, but don't lose the opportunity of discovering a new dimension to your dreams simply because these esoteric tools are unfamiliar to you.

## *IT'S ALL IN YOUR HANDS*

In palmistry, the Mount of the Moon, also called the Mount of Luna (at the base of your hand below your pinky and opposite your thumb) is the area of dreams. Most systems of palmistry agree that a well-developed Mount of the Moon indicates vivid imagination, creativity, and psychic ability. Even if you aren't recalling your dreams, various markings here, such as crosses, stars, and triangles, suggest that there's probably much activity you're not aware of. Palmistry books can help you understand how your dreams reveal themselves in the palm of your hand.

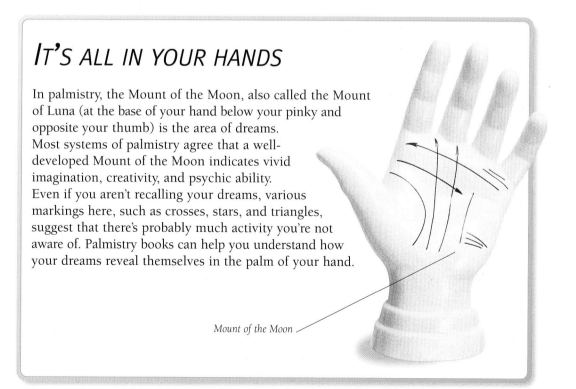

*Mount of the Moon*

# THE SCIENCE OF SIGNS

There are many points of intersection between astrology and dreams. Some researchers study the time, date, and place of a person's birth in conjunction with the time, date, and place of his or her dream to get interesting results. According to another method, since each sign of the zodiac belongs to one of four elements (fire, earth, air, or water), when your dream imagery is one of these elements, you can take a cue from what that element represents.

| Element | Astrological Signs |
|---|---|
| FIRE | Aries, Leo, Sagittarius |
| EARTH | Taurus, Virgo, Capricorn |
| AIR | Gemini, Libra, Aquarius |
| WATER | Cancer, Scorpio, Pisces |

■ **Sagittarius** *(the archer), the 9th sign of the zodiac, is a fire sign. "The fire burns strong and bright with lively enthusiasm and an infectious emotional level," write Julia and Derek Parker in DK's book* Parkers' Astrology.

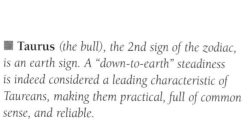

Serious practitioners of astrology don't claim to give you exact forecasts. As Julia and Derek Parker say in Parkers' Astrology, astrology can be "a sort of weather forecast, suggesting future trends." It can suggest the best time to look for a new job, but can't tell you when you might get it.

| Dream Representations | Meanings |
| --- | --- |
| Light, fire | Beginnings, excitement |
| Rock, soil | Groundedness, logic |
| Sky, clouds | Imagination, thought |
| Oceans, rain | Emotion, psychic ability |

■ **Taurus** *(the bull)*, the 2nd sign of the zodiac, is an earth sign. A "down-to-earth" steadiness is indeed considered a leading characteristic of Taureans, making them practical, full of common sense, and reliable.

# WHAT'S IN A NUMBER?

Numerology holds that every number has a meaning, so it follows
that the numbers in your dreams might have meaning as well. To begin,
according to numerological theory, every number is "reduced" by adding its digits
together until it is only one digit long. The number 123, for example, would be
reduced by adding 1+2+3 together, resulting in 6. The birth date June 7, 1958 would
be reduced by adding 6 (June) +7 + 1+9+5+8, to equal 36, which in turn would be
reduced by adding 3+6 to equal 9. Many books are devoted to numerology, so what
follows is much abbreviated. Still, if you recall a number from a dream, reduce it as
I've just shown, and then use the following table to determine its meaning.

| Number | Meanings |
|--------|----------|
| 1 | Beginnings, independence, taking the lead, pushing ahead |
| 2 | Balance, partnerships, cooperation, sharing, beauty |
| 3 | Imagination, creativity, joy, friendship |
| 4 | Hard work, stability, foundations, practicality |
| 5 | Energy, change, spontaneity, freedom, cleverness |
| 6 | Marriage, family, home, harmony, generosity |
| 7 | Solitude, reflection, retreat, research, rest, the occult |
| 8 | Management, leadership, material success, judgment |
| 9 | Philanthropy, compassion, tolerance, completion, fruition |

■ **Watch out** *for how a number appears
in your dream – as the number plate of a
car, as time on a clock, or as the address of
a house . . .*

# Dreams and the Tarot

While it's impossible to detail all the nuances of Tarot cards in one brief section of a book about dreams, it is possible for you to use Tarot cards as a way to explore dream imagery. That's because, like dreams, the Tarot is based on pictures and, again like dreams, the meaning of each card is limited only by your imagination. Also limited only by your imagination are the ways you can use the Tarot to help you with your dreams.

LOVERS     THE TOWER     KING OF CUPS

1 One exercise involves using Tarot cards to "illustrate" your dream (this is particularly good if you, like me, are "artistically impaired").

2 Another way you can use the Tarot is to simply look at a card that resonates for you. Very often, when a particular card seems to hold special meaning for you, spending some time looking at it will eventually remind you of a dream image you hadn't remembered and help you to recall that particular dream (or dreams).

## Tarot types

If you've never seen a Tarot deck, you might want to begin by examining several at your local bookstore. There are, quite literally, hundreds of Tarot decks from which to choose, from the traditional Rider-Waite deck to the contemporary Aquarian deck. One of my favorites is the Mythic deck, which incorporates imagery from Greek mythology.

■ **Simply looking** *at the Tarot card that you feel holds some meaning for you may lead you to recall a significant dream image.*

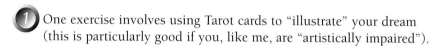

## Dreams and intuition

People who are naturally intuitive have long relied on their dreams as one of their guideposts. Lynn Robinson, author of *Divine Intuition*, notes that by their very nature psychic dreams can be difficult to document at the time they occur. In order to accept the intuitive guidance your dreams are offering you, Robinson suggests that, as you review what you've written about your dream in the morning:

*a)* Pay attention to how you feel about each dream image and scene

*b)* Underline those to which you respond most clearly and strongly

*c)* Consider how they relate to your present situation

*d)* Note any correlations that occur to you at the time

*e)* Once a week or so, go back through your dreams for that week and look for patterns you may have initially missed

As Robinson notes, "You may find that insights from several dreams can be put together to create a clear message for which you are waiting."

***In order to hear your intuitive voice telling you something you've got to be listening in the first place!***

■ **Dreams will help** *you to "see" yourself in a different way.*

## Your own inner compass

Ultimately, your best guide to interpreting dreams – both your own and those of others – is your own inner compass. Whether you choose to use specific esoteric tools to help you understand your dreams, whether your dreams are precognitive or personal, or whether you travel out of your body or stay safely in your own bed, what you make of your dreams is up to you.

At the very least, by now it's clear that dreams are certainly a tool for self-understanding, but that may well be only the beginning. It is possible that the connections we make with each other while we are dreaming and through our dreams may ultimately lead to greater human understanding and a more peaceful and hopeful future.

# A simple summary

✔ Psychic dreams are those that seem to herald future events or make connections with other people, times, or places while we are asleep. Their common thread is that they seem to contain information not available to us by ordinary means.

✔ Parapsychology is the branch of psychology that studies psychic phenomena, including clairvoyance, telepathy, extrasensory perception (ESP), and precognitive dreams.

✔ While waking life is measured in chronos, or clock time, dreams occur in kairos, also known as "holy time," such that we dream of people or events long gone or of events yet to happen.

✔ Psychic dreams seem to share certain signals that separate them from other dreams, such as the presence of someone who is deceased. However, you should always look for the simplest explanation first: most dreams are not psychic dreams.

✔ Precognitive dreams share the common element of occurring before the event they feature. Other types of psychic dreams are clairvoyant, telepathic, and extrasensory perception (ESP or sixth sense) dreams.

✔ Out-of-body experiences (OBEs) are similar to experiences recorded by those having near-death experiences (NDEs), and may be spontaneous or produced at will. However, some experts argue that an OBE experience is itself a dream.

✔ Esoteric dream tools include examining the astrological signs and elements, understanding the numerological significance of numbers, exploring the Mount of the Moon in your palm, mapping your dream with the help of Tarot cards, and using your intuition to understand more about your dreams.

✔ Ultimately, your best guide to interpreting dreams is your own inner compass.

# PART FOUR

## Dream Work

HERE, YOU'LL LEARN HOW various dream groups operate. We'll also explore the future of dreaming, including some new uses for your daydreams, the possibilities of collective and shared dreaming, and how forensic dreaming can help you achieve your greatest potential.

# Chapter 17

# Dream Work Groups

$S$ELF-DISCOVERY THROUGH your dreams is important, but another benefit of dream exploration is working with others on both your dreams and theirs. Deciding whether to be a part of a dream work group is a personal choice, as is deciding which type of group you might prefer: one led by Freudian, Jungian, or Gestalt analysts; one organized by laypeople; or one without any formal leader at all. The information here will help you make an informed decision about whether or not to join a dream group.

## In this chapter...

✓ **Why join a dream work group?**

✓ **Organizing a dream group**

✓ **Some simple do's and don'ts**

225

# Why join a dream work group?

*DISCUSSING DREAMS in groups is a natural outgrowth of Jung's collective unconscious, and* **dream work groups** *run the gamut from formal to informal, Freudian to Jungian to Gestalt, and daily to monthly. These days, you can even find a dream group online, join a dream group to work through a specific problem, or start your own dream group for your own specific purposes.*

> ### DEFINITION
>
> **Dream work groups** (*or dream groups*) *are groups of people who get together at a specific time to explore members' individual dreams. There are as many different types of dream groups as there are dream theories.*

## The advantages

While dreams are by their nature very personal, there are many reasons why you might want to join a dream group, not the least because it's a fun way to meet other people who share your interest in dreams:

**1** Other people's perspectives can provide you with keys to your dream imagery that you may have missed on your own

■ **A dream group** *that works well helps strengthen each member as an individual.*

**2** Dream groups led by professionals, whether Freudian, Jungian, Gestalt, or another discipline, can give you a structured framework within which to understand your dreams

**3** Working in a dream group reveals the archetypal imagery of dreams

**4** Long-term study of dreams in series (both your own and others') can be not only enriching but sometimes life-changing

*Dream group members must listen without interrupting, relate without coddling, understand without judging, and assist without needing to control. These attitudes help in other areas of life as well.*

■ **Don't run away** *from your fears as manifested in your dreams. If it's difficult to confront them alone, use your dream group's help.*

# Organizing a dream group

*IF YOU WANT to start a dream group yourself, it's a lot like starting any group. First, you find people who are interested in the same thing. It's probably not a good idea to include co-workers or family in your dream group. Many of your dreams may involve your relationships with them, and it's important to feel free to explore all the imagery and ideas in your dreams.*

## Starting up

Here are some ways in which you can form, or become part of, a dream group:

**1 Begin with acquaintances:** There may be enough interested people in your circle so that you won't need to reach out into the larger community for members.

**2 Put up fliers:** Depending on the type of group you're interested in, you can post your name and number at a local college or university, at the neighborhood coffee shop, at a bookstore, or any place where you know like-minded souls also go.

**3 Join an existing dream group:** If you're interested in working in a specific area, look in the Yellow Pages of your local telephone directory for therapists who lead dream groups. Asking around will lead to some people who know people who are already in dream groups (this happened when I solicited dreams for this book via e-mail). While more established groups are often closed to new members, new groups start up all the time, so get yourself on several lists that sound promising.

■ **Put up notices** *in places such as a bookstore window or on a cafe wall to get your dream group going.*

## Can I search online for dream-group partners?

The good news is that searching online is not nearly so impersonal as it was in the early days of cyber-connecting (see box "Dreaming online" below). However, the customary precautions that one should always take for any kind of online chatting or group formation should be observed.

## DREAMING ONLINE

Although I knew there was a lot of online dream work going on, I hardly expected the 590,000+ hits I got when I ran a google.com search for the phrase "dream group." Top hits included:

The Association for the Study of Dreams web site:
● www.asd.org

The dream group pages of:
● yahoo.com
● dreamgate.com
● dreamtree.com

Any of these sites are excellent places to start.

■ **If you're comfortable** *hanging out in chatrooms and surfing the web, you might like to try online dreaming.*

**INTERNET**

**www.dreamtree.com/ Community/StartDG.htm**

*On this site, people from all over the world post their names and e-mail addresses, from which you can either start a local dream group or work online.*

At his web site, www.jeremytaylor.com, dream researcher Jeremy Taylor notes that he's been pleasantly surprised by the degree of camaraderie and discovery that goes on in online dream groups. Concerns about lack of direct interaction seem to be unfounded, he notes. The important thing is the sharing of dreams in a spirit of growth and discovery, not just for the dreamer, but for all group members.

**Don't try getting into an online dream group if you're new to the cyberworld in general.**

■ **Dream group meetings** *can be as formal or informal as you care to make them.*

## Who?

Trust is king in dream group membership. After all, you are going to be sharing your deepest psychic information on an ongoing basis with the group members. Among the key considerations for dream group membership are the following:

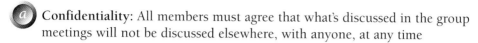 **Confidentiality:** All members must agree that what's discussed in the group meetings will not be discussed elsewhere, with anyone, at any time

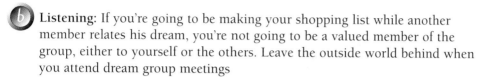 **Listening:** If you're going to be making your shopping list while another member relates his dream, you're not going to be a valued member of the group, either to yourself or the others. Leave the outside world behind when you attend dream group meetings

**Practicing:** Plan on working outside the group, both in studying dream theory and in recording your dreams

If you've got the group together but have no particular expertise (other than reading this book, of course!), it is best to make it clear at the outset that you're the organizer, not the expert.

## Where?

Whether you meet at your house, at someone else's house, at an office, or at the back of the local bookstore is something you'll want to establish at the first meeting. If the meetings are always going to be at the same person's home, a weekly fee can be used to pay for refreshments. Or, you may want to set up a schedule in which the meetings move from home to home, and the refreshments are brought by someone else every week. If you meet somewhere else, these may become discussion points, but they are things you'll want to consider at the outset.

*A local community room may not be the right place for your dream group. Sessions will often deal with intimate issues, and not everyone is happy dealing with them in a public setting, even if it's behind a closed door.*

## How long?

Sessions of 2 hours are most common: with six members, you can spend 20 minutes on each person's dream. Some groups meet for 3 hours to allow more time to explore each member's dream.

*Whether you meet weekly, biweekly, or monthly will be up to the group members. There is no hard and fast rule about it.*

## How?

There are several things to keep in mind while going about organizing a dream group:

**a** **Choosing a leader:** If you're good at organizing potluck dinners but hate getting up and thanking everyone once they're there, you may want to establish at the outset that you're not going to be the leader. If you've decided to have a group without a trained facilitator (and that's fine), the group will want to decide who will lead, whether formally or informally. You can also rotate who leads, with a different member in charge each time. Just be clear about it.

**b** **The size of the group:** Smaller dream groups (four to six members) seem to be most effective. If everyone expects to work on a dream at each meeting, a larger group would mean that no one's dream would be worked on thoroughly. On the other hand, too small a group can result in not enough diverse input.

**c** **Getting them to commit:** Many who have organized dream groups suggest that everyone be asked to make both a time commitment (such as 6 months) and a monetary commitment (anywhere from $1 to $10 a session) to ensure that the same group of people will stay together for a specific period of time.

■ **It may take** *a few meetings for all members of the dream group to feel comfortable with each other.*

## Some basic rules

Make it clear at your first meeting that there are certain criteria for membership and that all who attend the first meeting are not automatically part of the group. In this way, those who talk too much, listen too little, or push to control others can be gracefully eliminated.

***All members must understand that their mission is not to "interpret" each others' dreams but to ask the right questions so that others can interpret their dreams themselves.***

# THE TONE OF MEETINGS

One of the most important things you can do before you begin is agree on the tone of meetings. This includes everything from its format to how the group will deal with problem people (a friend calls them P.P.s). Some P.P. problems include consistently exceeding the allotted time one is given, being "too needy," talking too much, or being too controlling. There's also the flip-side P.P., who never talks, never shares a dream, or doesn't seem to be focused on the work at hand. Some ways to conduct dream group meetings:

### ⓐ Reviewing

*Many groups like to begin with a sort of "week-in-review," allowing each member to check in (I'll talk about this more in the next chapter, when I discuss "touching in").*

### ⓑ Sharing information

*There should be some time set aside for any "housekeeping" that needs attending to, as well as a time for sharing news, ideas, and any new books anyone's come across concerning dreams.*

### ⓒ Sharing individual dreams

*One way of sharing individual dreams is to go around the room, with each person relaying one dream, without comment from other members. A time limit can be set for this process.*

### ⓓ Which dream to discuss?

*The facilitator can now ask who wants to work on a dream this session. Who goes first will become a gut feeling among the group: perhaps someone had a particularly difficult week, which their dream addresses, for example.*

How a group actually works on an individual dream is something I'll be discussing in detail in the next chapter.

# Some simple do's and don'ts

*AS WITH ANY GROUP, whether a dream group or a sewing circle, laying down ground rules at the outset can avoid all sorts of problems later on. Most dream group facilitators agree on these basics, and so I've adapted the following from a number of sources:*

**a** **Show respect for the dreamer and the dream**: Even though the group will take part in it while it is being discussed, every dream "belongs" to its dreamer. Most groups agree to use phrases such as "If this were my dream . . . " when probing their own reactions to a dream's imagery.

**b** **Respect confidentiality**: Dreams reveal ourselves at our most vulnerable, childlike, open, and trusting, and for us to share them comfortably, the dream group must include a commitment to confidentiality. Nothing said within the group should be shared outside the group. Period.

**c** **Commit to attending, listening, and participating for the agreed period**: Being part of a dream group is not just about your own dreams, it's about the dreams of the others as well. Working with others' dreams involves listening carefully, asking questions, and then providing feedback. Every member of a dream group must do all three of these things for the group to be its most effective.

**d** **Respect the ground rules set up by the group**: Ground rules can cover everything from which psychological approach to dreams the group will use to whether the group is open to outsiders.

*Some groups like the idea of trying out new ways of exploring dreams together and include such experimentation as part of their meetings, while others prefer to stick with the tried-and-true. Whatever your group's ground rules, everyone should agree to stick to them.*

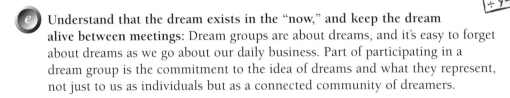

**e** **Understand that the dream exists in the "now," and keep the dream alive between meetings**: Dream groups are about dreams, and it's easy to forget about dreams as we go about our daily business. Part of participating in a dream group is the commitment to the idea of dreams and what they represent, not just to us as individuals but as a connected community of dreamers.

## Dream work groups work!

As Jeremy Taylor points out in *Where People Fly and Water Runs Uphill* (see *Further Reading* at the end of this book), "the vast majority of people are strengthened, liberated, revitalized, and deeply supported and affirmed by their experiences in dream groups." Working with others on your dreams can be scary, but like all such deep psychic work, the lasting benefits are well worth the effort and emotional risk you need to take.

■ **The benefits** *of working in a dream group spill over into other areas of life. You'll become better at working through problems and dealing with other people.*

# A simple summary

✓ Dream groups can be the next step in working with your dreams, with their benefits spilling over into other areas of your life as well.

✓ Respecting confidentiality, listening, asking questions, and providing feedback are key when working with dreams in groups.

✓ Dream group members should share a commitment to working together for a set period of time to learn about their dreams.

✓ Small dream groups of four to six members seem to work best, with sessions of 2 hours.

✓ One of the most important things you can do before you begin is agree on the tone of the meetings.

✓ Part of participating in a dream group is the commitment to the idea of dreams and what they represent, not just to each of you individually but as a connected community of dreamers.

✓ Working with others on your dreams can be scary, but like all such deep psychic work, the lasting benefits are well worth the effort and emotional risk.

# Chapter 18

# Dream Groups in Action

ALTHOUGH EVERY DREAM group is as individual as the people who are a part of it, exploring several dream groups in action can help you envision your own hopes and expectations. Dream group dynamics involve far more than the way people interact with each other – they also have to do with how we interact with our deepest selves. No matter what approach your group uses to interpret dreams, the possibilities for growth and greater understanding for all involved are quite possibly unlimited.

*In this chapter...*

✓ **Group dynamics**

✓ **Ways and means**

✓ **Is it right for you?**

TOGETHER WE WILL FIND OUR WAY

# Group dynamics

*GROUP DYNAMICS REFERS to the way people interact when they are with others. Some are natural controllers; some are organizers; some listen quietly; some insist on synthesizing the varied approaches of the others into a cohesive whole. Because, as dream analyst Jeremy Taylor puts it, "The mutual projections in a dream group almost invariably produce valuable insights for all involved," dream group dynamics take on added importance.*

## The downside of ritual

It's important to be aware of some of the possible pitfalls of group dynamics, as well as its inherent potential. The more frequently a group gets together (for any purpose, not just discussing dreams), the more likely the people involved will fall into comfortable, predictable patterns of communication. What's wrong with comfort? you may ask. The answer is that we begin to miss a lot when we're comfortable with others because we stop paying attention to *preconscious signals* such as body language and eye movement. We get used to each other's patterns.

### An example

Jeremy Taylor calls this phenomenon "repressive preconscious group collusion." This mouthful can be explained by an example. Suppose in a dream group, J. always uses her hands when she talks. If she starts punching a fist into an open palm when describing a particular dream, we may not pay close attention. Even though this particular use of her hands is not typical of J., we may miss it because as a group we've become complacent about how J. talks with her hands.

■ **For dream groups** *to be most effective, all members must be sensitive to each other's body language.*

# How not to let patterns take root

One simple way of dealing with such complacency is the natural attrition that occurs in any group. When one member leaves and another joins, the group will need to shift its rhythms and pay closer attention accordingly. If your group is so cohesive that this is unlikely, making sure these patterns don't become entrenched becomes still more important.

## Guest facilitators

Jeremy Taylor suggests periodically inviting "guest facilitators" to lead your group. Whether they come to introduce you to alternative approaches to dream work, or you invite them because of their experience in leading dream groups, outsiders (especially professional dream workers) are quick to pick up on group dynamics and group patterns of repression – and point them out.

## Shedding the patterns

A second way of avoiding preconscious patterns is to begin each dream group session with a timed writing or drawing exercise (5 minutes is enough) that forces a shedding of those patterns before you get down to the dream work. One example of such an exercise might involve what's called a "prompt," one word on which you focus until you begin writing. Any word can be a prompt: a noun, verb, adjective, even a conjunction. The most important thing in writing from a prompt is to not stop. For example, if your prompt is the word "potato," here are the various steps you can go through:

1. You'd write the word "potato" on a blank sheet of paper.

2. Then, if nothing else occurs to you, you would write the word again: "Potato. Potato. Potato."

3. Eventually, your mind will move on. Write down whatever occurs to you: "One potato, two potato, three potato," or, "Mashed potatoes are my favorite."

It's possible that what occurs to you will have nothing to do with a potato on the surface. That's fine. The purpose of this exercise is to shake off your regular patterns and move you into a more finely tuned mode that will make you more attentive to the others in your dream group (as well as to yourself).

■ **Pay close attention** *when others are relating their dreams so that you don't miss out on any nuances.*

## Patterns of projection

Anything anyone feels, says, or suggests about another's dream is, at its most basic, *projection*, and in a dream group, projection can be enormously helpful. The longer a dream group is together, the easier it is to see individual patterns of projections.

**DEFINITION**

The psychological term **projection** *refers to the assumption that another's reaction to something will be the same as one's own.*

*In an established group, it is easier to see individual patterns of projections, which in turn offer important clues about what carries emotional weight for each person.*

Our initial reactions to someone else's dream will always be subjective responses, but this is where the most profound personal connections are made. In fact, the topic of my graduate dissertation was the writer/reader connection. My conclusion was that such connections occur at a very personal level, no matter how universal their origin. For example, you are much more likely to feel something about the story of Anne Frank, one individual who died in the Holocaust, than about the number 6,000,000. In a similar way, universal connections are made on an individual level, and every suggestion made about someone else's dream is valuable to not only the dreamer, but to the person making the suggestion and the rest of the group as well.

■ **We relate better to universal** *tragedies through an individual's story rather than through the trauma suffered by a faceless multitude. Shown above is a monument to the victims of the Holocaust during World War II, in Stockholm.*

# Ways and means

*DREAM PIONEER Montague Ullman firmly believes that anyone can learn how to interpret dreams, anyone can lead a dream group, and anyone, even those without any formal training, can help someone else uncover the messages in his or her dreams.*

## The power of dreams

Part of Ullman's legacy to future dreamers are guidelines for teaching dream work to others, which begin with an explanation of why dream imagery carries potential healing power:

■ **In any group,** *each role will finally be assumed by the person most suited to it. This is true of dream groups as well.*

*a* **A dream is about your present life:** Ullman asserts that daily events touch on earlier emotional issues, and every night, your dreams set to work on them

*b* **A dream can recall past information about an issue as well as present data:** The imagery that dreams use to "show" you information usually comes from times past when you had similar feelings

*c* **Dreams do not lie:** One of the most fundamental truths about dreams is that they are inherently honest. Naïve, innocent, and trusting, our dreaming psyche reflects our subjective state

*According to Montague Ullman, we translate the dream into language, transforming "what originally was experienced in a sensory form . . . into a narrative form."*

The most important thing to be aware of about our dreams, Ullman notes, is what we took to bed with us before they began. "The dream is a continuation at night of feelings stirred up during the day," he says. Our work on a dream begins at the moment we translate the dream image into language. If we are in a dream group, the next step is to share that translation with the group.

## Touching in

Most dream groups begin with "touching in" – a short period of time in which each member can share information about his or her week. Touch-ins act as a sort of emotional week in review. Not only are all group members given the opportunity to talk about how they felt between the last meeting and this one, they can also analyze how they're feeling.

*Touch-ins don't need to be formal, but it's best that they be timed. No more than 4 minutes per member is usually enough.*

The meetings are not the place for working through particular difficulties, no matter how tightly knit the group may become.

*Don't turn touch-ins into individual therapy sessions, which they tend to become unless carefully timed and monitored.*

### Keeping in touch

Many groups have less emotionally laden touch-ins that also include sharing news and views about dreams and dreaming. This can be a good place to talk about how larger local and global happenings may have entered into peoples' dreams – incidents such as a murder or serious accident in the local community, or the events of September 11, 2001, when terrorists crashed planes into US World Trade Center and the Pentagon.

■ **Nightmares of planes** *crashing into buildings were reported from all over after the September 11 terrorist attacks in the US. Your dream group's "touch-in" may feature discussion of such a phenomenon.*

## Centering

A centering exercise is a good way for the group to come together after the unburdening of touching in, so that they can then concentrate on the work at hand. Centering exercises run the gamut from a statement said together aloud to a focused meditation in which each member moves from self to group in a conscious way. Jeremy Taylor cites the following as his favorite exercise:

"Hold hands in a circle . . . For the space of twelve in-and-out breaths the group holds hands in silence, breathing easily and deeply. What anyone does inside his/her own head is always their own business, but what I always recommend is this:

Visualize light entering your body on the in breath, so that as you continue to breathe and hold hands, you see yourself more and more vividly in your mind's eye becoming filled with light, from the soles of your feet all the way to your scalp and the tips of your hair, with the light flowing in and out your hands to the other members of the group."

## Dream sharing

At the conclusion of the centering exercise, dream sharing begins. Your group may choose to start the dream sharing session with each person relating a dream without comment from other members, as outlined in Chapter 17. Or the facilitator may ask who wants to work on a dream this week, and then select who will go first. Many facilitators use emotional issues from the touch-in as markers for whose dreams will be worked on in a given week.

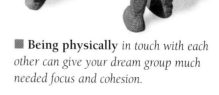

■ **Being physically** *in touch with each other can give your dream group much needed focus and cohesion.*

## Taking notes

It's a good idea to have someone take notes on each week's discussions. Most dream groups prefer not to tape-record the proceedings, as the members tend to be conscious of the recording device as they speak.

*Whether you write down notes or record the sessions is up to the group members to decide. Just remember, it's worth doing.*

■ **Even if a group** *member's dream feels strange, try to think of it as your own and interpret it accordingly (but only if the dreamer is open to the idea).*

## Group responses

Working on dreams in-depth varies substantially from group to group. The formality of group responses, for example, may be very different from group to group. Here are a few instances:

**a** Some go around the circle, with each group member asking the dreamer to clarify certain things before moving on to interpretation. (Going around the circle is a good way to make sure even the quieter members of a group have an opportunity to speak).

**b** All group members may accept the dream as if it were their own and interpret it from that perspective.

**c** You may have an open forum on the dream, with anyone and everyone calling out and discarding possible interpretations until the dreamer gets an "aha!" response. Often, the dreamer won't be the only one to have an "aha!" about his or her dream. One of the most exciting things about a dream group is the "aha!"s that occur from others' dreams.

*When the group has finished with one dream, it is often a good idea to take a moment to re-center before moving on to the next dream.*

## Professional interpretation

If the facilitator is a professional dream worker with a specific focus, dreams will be explored according to that discipline:

- **Freudian dream workers** will work to connect the dream to unconscious issues
- **Jungians** will explore archetypal patterns
- **Gestalt therapists** will encourage the dreamer to assume every role in the dream and then question each player's responses

# DEALING WITH INDIVIDUAL DREAMS

Most groups choose to time how long is spent on an individual dream. Either the facilitator or someone else can perform this task. When the allotted time is winding down, the facilitator will ask several questions to make sure the dreamer is comfortable with the direction the group has taken. These questions may include:

(a) Would you like to explore anything else about the dream?

(b) Are there any clarifying questions you would like to ask the group about your dream?

(c) Is there anything anyone else in the group would like to add? (Some facilitators solicit questions from those who have remained silent at this point.)

■ **Being a facilitator** *has as much to do with listening intelligently as with formal training.*

## Group dreaming

When dream groups have been together for some time, there's often a desire to venture into other types of dreaming. One such possibility is group dreaming, not to be confused with shared dreaming (discussed in the box on the following page). Simply put, group dreaming (or collective dreaming) is a method in which a group of people all work to dream about one particular person's problem or emotional issue.

Here's how group dreaming works:

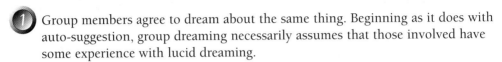 Group members agree to dream about the same thing. Beginning as it does with auto-suggestion, group dreaming necessarily assumes that those involved have some experience with lucid dreaming.

2 Group members then bring the resulting dreams to their next meeting and compare them.

One of the primary benefits of group dreaming is having others dream about an emotional problem that you haven't been able to resolve within your own dreams. I'll explore shared and collective dreaming more in Chapter 20, when we look at some of dreaming's potentials.

*Group dreaming usually benefits all who participate, because nearly all our difficulties have common roots.*

■ **Group dreaming** *can be of great help in sorting out an emotional problem that you haven't been able to resolve through your own dreams.*

# SHARED DREAMING

Shared dreaming is not the same as group dreaming, although it is often an outgrowth of it. When two people share a dream, both have the same dream, and see each other just as if they were awake.

Shared dreaming begins with the dreamers agreeing to "meet" at an assigned place in a dream. This can be the bed they share, a coffee place they frequent, the room where their dream group meets, or some fantasy place one (or both) has imagined. Like group dreaming, shared dreaming assumes some lucid dreaming experience, as the dreamers will need to exercise conscious control within their dreams to get to the meeting place.

When both dreamers "arrive," the mutual dream begins. Each dreamer will come away from a shared dream with his or her own point of view, but the commonality of what occurs within the dream suggests that shared dreaming is no fantasy.

**INTERNET**

www.lucidity.com/
LD9DIR.html

*This site offers lucid dreaming pioneer Stephen LaBerge's thoughts and suggestions for shared dreaming.*

■ **In shared dreaming,** *the two people concerned agree on a "meeting place" for the dream – a coffee shop, a park, or an imaginary place.*

## THE "NEGATIVE AHA!"

Perhaps one of the most interesting possibilities in dream group dynamics is the "negative aha!" This occurs when someone makes an observation about someone else's dream and the dreamer's response is, "No, not at all. It's entirely the opposite." That "opposite," however, is something that the dreamer would not have noticed had the group member not made the "wrong" suggestion so that the "negative aha!" could occur.

# Is it right for you?

*HOW DO YOU decide if a dream group is right for you? While the final choice depends on your individual personality, circumstances, and needs, here are some questions that might help you decide.*

■ **Are you sure** *you will be comfortable discussing your dreams, problems, and personal life with others?*

## The question is . . .

If the answer to any of these is in the negative, think twice before joining a dream group.

*a* Do I want others' input into what my dreams mean?

*b* Am I comfortable sharing my dreams with others?

*c* Do I clearly understand my reasons for joining a dream group?

*d* Do I want to help others work on their dreams as well as have others work with me on mine?

*e* Is there a particular psychological approach to dreams that I prefer?

## To sum up . . .

Only you can decide if a dream group is right for you. This quote from Jeremy Taylor's *Where People Fly and Water Runs Uphill* may help.

*Jeremy Taylor says: "Working with dreams in groups is a far superior method of raising consciousness and releasing the multiple creative energies, increased understandings, and gifts for living that dreams invariably bring."*

If you decide you're interested in working with someone else on your dreams, but aren't sure you want to do so in a group setting, you'll want to read Chapter 19, where you'll learn about one-on-one dream work.

## A simple summary

✔ It's important to be aware of the nuances of group dynamics, including what Jeremy Taylor calls "repressive preconscious group collusion," projection, and the "negative aha!"

✔ The longer a group is together, the easier it is to see individual patterns of projections, which in turn offer important clues about what carries emotional weight for each person.

✔ According to dream pioneer Montague Ullman, the most important thing to be aware of about our dreams is what we took to bed with us before they began.

✔ Most dream groups begin with "touching in" – a short period of time in which each member can share information about his or her week, followed by a centering exercise, which helps the group concentrate on the work at hand.

✔ Group dreaming involves everyone in the group dreaming about one person's problem.

✔ When two people share a dream, both have the same dream and see each other just as if they were awake.

✔ Only you can decide if a dream group is right for you.

# Chapter 19

# One-on-One Dream Work

I F YOU'RE INTERESTED in working with someone else on your dreams, but aren't sure you'd like to work in a group, one-on-one dream work may be your next step. One-on-one dream work doesn't have to be done with a therapist; you can work with your partner, a friend, or even an acquaintance you find online. Nor does one-on-one dream work need to be formal: it's as much about listening, paying attention, and intuition as it is about interpretative training.

## In this chapter...

✓ What's a dream interview?

✓ Preparing for a dream interview

✓ Selecting a partner

✓ A matter of style

✓ Your dream/your self

COME FACE-TO-FACE WITH YOUR HIDDEN SELVES

# What's a dream interview?

ONE-ON-ONE DREAM WORK *often begins with a **dream interview**, a simple method that can help you and your **dream partner** work on interpreting a dream. Dream expert Gayle Delaney, PhD, suggests six steps for a dream interview that you can use as stepping stones toward developing your own approach.*

## SIX STEPS TO A DREAM INTERVIEW

**1  Describe . . .**

*the dream elements, being sure to include feelings about each element. For instance, if the picture shown here was your dream image, you would describe not only the raven but also your indifference toward it.*

**2  Review . . .**

*each description, being careful to use the same words (words are often subliminal triggers).*

THE RAVEN BY DAVID INSHAW

**3  Bridge . . .**

*from each image to the dreamer. Questions in this step can include "Does this image remind you of something about yourself?" or "Can you connect this to something going on in your life?"*

**4  Verify and clarify . . .**

*the strength of each bridge. You might phrase such a question, "How does this remind you of this person/feeling/place?"*

**5  Summarize . . .**

*each description and bridge, both as you go along and when the interview is finished. The summary stage is where both dreamer and interviewer often add spontaneous thoughts or ideas that hold the keys to various dream images.*

**6  Reflect . . .**

*on what the dream interview has revealed about the dream. Don't come to any immediate conclusions. Agree to meet in a week to discuss your thoughts in more detail.*

# Preparing for a dream interview

*THE MOST IMPORTANT thing to bring to a dream interview is a recent dream. While this may sound obvious, you'll want to select a dream that left you with some sort of feeling when you awoke, whether uneasiness, resolution, anger, or another strong reaction. If you recorded the dream in your dream journal as soon as you awoke, you'll want to bring this written document along to work from as well.*

## In the beginning

Some dream experts suggest that, at least when you first begin dream interviewing, you do some further work with the written dream before the actual dream interview takes place.

■ **It makes sense** *to work on your chosen dream before you start analyzing it with a dream partner.*

Gayle Delaney, for example, suggests diagramming the dream, using a different type of mark for each dream element (see Chapter 7 for details).

*Dream elements include settings, people and animals, objects, feelings, and action. You can use iconic markings such as a house or tree for each setting, or use a different style, such as bold face, for different elements (see Chapter 7).*

## Making sense of your dream

You can also use your dream journal for free association, working with each dream element individually and seeing where it leads you, or for more experimental excursions, questioning each element. You might ask, for example, if the "you" in your dream is yourself or your father, or if the "father" in your dream is actually your spouse. This may well be the kind of dream work that you've already been doing on your own. In fact, it's often when you feel you've gone as far as you can by yourself that you will want to begin working with a dream partner.

# Selecting a partner

*WORKING WITH A DREAM partner brings a fresh point of view to your dream imagery. That said, the single most important attribute of a dream partner (including you) is the ability to listen. This means that, when a dream is first reported, there should be no interruptions, no judgments, and no mind-wandering. Both the dreamer and the dream partner should focus on the dreamer's narration of the dream. Only after the dream has been related for the first time should the dream partner begin the dream interview.*

## The ideal partner

You've probably heard the adage, "You can pick your friends, but you can't pick your family." The good news is that you can pick your dream partner, and you should give this relationship the same careful scrutiny you would any meaningful partnership.

*You should not impose your own meanings on someone else's dream imagery. Make suggestions and share how particular images make you feel, but always be clear that these arise from your own reactions to the dream, not the dreamer's.*

Some people find that a good friend or loved one is already at the same point in his or her dream work, and form a dream partnership without even trying. Others find dream partners when they take a class on dreaming through a local continuing education program, or through college or university dream networks.

*Don't feel pressured into selecting a dream partner with whom you feel uncomfortable in any way. Take your time. When you find the right dream work partner, you will know.*

## A personal choice

Sharing your dreams is deeply personal work, and choosing a dream partner is a personal matter. Deciding whether you want to work with a layperson like yourself, with a friend or relative, or with a dream work professional is similarly a very personal choice. In the following section I'll give you some guidelines to help you make this decision.

**INTERNET**

**www.dreamtree.com**

*Click on the icon for "Dreamworkers" at the bottom of this interactive web page for listings of both online and offline potential dream partners.*

## Choosing a friend or loved one

Choosing someone you already know is a logical choice for a number of reasons, the main one being that they already know you.

*(a)* When you work with a dream partner who knows you, they often have information about you and your life that someone you know less well will not, unless you choose to tell them. Information like this can lead to insights about your dreams that you yourself might miss.

*(b)* In addition, a friend or loved one cares about you, and vice versa. This means that you will care about each other's dreams and the potential for healing and wholeness they provide.

### The other side of the coin

These same pluses, however, also translate into minuses:

*(a)* What happens when your dream work partner appears in a dream in a less-than-flattering light? Will your partner (and you) be able to separate the dream character from the dream partner?

*(b)* What if one of the issues your dream chooses to focus on is connected with your dream partner? Will the two of you see it, acknowledge it, and be willing to work with it?

*(c)* And don't forget about those preconscious signals I told you about in Chapter 18! When you are comfortable with someone, you are likely to miss out on the significance of their body language, eye movements etc., because you are so used to them.

■ **There are both** *pros and cons to working on your dreams with people close to you.*

# AS FOR ME . . .

My best dream partners have always been my closest friends – and my closest friends have always made natural dream partners. I've never needed to actively seek out dream partners – or do dream work in any formal way, in fact – because dream work is a part of nearly every friendship I have.

## Working with a dream expert

If your spouse can't fix a dripping faucet or a squeaky brake, you probably have the phone number for a good plumber or your favorite mechanic posted near your phone. There are times when you have to turn to an expert, and in dream work, this time comes:

**a)** If your friends aren't interested in dreams the way you are, in which case you may not find a friend willing or able to be a good dream partner

■ **If your dreams** *involve the people close to you, you may not feel comfortable discussing the dreams with them.*

**b)** If your dreams are touching on issues you would feel more comfortable discussing with someone who's been trained to help with them

*Friends and family are great for dream work, but there are times when someone who's been trained to work with dreams is the way to go.*

## Going with a pro

Choosing a dream work expert to work with should be approached with the same careful analysis of style, skill, and sense of connection that you would bring to any professional relationship. If you're reserved and serious, you're not going to pick a doctor who jokes about your health.

*You'll want to find a dream worker whose approach to dreams and dream work meshes with your own.*

## Already working with a psychotherapist?

If you're already working with a psychotherapist, dream work may already be part of the work you're doing.

**a** Some therapists rely heavily on dream interpretation as part of treatment; others believe dreams have little value in psychoanalysis

**b** If you like the work you and your therapist are doing, but dreams have not been a part of it, ask your therapist how he or she feels about dream work, and if he or she would be interested in helping you work with your dreams

**c** If your therapist is not interested or doesn't feel comfortable with the idea, ask if there's someone else he or she would recommend for you to work with to do so

**d** If your therapist feels dream work would be counterproductive, you may need to decide how important dream work is to you at this point. You may decide to start seeing a different therapist who is more interested in dream work

Having said all that, let me remind you once again that one-on-one dreamwork (something I've been doing for over 30 years) is as much about listening, paying attention, and intuition as it is about interpretative training. It's not necessary to go to a therapist, but if you decide you need to, or if you simply can't find a suitable dream partner, then go ahead. The following section can help you decide which type of analysis works best for you.

■ **It's important** *to choose a therapist who believes that analyzing dreams can be useful in psychotherapy.*

# A matter of style

*WHETHER YOU DECIDE to work with a friend, a loved one, a trained dream worker, or a professional, you'll want to consider what style of dream analysis feels most comfortable to you. In Chapter 18, I discussed Montague Ullman's approach, which synthesizes Freudian, Jungian, and Gestalt theories. I explained these dream pioneers' theories in Chapter 2. Now let's take a closer look at how each of their therapeutic approaches works with a dream.*

## LAYER BY LAYER

While every approach to dreams will phrase it slightly differently, it may be helpful for you to think of your dream as a layered reflection of your self: the conscious layer, the preconscious layer, the personal unconscious layer, and the collective unconscious layer.

**The conscious layer:** *this is the "I," the outward layer that interacts with the larger world (in Freudian terms, the ego)*

**The preconscious layer:** *this is the readily accessible area of your mind where you store facts, memories, ideas, and thoughts*

**The personal unconscious layer:** *this is the less accessible area where you store hidden memories, repressed emotions, and instinctive reactions (in Freudian terms, the id)*

**The collective unconscious layer:** *this layer, according to Jung, connects you to everyone else, and is part of what genetically makes us human. It's here you'll find myth, history, and belief systems*

## Decoding dreams

The dreaming mind accesses both the preconscious layer and the collective unconscious layer of the psyche for images, which it then uses to translate the material of the personal unconscious layer for the conscious layer. Dream work, quite simply, is a way of helping the conscious layer understand these "coded" messages.

*After you've reviewed the key elements of each style of dream interpretation, you may come to a synthesis of your own. As for me, I believe there are only two things to remember when you approach a dream: trust yourself and relax.*

## Freud and dreams: uncovering hidden content

As you'll recall from Chapter 2, Freud divided the dream into two levels: a surface content he called "the manifest dream," and a hidden content he called "the latent dream." Freud believed that dreams were a way of dealing with suppressed instinctual urges, and that five distinct processes were at play in the censoring process of working with dreams:

- Displacement
- Condensation
- Symbolization
- Projection
- Secondary revision

*Freudian dream work involves removing the censoring material put in place by one of these processes to reveal the underlying unconscious material, often repressed since childhood, at its root.*

■ **Freudian dream work** *assumes that, much like an island, most of the substance of your dream is hidden, with only the upper surface showing.*

## Jung and dreams: compensation and individuation

Jungian dream analysts disagree with Freudian dream theory at a fundamental level: Rather than attempting to *hide* the unconscious material, Jung wrote, dreams are messages attempting to *communicate* what the unconscious can teach the conscious. In Jungian theory, dreams serve two purposes: compensation for waking imbalances; and individuation, an effort of the individual psyche to achieve wholeness. Dreaming, according to Jung, is part of the larger process of self-discovery and learning about our personal potential.

*Rather than employ Freudian free association, Jung proposed what he called direction association. This method focuses on the material of the dream itself, image by image, feeling by feeling.*

Process is an important part of Jungian dream work, both in processing what's going on in our daily lives in our dreams, and in a process-oriented approach to dream work itself, which takes place over a long period of time. One of the assumptions of Jungian dream work is that the dream is part of a larger individual psyche, the individual part of a larger collective psyche, and the collective psyche part of an ultimately interconnected universe. Jungian dream interpretation, then, focuses on seeking individual wholeness, while at the same time working toward larger connections.

■ **Jungian dream work** *seeks wholeness for your self, so that your self can find its place in the world.*

## Perls and dreams: the layered personality

Gestalt dream pioneer Fritz Perls suggests that the layers of a dream reflect the layers of the personality, which are outlined by Perls as: the cliché – or superficial – layer; the role-playing layer; the defensive layer; the implosive layer; and the explosive layer.

*According to Perls, the deepest dream work occurs between the implosive layer and the explosive layer, where the dreamer moves from denial, to strong emotion (often grief or anger), to freedom of expression.*

The key to Gestalt dream therapy is discovery rather than interpretation, feedback rather than analysis. In one-on-one Gestalt dream work, your dream partner will encourage you to assume various roles within your dream, engage in dialogues with your dream personas and dream objects, and continue the dream itself to discover what your dream has revealed about your self.

# Your dream/your self

*WHILE WORKING WITH* another can help *you see elements of your dreams you may have missed, you are always the ultimate authority on your dreams and their meaning. Throughout this book, I've freely interpreted others' dreams, just as you and your dream partner will do as you work on each other's dreams. Always remember, however, whether working with a partner, a therapist, in a group, or on your own, that your dreams are yours and no one else's.*

A dream is like walking through a door into rooms you have not been in before. How you perceive what you find in those "rooms" – and what you do with it – are part of the joy of self-discovery that comes when you begin to work with a new dream.

■ **Every dream offers** *an opportunity to walk through an open door and discover a landscape that has been there all along.*

## A simple summary

✓ A dream interview is a method for focusing on the personal meaning of a dream.

✓ Working with a dream partner brings a fresh point of view to your dream imagery.

✓ Deciding whether to work on your dreams with a friend, loved one, dream expert, or professional is a personal choice.

✓ Understanding the various approaches to dreams can help you synthesize your own approach to dream work. Freudian dream work focuses on uncovering the unconscious; Jungian on individual and collective wholeness; Gestalt on self-discovery.

✓ Your dreams belong to you and no one else.

# Chapter 20

# Dreaming in the 21st Century

THE POSSIBILITIES FOR DREAMS don't end with your self-understanding: dreams can also aid in global understanding, which is what much of 21st century dream theory involves. Like everything, however, the roots of future dreaming begin in the past, taking what has been learned, and applying it to both the present and the future. By discovering the ways we are alike, rather than what separates us, dreams may well be a way in which humanity can ultimately unite. In the end, the future of dreams and dreaming is up to each of us – and to all of us.

## In this chapter...

✓ Dreaming awake

✓ Dreaming the future, dreaming the past

✓ Dreaming on your own

"NO MAN IS AN ISLAND UNTO HIMSELF . . ."

# Dreaming awake

*THROUGHOUT THIS BOOK, I've focused almost exclusively on the dreams you have when you are asleep. If you're like most people, however, you've likely spent a great deal of your waking time dreaming, too. But while you've probably daydreamed about everything from your next encounter with Jennifer Aniston or Brad Pitt to how you're going to tell your boss what you really think of him or her, you may not have considered the problem-solving possibilities of conscious dreaming.*

## Conscious dreaming

*Conscious dreaming* offers problem-solving assistance to the attentive waking dreamer as well as to the lucid dreamer because, as dream expert Louis M. Savary, STD, PhD, notes, "dreams can help you clarify and live up to your ultimate values." This means that paying attention to the uncensored stories you create in your daydreams can not only help you imagine solutions to problems, but explore ways of implementing those solutions as well.

**DEFINITION**

**Conscious dreaming,** *sometimes used as another name for lucid dreaming, refers to using the subconscious as a problem-solving tool.*

## Simple steps to conscious dreaming

One way of trying some conscious dreaming of your own is with the following exercise. Once you've tried conscious dreaming a few times, you'll no longer need to follow these steps precisely. They're presented merely as a guideline; you can use, or not use, your daydreams however you wish.

1. Write down the problem on which you want to work. Be as detailed as you wish, but be sure to state the specific nature of the problem as clearly as possible; not just "My boss is driving me crazy," but "My boss is driving me crazy because she always waits until I'm ready to leave to hand me a rush job."

■ **Everybody tends to** *let his or her mind wander during the course of a humdrum day, and this can be an important step toward conscious dreaming.*

**2** Once you've written down the problem, let your mind wander. You probably already know when and where this is most likely to happen. Is it when you stretch out on the couch after dinner? When you're supposed to be working at your desk but are instead staring at the wall? Simply begin with the problem as you've stated it and allow your mind to wander.

**3** Without working consciously to direct your thoughts, pay attention to where they go. Some will clearly be fantasy: The higher-ups suddenly realizing your boss is driving you crazy and firing her is probably not something very likely to occur, for example. Writing a letter to your boss's superior is something that could be done, however. If your daydream takes you there, pay attention to what you say in that letter. I'm not saying you should write it or, God forbid, send it. Just pay attention to what you write in your imagined letter.

■ **Fantasizing that** *the boss who troubles you is punished is natural wish-fulfillment.*

**4** After freely daydreaming for 5 to 10 minutes, stop and write down what you've thought about your problem so far, both the absurd and the sublime.

**5** Now, answer this question: is there something in what I've just written that I can use to help me solve my problem?

## It all adds up

It's quite likely that the answer to this question is yes. Let's say that in the letter to your boss's boss in your daydream, you mentioned that the reason she waits until 5 p.m. to put work on your desk is because she's the type of person who solves problems as they occur and so spends all day solving problems rather than attending to the work she should be doing. From this, you can ask a new question: What could be done so that your boss would attend to the work she should be doing? Could you recommend a new position, someone who would handle the daily problems and free your boss to do what she's supposed to be doing? Would weekly department meetings help? When you've identified a new question to daydream about, you can start over, continuing until you arrive at a solution that you not only know will work, but that you can help make happen.

## Trivia...

*Many writers report the sensation of having a story "write itself," or of having a character take over a story's direction. Similarly, many artists have talked about beginning a painting with an idea of an image and then having the image take over the painting. Both of these scenarios illustrate the idea behind conscious dreaming – paying attention to the subconscious, and, when appropriate, allowing it to lead the way.*

# Dreaming the future, dreaming the past

*IN CHAPTER 16, we explored future dreaming from a New Age perspective, including the possibilities of telepathic, clairvoyant, and intuitive dreams. But dreaming the future is not just about forecasting; it's about imagining possibilities. Can you imagine, for example, meeting others in your dream who are dreaming the same dream at the same time?*

## Past continuous

If you have already experienced a lucid dream or a shared dream, you know that such dreams are possible. Now, let us take this idea to its next level: a dream as a place where we could use archetypes to forge greater human understanding. That is the potential of collective dreaming.

But the future of dreaming isn't just about, well, the future; it's also about the past, specifically your own past. Research now suggests that Freud wasn't entirely wrong when he posited that all dreams have their roots in childhood trauma. In fact, by using dreams as forensic tools, we may be able to uncover mysteries of the past that continue to haunt us in the present.

■ **Freud posited** *that our personalities are trapped in our childhood traumas.*

## Forensic dreaming: was Freud right?

Forensic dreaming offers the opportunity to unravel mysteries of the past that continue to impinge on the present. Sound Freudian? To a certain degree, forensic dreaming does take the interpretation of dreams back to its beginning at the turn of the previous century when Freud published his landmark book.

■ **In forensic dreaming,** *fragments of our past can be brought together to make a comprehensible whole.*

## The voices within

In order to illustrate how forensic dreaming works, for the last dream of the book, here's one of my own:

*Little tiny Kait (my daughter) kept running away, wanting to do what seemed to me to be foolish, foolhardy things. First, she ran away from home through a field, but I ran after her and tried to stop her. Then she and I were huddled on a cliff-side. She wanted to leave me there and jump, and even though I knew she'd be safe if she did (this was a very Biblical-looking vantage point), I didn't want her to jump.*

*When I told Bob (my husband) about this, in the dream, I told him it seemed as if it would be okay because it turned out she wasn't her little self anymore, but her "bigger self, who she'd been all along." Then she was getting away from me yet again, and I knew I had to go after her, but she called on the phone and said, "I'm leaving for Israel. I leave at 11:30 and you can't stop me."*

*"What about your loans I co-signed for?" I screamed. "What about telling Diane (her landlady, though this isn't her name)? What about your father? What about ME?" I thought she'd known about responsibility, I told her, quaking, shaking. I'd trusted her, I said. And I was furious, telling it all to Bob in the dream.*

**INTERNET**

www.forensic-psych.com/articles/artDreams.html

*Learn how researchers have narrowed the gap between Freudian dream theory and brain research by reading the article posted at this web site.*

## The heart of the matter

When I woke up (I was staying at a friend's, and her puppy woke me with happy licking), I was still shaking, furious about how irresponsibly Kait was behaving. At once, I realized that the "Kait" in the dream was really me: my internalized parent had disguised herself as me to remind me how important she (the parent) was.

### Analysis

The night before I had this dream, two friends and I had a marathon Tarot card session, during which we each got to the heart of a matter we'd been avoiding. In my case, I wondered why whenever I came close to my goal of publishing fiction, something seemed to happen to undo it. It was as if, I said, I were standing in my own way. As we talked, I realized that I still carried childhood messages from my internalized "parents," which told me that wanting to publish fiction was selfish and irresponsible.

Even though I had realized this was not the case, my dream self tried to convince me otherwise. In this forensic dream, "little tiny Kait" was my creative self, the me that needs nurturing, faith, and trust – as well as that internalized parent, who, of course, is also a very caring and concerned aspect of myself.

■ **Dreams can help** *unearth deep mysteries of our past and bring to the fore our subterranean selves.*

## TAKE CARE

(a) Forensic dreams can reveal long-buried memories, especially when you are working with a friend or therapist to uncover the root of a deep-seated problem. It is hard emotional work, and you shouldn't attempt it unless you feel comfortable – and ready – to tackle the tough core issues in your life

(b) Another danger in forensic dreaming is a false memory, such as a recalled incest that never occurred

*As you use your dreams to heal yourself, remember that dreams work in metaphor and image, not waking reality.*

## Collective dreaming: taking Jung to the next level

Why dream alone when we can dream together? Collective dreaming, which I introduced in Chapter 18, has the potential to take Jungian archetypes to the next frontier: a place where more than one dreamer can meet among shared dream imagery to achieve collective understanding.

*Collective dreaming isn't new; in fact, it's ancient. Many cultures have collective dreaming at their cores, including the Senoi, Australian aboriginal tribes, Hindu mystics, and shamanic healers.*

Collective dreams share corresponding dream elements, and usually begin when two or more people arrange to meet in a dream at the same time, then separately remember the details of their dreams when they awaken. Collective dreams are divided into a number of categories:

*a* **Mutual dreaming** involves two dreamers agreeing to meet in a dream

*b* **Synchronous dreaming** occurs without prior arrangement between the dreamers

*c* **Telepathic dreaming** involves an awake sender and a sleeping receiver. The sender transmits target material via his or her mind to the receiver

*d* **Parallel dreaming** is not the same dream, but rather when two people simultaneously dream of each other

*e* **Shared dreaming** is when two dreamers meet in the same dream place and experience similar events

## Collective unconscious to "collective unconsciousness"

Dream educators Linda Lane Magallon and Barbara Shor believe that shared dreaming pushes beyond the Jungian collective unconscious "to forge a collective unconsciousness."

*Collective unconsciousness means that the possibility exists for a new level of trust among people, as more and more unconscious myth and image is shared in dreams.*

Magallon and Shor note, "Shared dreaming awakens our capacities for compassionate understanding and clear communication. This awakening may well be a necessity if we are going to evolve beyond divisive fears and mistrust, as well as illness, pollution, and other challenges that threaten not only our personal survival but the Earth's."

■ **Our dreaming consciousness** *has as much to do with our individual self as with collective humanity.*

# Dreaming on your own

*DESPITE THE STRIDES made in the last hundred years, the potentials of dreams and dream work are only now beginning to be explored and understood. Still, the possibility that our dreams can help us create a more hopeful tomorrow through the human interconnection they provide cannot be denied.*

## Beyond the individual self

This possibility is heralded in the words of dream pioneer Montague Ullman: "It is as if, while awake, we tend to lose sight of our basic interconnectedness, focusing more on our discreteness and our separateness. Asleep, we turn our attention to the reality of our interconnectedness as members of a single species. In this sense we may regard dreaming as concerned with the issue of species-connectedness. From the perspective of where we are today it would seem that the human species can endure only if it succeeds in overcoming the fragmentation that has resulted from the play of historical forces . . . Perhaps our dreaming consciousness is primarily concerned with the survival of the species and only secondarily with the individual."

*Our dreams may well be the frontier where we rediscover our human interconnectedness. But it first begins with each of us. So, close your eyes, breathe deeply, and take the first step: dare to discover your dreams.*

## A simple summary

✔ Conscious dreaming offers problem-solving capabilities to the attentive waking dreamer.

✔ Collective dreaming has the potential to take Jungian archetypes to the next frontier: a place where more than one dreamer can meet among shared imagery to achieve collective understanding.

✔ Forensic dreaming can help us understand how the past continues to influence us today, as well as uncover hidden mysteries that can help us heal.

✔ Our dreams may be the frontier where we rediscover our human interconnectedness. Take the first step: dare to discover your dreams.

# More resources

## Further reading

*A Little Course in Dreams*
Robert Bosnak
Boston: Shabhala, 1988

*A Primer of Jungian Psychology*
Calvin S. Hall and Vernon J. Nordby
New York: New American Library, 1973

*Breakthrough Dreaming*
Gayle Delaney
New York: Bantam, 1991

*Creative Dreaming*
Patricia L. Garfield, PhD
New York: Fireside, 1995

*Dream Power*
Ann Faraday
New York: Berkley, 1980

*Dream Thinking: The Logic, Magic, and Meaning of Your Dreams*
Alex T. Quenk and Naomi L. Quenk
Palo Alto: Davies-Black Publishing, 1995

*Dreams That Can Change Your Life*
Alan B. Siegel
Los Angeles: Jeremy P. Tarcher, 1990

*Dreamtime and Dreamwork*
Stanley Krippner, ed.
New York: Jeremy P. Tarcher/
Perigee, 1990

*Dreamwork for the Soul*
Rosemary Ellen Guiley
New York: Berkley, 1998

*Exploring the World of Lucid Dreaming*
Stephen LaBerge and Howard Rheingold
New York: Ballantine, 1990

*Healing Dreams*
Mark Barasch
Riverhead, 2000

*How to Get a Good Night's Sleep*
Norman Ford
New York: Barnes & Noble, 2000

*In Your Dreams*
Gayle Delaney
San Francisco: HarperSanFrancisco, 1997

*Let Your Body Interpret Your Dreams*
Eugene Gendlin
Wilmette, Illinois: Chiron Publications, 1986

*Lucid Dreaming*
Stephen LaBerge
Ballantine, 1998

*Memories, Dreams, Reflections*
C.G. Jung
New York: Vintage, 1989

*Our Dreaming Mind*
Robert L. Van de Castle
New York: Ballantine, 1994

*Pregnancy & Dreams*
Patricia Maybruck
Los Angeles: Jeremy P. Tarcher, 1989

*The Dimensions of Dreams*
Ole Vedvelt
New York: Fromm International, 2001

*The Dream Encyclopedia*
James R. Lewis
Detroit: Visible Ink Press, 1995

*The Dream-Working Handbook*
Helen McLean and Abiye Cole
London: Carlton Books, 2001

*The Emerging Mind*
Karen Nesbitt Shanor, ed.
Los Angeles: Renaissance Books, 1999

*The Healing Power of Dreams*
Patricia L. Garfield, PhD
New York: Fireside, 1992

*The Interpretation of Dreams*
Sigmund Freud
New York: Quality Paperback Book Club, 1995

*The Secret Language of Dreams*
David Fontana
San Francisco: Chronicle, 1994

*The Wilderness of Dreams*
Kelly Bulkeley
Albany: SUNY Press, 1994

*The Wordsworth Dictionary of Dreams*
Gustavus Hindman Miller
Ware, Hertfordshire: Wordsworth, 1995

*What Your Dreams Can Teach You*
Alex Lukeman
St Paul: Llewellyn, 1990

*Where People Fly and Water Runs Uphill*
Jeremy Taylor
New York: Warner, 1992

# Journals and magazines

*Dreaming*
Human Sciences Press, Inc.
233 Spring Street, New York
N.Y. 10013-1578
Phone: Journal Customer Service at (212)
620-8468, 8470, 8472, or 8082
*asdreams.org/idxjournal.htm*

Brought out by the Association for the Study of Dreams, *Dreaming* is a quarterly, multi-disciplinary journal that publishes scholarly articles related to dreaming from any discipline and viewpoint. This includes biological aspects of dreaming and sleep/dream laboratory research; psychological articles related to dreaming; clinical work on dreams regardless of theoretical perspective (Freudian, Jungian, existential, eclectic, etc.); sociological, anthropological, and philosophical articles related to dreaming; and articles about dreaming from the arts and humanities.

*Dream Time*
Association for the Study of Dreams
Information Office, P.O. Box 1166
Orinda, CA 94563
Phone: 925-258-1822 Fax: 925-258-1821
*E-mail: asdreams@aol.com*
*asdreams.org/idxmagazine.htm*

*Dream Time* magazine is an information service and forum for ASD members, special issues of which are available to the public. These issues cover topics such as children's dreams, and dreams and spirituality. The online section includes news about conferences and other meetings and events, articles on dreams and dreaming, as well as research abstracts of past issues and special columns on dreams and film, Cyberspace, and books.

# Organizations

*Novato Center for Dreams – Dream Library & Archive*
　　Novato, CA 94947
　　Phone: (415) 898-2559
　　*members.aol.com/dreammzzz/ncdarch.htm*

Located in Novato, California, 30 minutes north of San Francisco, the center houses a collection of dream books, periodicals, tapes, and other materials. Their Reference Library contains over 1400 titles on dreams in categories ranging from master's and doctoral theses to foreign language material and books for children. The Lending Library offers more than 150 dream books available online or by mail. The Dream Archive has articles, resumés, business cards, slides of dream art, and hundreds of assorted flyers.

*The Lucidity Institute*
　　2555 Park Blvd, Suite 2, Palo Alto
　　CA 94306-1919
　　Phone: 1-800 GO LUCID (465-8243)
　　or +1 650-321-9969
　　*E-mail: info@lucidity.com*

Founded in 1987 by Dr. Stephen LaBerge, the Institute supports research on lucid dreams and helps people learn to use them to enhance their lives. Members explore the world of lucid dreaming by participating in experiments described in the Institute's newsletter, *NightLight*, which features a variety of articles including discussions of research and new developments in consciousness. Workshops and training programs are available periodically. The Institute sells books, scientific publications, tapes, and lucidity induction devices.

*The D.R.E.A.M.S. Foundation, Canada*
Box 513 Snowdon
Montréal, QC
Canada H3X 3T7
Phone/Fax: (514) 990-2113
*E-mail: info@dreams.ca*

The D.R.E.A.M.S. (Dream Research and Experimental Approaches to the Mechanisms of Sleep) Foundation is a non-profit organization operating in collaboration with the Dream and Nightmare Research Laboratory at Montreal's Sacré-Coeur Hospital.

The foundation's aims are: To inform both the public and health/ science professionals about the nature of dreams and their practical applications in relationship to overall health and well-being; support ongoing research into dreams and non-pharmaceutical treatments for sleep and dream disorders; contribute to the training and education of students and researchers in these fields; provide funding for both fundamental and clinical research in these fields; contribute to improved treatment of patients with dream-related disorders; and encourage research into both normal and abnormal dreaming and sleep processes.

# Dream-related courses

## ASD list of Graduate Studies in Dreams
www.asdreams.org/subidxedugraduatestudies_98.htm

The Association for the Study of Dreams maintains a list of Universities, Colleges, and Institutions that offer graduate level classes, courses, and certification.

## DreamGate's History of Dreams online course
dreamgate.com/class

A six-week course that surveys the history of dreams, dreaming, and dreamwork. The course covers dream anthropology, dreams in ancient civilizations, dreamwork in Freud, Jung, Adler, Perls, Gendlin, grassroots dreamwork, lucid dreaming, mutual and *psi* dreaming, and many other modalities. Participants can join an online dreamgroup that has been developed for fun as well as insight. It starts the first day of each new month and you can sign up online.

## JFK University – Certificate in Dream Studies
Phone: (925) 258-7322 for a personal appointment
www.jfku.edu/holistic/hs-dream.html

JFK in Orinda, California, offers a graduate program in Consciousness Studies that includes a 36-unit Certificate in Dream Studies. Offering more than 15 courses that directly and indirectly address the study of dreams, this Certificate is said to be designed for students and professionals who desire to work with and explore dreams for use in education, research, consulting, and writing.

## The Haden Institute
1819, Lyndhust Ave.
Charlotte, NC 28203-5103
Phone: (704) 333-6058
Fax: (704) 333-6051
www.hadeninstitute.com

Offers Jungian counseling and teaching designed to foster spiritual growth. Most events are held in and around Southeastern United States. The Institute offers National Training for Certified Dream Group Training. The dream courses are designed to be done from home and meetings are held three times a year.

# Web sites

*THE ONLY ASPECT of dreaming you won't find online is the dreaming itself. Whether it's solace from nightmares, resources for dream journaling, or potential shared dreaming partners, Internet sites for dreamers are just a click away. Here's a selection to get you started.*

### members.tripod.com/~045tu/sen.htm

Can't get a handle on what a particular dream landscape or scenery means? This contemporary dream landscape dictionary can give you linguistic clues toward understanding the metaphors of your own dream places.

### oz.sannyas.net/quotes/chakra10.htm

For a more esoteric approach to chakras and dreams, try this web site, where you'll find a detailed analysis of dreams and their chakra connections.

### thriveonline.oxygen.com/serenity/experts/dream/pregnancy.html

Online help is just a click away at this up-to-the-minute site that explores the connections between dreams and pregnancy. You'll also find nearby help for other life transition dreams.

### www.asdreams.org/subidxedubookhelp.htm

This site has links to numerous dream sites, as well as a listing of books about dreams and dreaming.

### www.asdreams.org/nightma.htm

The Association for the Society of Dreams (ASD) provides a web page that answers "Common Questions About Nightmares." You can also link to the ASD homepage from this site, of course.

### www.avcweb.com/dreams/colour-in-dreams.htm

This web site provides a Color Healing Chart and suggestions for examining possible meanings for the colors in your dreams. Read it for fun or print it out for future reference!

### www.css.to

The Canadian Sleep Society web site provides information about sleep centres and offers sleep links and sleep related news and articles.

### www.dreamgate.com/dream/articles_rcw/ed2-2inc.htm

Learn more about everyday creative dreaming in this article by ASD member Richard Wilkerson.

### www.dreamgate.com/dream/library/idx_psi.htm

Link to a variety of web sites and articles about psychic dreaming from this all-encompassing link.

### www.dreamgate.com/dream/resources/online_c.htm

Here you'll find an online dream resource list as well as links to many other dream sites.

### www.dreamresearch.ca/rem/symbols.html

At this site you will find tools for developing your own methods of interpreting your dreams, rather than a reductive dream dictionary.

### www.dreams.ca

The Dreams Foundation web site provides information on dreams and their practical application and interpretation. It also offers dream resource links and events and workshops.

### www.dreamtree.com

Click on the icon for "Dreamworkers" at the bottom of this interactive web page for listings of both online and offline potential dream partners.

### www.dreamtree.com/Community/StartDG.htm

Dreamtree.com offers regional dreamers' discussion lists. People all over the world post their names and e-mail addresses, from which you can either start a local dream group or work online.

### www.dreamweavers.org

Get your own Jungian dream analysis online at this web site. You can also learn more about Jungian dream analysis here.

### www.forensic-psych.com/articles/artDreams.html

Learn how researchers have narrowed the gap between Freudian dream theory and brain research at this web site.

### www.lucidity.com

This is the web site of the Lucidity Institute, founded by Stephen LaBerge. It offers a detailed introduction to lucid dreaming, excerpts from Stephen LaBerge's books, articles, FAQs, links, and more.

### www.lucidity.com/LD9DIR.html

This site offers lucid dreaming pioneer Stephen LaBerge's thoughts and suggestions for shared dreaming.

### www.nauticom.net/www/netcadet/nltjk.htm

Run by an ASD-affiliated "dream journalist," this page is on Long Term Journal Keeping and links you to useful articles such as "advice on writing your dreams."

### www.sawka.com/spiritwatch/bio.htm

This web page is a good introduction to dream researcher Jayne Gackenbach's work on dreams.

### www.sawka.com/spiritwatch/tableof.htm

Scholarly papers on a variety of lucid dreaming and dream control topics by a who's who of dream experts and researchers can be found at this web site.

### www.shpm.com/qa/qadream/qadream45.html

Richard Wilkerson, who writes the Cyberphile column for the Association for the Study of Dreams newsletter, answers questions about creative dreaming at this direct link. You'll find answers to other questions about dreams and their potential at his online SelfhelpMagazine.com.

### www.sleepfoundation.org

Want to know more about sleeping or not sleeping? Go to the National Sleep Foundation's web site for up-to-the-minute information on research and resources.

# A simple glossary

**Anima** Refers to the psyche's female personality traits.

**Animus** Refers to the psyche's male personality traits.

**Archetypes** Called "mythological motifs" by Carl Jung, these are symbolic ideas that arise from the collective unconscious and appear repeatedly in story, myth, and dream. *See* Collective unconscious.

**Ascended master** Someone who advanced so far spiritually in their physical life that they escaped the cycle of life-death-life and can now manifest at will. According to legend, the ascended master Babaji achieved this feat at the age of 14.

**Chakras** According to yogic tradition, these are the body's energy centers, each located at a major nerve plexus. When your chakras are functioning well, you will feel healthy and whole. Chakra dysfunctions are often signaled first in dreams.

**Cognitive process** A fancy term for thinking invented by Calvin Hall. By calling dreaming a cognitive process, Hall was suggesting that dreaming is, quite simply, another way of processing thought.

**Collective unconscious** A concept introduced by Carl Jung that acknowledges the universal symbolism found within myths from diverse cultures. These symbols are also the language of the unconscious and hence, of dreams.

**Conscious dreaming** Sometimes used as another name for lucid dreaming, for our purposes this refers to dreaming awake and utilizing the subconscious as a problem-solving aid.

**Creative dreaming** A way of using dreams to work with unresolved issues from our waking lives.

**Creative visualization** A way of seeing something in your mind's eye in order to work with it before it actually occurs.

**Depth psychology** Involves probing the unconscious to discover the roots of conscious behavior.

**Dream dictionaries** Alphabetically arranged guides that connect dream images to specific symbols. Dreaming of a baby, for example, might signify pregnancy.

**Dream incubation** Actively seeking a dream to fulfill a specific purpose, such as healing or advice.

**Dream interview** A method for focusing on the personal meaning of a dream.

**Dream partner** Someone with whom you work on your dreams.

**Dream persona** Someone who represents you in your dream. While most often you are yourself, there are times when you are "played" by someone else, such as an actor or television star, or someone from waking life whose characteristics represent the you in your dream.

**Dream work group (or dream group)** A group that gets together at a specific time to explore its members' individual dreams. There are as many different types of dream groups as there are dream theories.

**Dreams** Narratives experienced while one is asleep, consisting of a mixture of "real" and "unreal" events. *Webster's New World Dictionary* calls a dream "a sequence of sensations, images, thoughts, etc., passing through a sleeping person's mind."

**Dream signals** Your own frequently occurring dream images.

**Dreamsigns** Fantastic elements within your dream that can alert you to the fact that you are dreaming.

**Dreamtime** The name given to the heroic parallel reality from which Australian aboriginals come and to which they return. Rituals performed in the present life reenact these heroes' journeys in order to keep the connection between past, present, and future realities one.

**Dualism** The philosophical system that holds that while humans' physical bodies function as other animals' bodies do, their minds are controlled by a nonphysical soul.

**Ego** The portion of the psyche that experiences the external world; the conscious, in other words.

**False awakening** The sensation of waking and doing things when in fact you are still dreaming.

**Free association** A method of talking in which one thing leads to another without conscious thought.

**Group dreaming (or collective dreaming)** A method in which a group of people all dream about a particular person's problem or emotional issue.

**Hero's Journey** According to mythologist Joseph Campbell, this is an archetype for life itself. Beginning with a call to adventure, the journey continues through a series of challenges and struggles to victory and resolution. Epics from *Gilgamesh* to the *Odyssey* to Shakespearean tragedies to present-day films follow this formula – as do many of our dreams.

**Holistic** All-of-a-piece. When we refer to the self as a holistic being, for example, we are saying that our minds and bodies are part of an interconnected whole.

**Id** The psychological term for the portion of the psyche concerned with pleasure and desire. Freud believed this was the realm of the unconscious.

**Latent dream** According to Freud, this is the level of a dream containing the dreamer's repressed desires. *See* Manifest dream.

**Light-pens** Pens that include a light that shines directly onto the page on which you are writing, so that you may record your dream at night without turning on a room light. Dream researcher Jeremy Taylor and his wife attach disposable ballpoint pens to small flashlights and have found them to be quite effective.

**Lucid dreaming** Being aware that you are dreaming while you are dreaming.

**Manifest dream** According to Freud, this is the level of a dream containing its surface meaning.

**Narrative** A term for the process of telling a story or series of events. A dream narrative, then, is your telling of a dream's story.

**Neuroses** Mental disorders that give rise to symptoms such as anxiety, compulsion, phobia, or depression.

**Nightmares** Disturbing dreams that often force partial awakening because of the disturbing emotions invoked by the dream, especially fear and anxiety.

**Persona** The mask each of us wear to face the world.

**Precognitive dreams** Dreams that share the common element of occurring before the event they feature.

**Preconscious signals** Messages we send to each other without being consciously aware of them, including body language, eye contact and movement, and the ways we stand and move.

**Projection**  A psychological term that refers to the assumption that another's reaction to something will be the same as one's own.

**Psyche**  From the Greek word for soul, this refers to the whole complex entity of the human mind.

**Psychic dreams**  Also sometimes called psi dreams, anomalous dreams, or New Age dreams, may be clairvoyant, prescient, telepathic, or precognitive. Their common thread is that they seem to contain information not available to us by ordinary means.

**REM (rapid eye movement) sleep**  The period of sleeping during which our eyes move rapidly. While it is not the only time we dream during the night, it is often when our most vivid dreams occur.

**Repression**  The psychological mechanism by which we withhold unconscious information from our conscious minds.

**Shadow**  Refers to personality traits opposite those we reveal via our persona.

**Sleep latency**  Refers to the period of time between going to bed and falling asleep.

**Spiritual dreaming**  This can be as simple as a dream that provides you with a new understanding of something, or a far more profound and mystical encounter with higher powers or forces beyond your waking knowing that changes your understanding of yourself and the world in some way.

**Spontaneous creative dreaming**  Occurs without conscious dream incubation to solve a problem. In this type of creative dreaming, dream solutions occur even though the dreamer has not actively sought them.

**Superego**  The psyche's censor, enforcing moral codes for the ego, and blocking unacceptable impulses of the id.

# Index

# Acknowledgments

## Author's acknowledgments

There are two literatures of dreams: the written texts, and the dreams themselves. I have been fortunate in both the many books that have been written about this subject (see Further Reading at the end of this book for some of them), and in the many dreamers who chose to share their dreams with me (and you): Frank Giardina, Lori Johnson, Kaitlin Kushner, Joshua Lenard, Hope Bussey McKenzie, Gail Rubin, Donna Smith, Eileen Stanton, Pari Noskin Taichert, and Kristy Yazzie. To all, thank you.

Thanks also to the ever gracious and always witty Jennifer Williams at DK in New York; to Lynn Northrup, who's edited enough of my books that it's possible she edits my dreams; to Lynn Robinson, for making the not-so-psychic connection that resulted in me writing this book; to Pari Noskin Taichert and Joanie Luhman, friends extraordinaire; and, as always, to Bob and Kait. Dedicated to the memory of my dear friend Bette Casteel, also a writer and dreamer, and my dog Too, both of whom died during the writing of this book.

## Publisher's acknowledgments

Dorling Kindersley would like to thank the following for their kind permission to reproduce their photographs:

Alistair Duncan; Andy Crawford / Kit Houghton; Brain Pitkin; Brian Cosrrove; Gables; Guy Ryecart; Jake Fitzjones; Joe Cornish; John Bulmer; Peter Wilson; Ray Moller; Sam Lloyed; Science Museum / London; and Stephen Oliver.

Dorling Kindersley India would like to thank Anita Roy and Ira Pande for editorial help.

## Picture credits

**Picture research:** Anna Grapes
**Picture librarians:** Jonathan Brooks,
David Saldanha

The publisher would like to thank the following
for their kind permission to reproduce their
photographs: (Abbreviations key: t=top, b=bottom,
r=right, l=left, c=centre, BAL=Bridgeman Art
Library, London/New York)

12: Musée Delacroix, Paris; 14: British Museum;
17: *Goanna Dreaming*, 1996 © Michael Tommy
Jabanardi; 20: BAL/Casper David Friedrich/
Hamburg Kunsthalle, Hamburg, Germany;
22: Scala/Henri Rousseau/The Museum of Modern
Art, New York. Gift of Nelson A Rockerfeller;
24: Getty/Bruce Ayres; 26: Corbis/Hulton-Deutsch
Collection; 27: BAL/Salvador Dali/ Ex-Edward
James Foundation, Sussex, UK, Gala-Salvador Dali
Foundation, DACS London 2002; 30: BAL/JAD
Ingres/Louvre, Paris, France; 36: Corbis/
Burstein Collection; 37: Michel Zabe/INAH (tr);
39: BAL/Peter Layzell/Private Collection/Portal
Gallery Ltd; 42: SPL/Sam Ogden; 53: BAL/Odilon
Redon/Giraudon/Musee d'Orsay, Paris, France;
54: BAL/Goya/Private Collection (br); 56: Getty/
Tony Cordoza; 64: BAL/Magdolna Ban/Private
Collection; 65: British Library; 86: Getty/Sean
Murphy (br); 93: English Heritage; 102: RHPL/A
Woolfitt; 110: Getty/Romilly Lockyer; 115: Corbis
Stock Market/Gerhard Steiner; 117: Getty/Mark
Douet; 118: Getty/ Howard Kingsnorth; 120: BAL/
Henry Fuseli/The Detroit Institute of Arts, USA;
Founders Society purchase with Mr and Mrs Bert L
Smokler and Mr and Mrs Lawrence A Fleischman
funds; 128: Getty/Alberto Ruggieri; 134: Getty/
Marion Peck; 142: Photonica/Kamil Vojnar;
145: Getty/Bill Crump; 150: Photonica/Kamil
Vojnar; 156: Powell-Cotton Museum; 160: John
Hedgecoe; 162: Kobal Collection/Universal 1982;
164: Photos 12/Universal Pictures, 1935;
165: Photos 12/Edvard Munch/ Nasjonal Galleriet,
Oslo, Norway/Munch Museum – Ellingsen Group,
BONO, Oslo, DACS London 2002; 166: Ronald
Grant Archive/Paris Europa/HISA/FI-C-IT, 1962
(t); 166: Photos 12/FC (Rome)-PECF (Paris), 1973
(b); 167: Redferns; 169: NASA; 174: Getty/Romilly
Lockyer; 179: BAL/Odilon Redon/Rijksmuseum
Kroller-Muller, Otterlo, Netherlands; 190–191:
Getty/Stuart McClymont; 202: National Museum,
New Delhi; 212: Kobal Collection/Carolco
Pictures/TriStar Pictures, 1989; 214: Getty/Ken

Chernus; 218: Peter Lawman; 219: Peter Lawman;
226: Getty/Tomek Sikora; 227: Getty/Howard
Kingsnorth; 236: Getty/Jump Run Productions;
245: Getty/Zigy Kaluzny; 246: Corbis Stock
Market/Jon Feingersh; 248: Getty/Color Day
Production; 252: BAL/David Inshaw/Private
Collection; 262: BAL/Maurice Chabas/Petit Palais,
Musee des Beaux-Arts de la Ville de Paris, France;
265: Getty/Andrew McCaul;

All other images © **Dorling Kindersley.**
For further information see:
**www.dkimages.com**